T0367956

LITE LEADERSHIP
Theory and Practice

BENNETT ANNAN, PsyD, EdD

WESTBOW
PRESS®
A DIVISION OF THOMAS NELSON
& ZONDERVAN

WestBow Press books may be ordered through booksellers or by contacting:

WestBow Press
A Division of Thomas Nelson & Zondervan
1663 Liberty Drive
Bloomington, IN 47403
www.westbowpress.com
844-714-3454

ISBN: 978-1-6642-3338-6 (sc)
ISBN: 978-1-6642-3339-3 (hc)
ISBN: 978-1-6642-3337-9 (e)

Library of Congress Control Number: 2021909254

Print information available on the last page.

WestBow Press rev. date: 7/2/2021

This book is dedicated to my two daughters
AMANDA ANNAN-DANQUAH,
and
THELMA ANNAN
both of whom have loved me unconditionally all through the years

leader *noun*
lead·er | \ ˈlē-dər\

2: A PERSON WHO LEADS
(Source: merriam-webster.com)

leaderlite *newly coined noun*
lead·er·lite | \ ˈlē-dər-līt \

1: A HOLISTIC LEADER
(Source: the author)

CONTENTS

LEADERSHIP AND MANAGEMENT: THE DIFFERENCES

> Management is doing things right; leadership is doing the right things.
>
> —Peter Drucker

> Austrian-born American management consultant, educator, and author, whose writings contributed to the philosophical and practical foundations of the modern business corporation. He was also a leader in the development of management education, and he invented the concept known as management by objectives.
>
> —*Encyclopædia Britannica*

Many scholars and researchers confuse the meanings of "leader" and "manager." What is more interesting is they use these words interchangeably. Leaders and managers typically play two distinct roles in any organization. These roles occasionally intertwine, and I believe this is the source of the confusion.

The following section describes the differences and similarities between the two roles and the overlap that sometimes occurs. Lite leaders need to understand the main components of each role as well as the relationship between them. Leadership and management roles are essential to every workplace, and thinking otherwise could be a perilous mistake.

DEFINITION OF LEADERSHIP

The definition of leadership is difficult to establish clearly; in the years of leadership studies, there have been many diverse definitions of this term. Stogdill (1974) wrote that there are almost as many definitions of leadership as there are people who have attempted to define the concept.

The New International Webster's Vest Pocket Dictionary (2003) defined leadership as "a guide; one in command; a person of influence or importance; that which precedes or joins." This definition does not take into consideration the purpose and the distinctive features of leadership but merely considers leadership with respect to the position (individual or collective), tenure, and ability of leaders.

The management guru Peter Drucker proclaimed that "the only definition of a leader is someone who has followers" (Drucker 1996, 8). According to Carly Fiorina, the former chief executive officer of Hewlett-Packard, "Leadership is a performance. You have to be conscious about your behavior, because everyone else is" (Hardy 1999, 138). Hollander (1978) described leadership as a two-way process of influence between a leader and followers. Lucas (2003) stated that, contrary to popular opinion, leadership is not supposed to be about deciding where other people should go. It's about finding out where they want to go and then helping them get there.

John C. Maxwell (1998) summed up his definition of leadership in *The 21 Irrefutable Laws of Leadership* as nothing more and nothing less than influence. His concept of influence refers to the power that the leader has over subordinates and the ability of the leader to influence others—those who would consider themselves followers and those outside that circle.

The Leadership Development Center (2004) of the Diocese of Rochester defined leadership as the process of influencing the behavior of other people toward the goals of the group in a way that fully respects their freedom. The emphasis on freedom is important. The Development Center believes that the greatest Christian leader, Jesus Christ, might have used this form of leadership in his teachings because even though he influenced many diverse people during his ministry, he did not compel anyone to follow him.

The definition that is used by the Christian Leadership World describes leadership as enabling a group to engage in the process of developing, sharing, and moving into vision and then living it out (The Teal Trust 1998). This group of Christians also believes that the enabling process is not possible unless it is linked with the leader's character and integrity in building up the trust necessary for leadership to be exercised over a period of time.

Warren Bennis's definition of leadership places much more emphasis on the individual capability of the leader. He proclaimed that leadership is a function of (a) knowing oneself, (b) having a vision that is well communicated, (c) building trust among colleagues, and (d) taking effective action to realize one's own leadership potential (Hoenig 2000). Thus, leaders should know themselves very well before they can lead others. This requires thoughtful, reflective self-assessment. Leaders have to take some time off to identify their strengths and weaknesses, analyze them, and develop a self-improvement plan. They then have to build on their strengths and work on developing and/or improving what they consider their drawbacks (Leadership Development Center 2004).

John Gardner (1990), in his book *On Leadership*, said leadership is the process of persuasion and example by which an individual (or leadership team) persuades a group to take action that is in accord with the leader's purpose or the shared purposes of all. Robert Greenleaf's (1970) servant leadership is a practical philosophy that supports people who choose to serve first and then lead as a way of expanding service to individuals and institutions. Finally, leadership can be defined as "a process whereby an individual influences a group of individuals to achieve a common goal" (Northouse 2004, 3).

Some common themes can be seen among these definitions, such as influencing followers. The most common ideas include "exerting influence, motivating and inspiring, helping others realize their potential, leading by example, selflessness and making a difference" (The Teal Trust 1998).

In my opinion, there are four principles that define what it means to lead. Leadership is influence, it determines results, it requires followers, and most importantly, it improves the lives of followers.

DEFINITION OF MANAGEMENT

There are various views as to how to define management. Traditionally, the term *management* refers to activities often performed by a group of people engaged in planning, organizing resources, leading, and controlling and coordinating functions of an organization.

Planning includes identifying goals, objectives, methods, resources needed, responsibilities, and dates for completion of tasks. Examples of planning include strategic planning, business planning, project planning, staffing planning, and advertising and promotions planning.

Organizing resources is the function of management that involves creating ways and means to achieve the goals of the organization in an optimum fashion. Examples include organizing new departments, human resources, office and file systems, and reorganizing businesses.

Leading includes setting direction for the organization, groups, and individuals and influencing people to follow that direction. Examples include establishing strategic direction (vision, values, mission, and/or goals) and championing methods of organizational management to pursue that direction.

Controlling or coordinating involves manipulating and directing the organization's systems, processes, and structures to reach the goals and objectives of the organization effectively and efficiently. This includes an ongoing collection of feedback and monitoring and adjusting systems, processes, and structures accordingly. Examples include use of financial controls, policies and procedures, performance management processes, and measures to avoid risks (McNamara 2003).

Another common view is that management is getting things done through the efforts of others, especially employees. Yet another view, quite distinct from the traditional view, asserts that the job of management is to support employees' efforts to be fully productive members of the organization and citizens of the organization or the community. However, to most employees, the term "management" probably means the group of people (executives and others) who are primarily responsible for making decisions in the organization. In a nonprofit, the term "management" might refer to all or any of the activities of the board, executive director, and/or program directors (McNamara 2003).

According to some writers, teachers, and practitioners, the traditional view of management is outmoded. Another interpretation of management is that it needs to focus more on leadership skills—for example, establishing and communicating visions and goals and guiding others to accomplish them. Some claim that leadership must be more facilitative, generally participative, and empowering. Some assert that this really isn't new or a change in the management functions approach. Instead, it is reemphasizing certain aspects of management (McNamara 2003).

Now that we have looked at the definitions of leader and manager, it is time to look at the differences between the two roles in any workplace or organization.

THE DIFFERENCES BETWEEN LEADING AND MANAGING

Leadership and management operate together, but they are different in several ways. While leadership is the art of influencing people, management is the science of achieving tasks.

Another difference between a leader and a manager comes from the idea that the person in the top-level position in an organization is at least responsible for setting or pursuing the overall direction of the organization. This level of management is often referred to as the leadership of the organization—a term that has also been used to refer to those who embrace and lead change in organizations for the betterment of all stakeholders—because of the recent focus on the need for transformational leadership to guide organizations through successful change.

I will use the following criteria to further illustrate the differences between leaders and managers: strategic planning and strategic management, change and change management, and push-and-pull philosophy.

STRATEGIC PLANNING AND STRATEGIC MANAGEMENT

Strategic planning is a future-oriented activity that tends to determine the organizational strategy and is used to set priorities. It is much more likely to be created by leaders of the organization. In other words, leaders plan the strategy to establish the overall objectives of the organization, frame policies, and most importantly, assist in the determination of the organizational strategy to meet competition, survive, and grow in the market. In strategic planning, leaders use analytics to focus on making optimal strategic decisions (Surbhi 2017).

On the other hand, strategic management—a bundle of decisions or moves taken in relation to the formulation and execution of strategies to achieve organizational goals—is much more likely to be implemented by managers of the organization. Managers focus on the process that (a) helps the organization to assess its internal and external business environment, (b) forms strategic vision, (c) sets objectives, (d) establishes direction, (e) and formulates and implements strategies that are aligned with the achievement of the goals of the organization. In this process, they tend to use management by results because management is an action-oriented activity. Managers are all about producing strategic results (new markets, new products, new technologies, etc.; Surbhi 2017).

All in all, strategic planning, which involves the identification of actions to be taken, is drafted by leaders of the organization. Strategic management is implemented by managers and involves identification of (a) the individuals who will perform the actions, (b) the right time to perform the actions, and (c) the way to perform the actions.

CHANGE AND CHANGE MANAGEMENT

Keth (2015) argues that, although there is some difference between change and change management, the two approaches are similar in introducing change in an organization. A common axiom that humankind has learned from evolution—adapt or die—can be applied to organizations, as change is inevitable for any organization to cope with changing environments. This is because change, if properly approached, drives any organization to a desired future state.

The key difference between these two terms, "change" and "change management," is that, while leaders create, lead, and enable the process of change to attain a desired future state of well-being, managers tend to apply the set of processes, mechanisms, and tools in enabling an organization to transition it from the present state to a future desired state (Keth 2015).

Another difference between change and change management is that leaders are associated with the urgency of change and expansive change, whereas aspired new vision is broad. To accomplish the vision, leaders (a) develop new approaches or think out of the box, (b) identify better, quicker, and cheaper avenues to do things, (c) make people buy into the change and transform them as followers of change, and (d) encourage others to value change (Keth 2015). The leadership qualities required to make change happen are not common among all leaders, and Keth (2015) argued that charismatic leaders who have high interpersonal relationship skills in leading people are often associated with change.

In an event of a change, leaders drive the change and make employees accept it. Managers, on the other hand, use a set of processes, mechanisms, and tools that are designed to assist the change for a smooth transition. They also monitor the change process through the application of these tools. Change very often comes with resistance, and managers are obliged to ensure that such disruptions do not happen by keeping the change process in control (Keth 2015).

In general, some believe that leaders exist only the top levels of organizations, and that managers can be found in the levels farther down. Others believe that leaders occupy, or should occupy, positions throughout the organization, but still use the term leaders mostly to refer to the top positions in the organization. Others, including myself, believe that managing and leading occur at many organizational levels (McNamara 2003).

A more classic difference between a leader and a manager was famously pointed out by Peter Drucker (1996): leaders do the right things and managers do things right. Bennis and Nanus (2004) put it this way: "Managers work toward the organization's goals, using its resources in an effective and efficient manner" (75). In a traditional sense, large organizations may have different levels of managers, including top managers, middle managers, and first-line managers (sometimes referred to as front-line managers; McNamara 2003). According to Bennis and Nanus (2004), the distinction is crucial, and the difference may be summarized as activities of vision and judgment—*effectiveness*—as opposed to activities of mastering routines—*efficiency*.

The correlation between leadership and management is an unending debate. For example, does a leader need to have good management skills in order to be successful? Does a manager have to be a great leader to be effective? More so, what is the difference between leadership and management? Table 1.1 offers a comparison of these two terms.

Table 1.1
Leadership Versus Management Comparison Chart

	Leadership	Management
Definition	Leadership means "the ability of an individual to influence, motivate, and enable others to contribute toward the effectiveness and success of the organizations of which they are members."	Management comprises directing and controlling a group of one or more people or entities for the purpose of coordinating and harmonizing that group toward accomplishing a goal.
Personality types	Often called brilliant and mercurial, with great charisma. Often seen as loners and private people. Comfortable taking risks, sometimes seemingly wild and crazy risks. Almost all leaders have high levels of imagination.	Tend to be rational, under-control problem solvers. Often focus on goals, structures, personnel, and availability of resources. Personalities lean toward persistence, strong will, analysis, and intelligence.
Orientation	People-oriented	Task-oriented
Focus	Leading people	Managing work
Outcomes	Achievements	Results
Approach to tasks	Simply look at problems and devise new, creative solutions. Using their charisma and commitment, they excite, motivate, and focus others to solve problems and excel.	Create strategies, policies, and methods to create teams and ideas that combine to operate smoothly. Empower people by soliciting their views, values, and principles.
Approach to risk	Risk-taking	Risk-averse
Role in decision-making	Facilitative	Involved
Styles	Transformational, consultative, and participative	Dictatorial, authoritative, transactional, autocratic, consultative, and democratic
Power through	Charisma and influence	Formal authority and position
Organization	Leaders have followers	Managers have subordinates
Appeal to	Heart	Head

All in all, according to Diffen.com (n.d.), managing and leading are two different ways of organizing people. While leadership is about setting and spearheading a new direction or vision for an organization, management is about controlling or directing subordinates and resources according to principles or values that have already been established. Also, whilst the leader uses passion and stirs emotions, the manager uses a formal, rational method.

PUSH-AND-PULL PHILOSOPHY

Another difference between leadership and management can be well understood by examining the push-versus-pull philosophy. While management uses the push philosophy, leadership uses the pull philosophy (see figure 1.1).

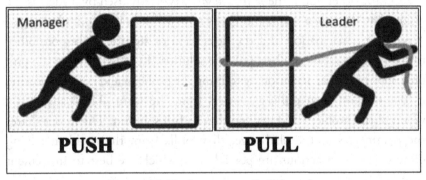

Figure 1.1. Push-versus-pull philosophy.

The *push philosophy*, typically used by management, is the classic vision of "I'm the boss, do what I tell you." It is directive, and it holds authority closely. The push philosophy sees a problem, creates a solution, and then pushes the action steps on to the team. There is little focus on coaching or development of the members of the team.

The push philosophy (Ingels 2014) drives the "how, who, and what" parts of the process. It does not tend to share the "why," as the framing of the problem and the needs of a solution remains with them. It also drives a solution and drives tasks to provide the solution. The team, in this scenario, executes the actions they are given without deep knowledge of the problem at hand or their role in providing a solution. Subordinates are kept on task in order to be productive.

This push philosophy can be very efficient. There is no interaction, and the team moves directly to task. The downside to the style is a lack of participation from those executing the task. Their understanding of the role and assistance in creating the solution is limited to the simple execution of their instructions. This means that the task is implemented quickly, but there is limited understanding and depth of the role. Those utilizing the push philosophy remain responsible to delegate 100 percent of the solution to their subordinate team members (Ingels 2014).

The push philosophy can also be very frustrating for those being managed under this style, as they are not participating in their roles, not being challenged to develop, and likely not clear on where they are truly adding value to part of a larger process (Ingels 2014).

On the other hand, the *pull philosophy* typically used by leaders is the vision that "We are a team, and here's how will we tackle our challenge." It requires participation and the delegation of significant responsibility to the team to create the best possible solution. Leaders utilizing the pull philosophy seek participation by framing the problem and communicating it to the team, then pulling answers from the team. The leader has a vision of the problem and may not have a full solution. The leader shares the parameters of the challenge, then pulls from the problem-solving discussion which actions are possible and which are best to implement (Ingels 2014).

The pull philosophy describes to the team the "why" of the problem, which drives the discussion of "who, how, and what." It drives participation, which requires the team to understand their roles and where they are expected to add value to the process (Ingels 2014).

The leader who uses the pull philosophy presents the problem(s) and asks for solution recommendations to the challenge presented. In other words, the leader (a) pulls from the resources and knowledge of the entire team, (b) shares experience and knowledge relevant to the challenge, and (c) guides and facilitates relevant discussion. Team members without the skill to participate effectively often struggle to retain focus and become frustrated and enter facilitation management and skills development. Suggestions are received and discussed by the leader and the implementation team. A viable option is reached, and the leader then works with the team to develop reasonable expectations and time targets (Ingels 2014).

THE SIMILARITIES BETWEEN LEADING AND MANAGEMENT

Leadership and management have similarities that cause people to confuse them as synonyms and interchangeable. Nderitu (2017) offered four similarities between leadership and management.

ROLES

Both leadership and management roles have one primary concern, and that is to allocate existing resources in a way that can be used efficiently. In addition, they both share the ultimate goals of maximizing profits and establishing a robust bottom line.

INFLUENCE

Both leadership and management roles involve influencing the work structure and environment. It is required that both the leader and the manager lead by example; thereby, both roles influence their followers and subordinates respectively to either perform well or poorly. Followers of the leader and subordinates of the manager operate or work according to their spirit.

VISION

Both leadership and management roles are anxious with achieving a goal—creating a plan and meeting deadlines to accomplish the goal. Each of them focuses and works toward a specific set vision of the organization.

WORKING RELATIONS

Both leadership and management roles involve working with people—leaders work with their followers, and managers work with their subordinates. In order to achieve the best working relationships with these people, they both have to strive to be ahead of them in order to determine the way forward.

SUMMARY

In *On Becoming a Leader*, Warren Bennis (1989) wrote extensively about the differences between the roles of leadership and management. These differences are outlined in table 1.2.

Table 1.2
Differences Between the Roles of
Leadership and Management

No.	Role of Manager	Role of Leader
1.	Administers	Innovates
2.	A copy	An original
3.	Maintains	Develops
4.	Relies on control	Inspires Trust
5.	Has a short-range view	Has a long-range perspective
6.	Asks how and when	Asks what and why
7.	Imitates	Originates
8.	Focuses on systems and structure	Focuses on people
9.	Is the classic soldier	Is his own person
10.	Accepts the status quo	Challenges the status quo
11.	Does things right	Does the right things
12.	Has their eyes on the bottom line	Has their eyes on the horizon

Note. Adapted from Warren Bennis's 1989 book, *On Becoming a Leader*.

REFLECTION PAPER ON PROFESSIONALISM, ETHICS, AND CONSULTING

Based on my previous knowledge and experience in consulting and that which I derived in the assigned readings for class, this reflective essay has afforded me the opportunity to engage with and clarify my consulting perspectives.

Block (2011) stated that "a consultant is a person in a position to have some influence over an individual, a group, or an organization but has no direct power to make changes or implement programs." (2). To be a successful consultant, one must have three kinds of skills: (a) technical, (b) interpersonal, and (c) consulting skills. In addition, the skill of identifying and verbalizing issues around trust, feelings, responsibility, and the needs of the consultant are an important dimension to consulting success (Block 2011). For some time, I had thought that my mechanical engineering skills would no longer be helpful in my burgeoning professional consulting career, but I have found out that I was wrong. Today, I am happy to learn that possessing a technical skill or expertise such as mechanical engineering is the foundation for success as a consultant.

Technical skills are important because "if we didn't have some expertise, then people wouldn't ask for our advice" (Block 2011, 5). In addition, interpersonal skills are also very important as they help the consultant interact and function with people (Block 2011). Interpersonal skills help the consultant to build and maintain relationship, and they also help consultants listen; articulate ideas; provide support; and disagree directly, respectfully, and reasonably (Block 2011). I have learned this skill from Carl Rogers's (1986) theories, and I believe that the quality of the relationship is the critical variable—and not what is said or done.

Consulting skills are important too because each consulting project—whether it lasts ten minutes or ten months—goes through five phases. Knowing that the steps in each phase are sequential and skipping one, or assuming it has been taken care of, can land the consultant in trouble (Block 2011).

To further develop the aforementioned qualities, the consultant must first strive to maintain an equal balance in the attention given to the content of the problem and the feelings about the interaction that is taking place when working with the client (Block 2011). In other words, you would "do what you say you would do," according to Kouzes and Posner (2002). Secondly, the consultant must become comfortable articulating how the relationship is going, and thirdly, they must grow more skillful in putting one's sense of the relationship into words to avoid triggering client defensiveness (Block 2011).

Furthermore, ethics are critically important in consulting, and a lack of ethics can put the consultant's reputation at risk (Greiner and Poulfelt 2010). One important ethical guideline I would adhere to is the need to be authentic—putting into words what I experience with the client (Block 2011) and doing what I say I am going to do (Kouzes and Posner 2002). Block (2011) asserted that "this is the most powerful thing you can do to have the leverage you are looking for and to build client commitment" (37). I would also make sure that my mission statements, vision, values, and strategy are fully aligned at all times. I would refrain from doing things to make short-term profits that could put my reputation at risk (Greiner and Poulfelt 2010).

Some professional and ethical behaviors I will be committing to gain leverage would include getting involved; sticking to the assigned role; reaching out for responsibility; doing whatever it takes to get the job done; being a team player; being observant, honest, and loyal; really listening to the client's needs; and taking pride in my work (Greiner and Poulfelt 2010).

Having had a chance to reflect on my consulting skills, I am confident that I have what it takes to be a successful and happy professional consultant.

REFERENCES

Bennis, W. (1989). *On Becoming a Leader* (1st ed.). Reading, MA: Addison-Wesley.

Bennis, W., and Nanus, B. (2004). *Leaders* (2nd ed.). New York, NY: HarperCollins.

Block, P. (2011). *Flawless Consulting: A Guide to Getting Your Expertise Used* (3rd ed.). San Francisco, CA: Pfeiffer.

Diffen. (n.d.). *Leadership versus Management*. Retrieved January 1, 2020, from https://www.diffen.com/difference/Leadership_vs_Management.

Drucker, P. F. (1996). "Leaders Are Doers." *Executive Excellence, 13* (4), 8.

Gardner, J. W. (1990). *On Leadership*. New York, NY: Free Press.

Greenleaf, R. K. (1970). *The Servant as Leader*. Indianapolis, IN: Robert K. Greenleaf Center.

Greiner, L., and Poulfelt, F. (Eds.). (2010). *Management Consulting Today and Tomorrow*. New York, NY: Routledge.

Hardy, Q. (1999, December 13). "All Carly, All the Time." *Forbes, 164* (14), 138–144. https://www.forbes.com/global/1999/1213/028_01.html.

Hoenig, C. (2000). *Leadership Development Center*. Retrieved from http://www.leadership.buffalo.edu.

Hollander, E. P. (1978). *Leadership Dynamics: A Practical Guide to Effective Relationships*. New York, NY: Free Press.

Keth. (2015, August 2). "Difference between Change Management and Change Leadership." *Difference Between*. Retrieved from https://www.differencebetween.com/difference-between-change-management-and-vs-change-leadership/.

Kouzes, J. M., and Posner, B. Z. (2002). *The Leadership Challenge* (3rd ed.). San Francisco, CA: Jossey-Bass.

Leadership Development Center. (2004). *Resources—Tips and Tricks*. State University of New York at Buffalo. Retrieved from http://www.leadership.buffalo.edu/tips1.shtml.

Lucas, P. J. (2003). *January 2003 Quotes*. Retrieved from http://www.cumarketing-strategies.com/tip_quote.htm.

Maxwell, J. C. (1998). *The 21 Irrefutable Laws of Leadership*. Nashville, TN: Thomas Nelson.

McNamara, C. (2003*). Common Terms, Levels and Roles in Management*. Retrieved from http://www.managementhelp.org/mgmnt/defntion.htm.

Nderitu, G. (2017, November 23). *Similarities between Leadership and Management*. Retrieved from https://www.knowswhy.com/similarities-between-leadership-and-management/.

Northouse, P. (2004). *Leadership Theories and Practice* (3rd ed.). Thousand Oaks, CA: Sage.

Rogers, C. (1986). "Carl Rogers on the Development of the Person-Centered Approach." *Person-Centered Review, 1*, 257–259. Retrieved from http://adpca.org/journal.

Stogdill, R. M. (1974). *Handbook of Leadership: A Survey of Theory and Research*. New York, NY: New York Press.

Surbhi, S. (2017, March 26). *Difference between Strategic Planning and Strategic Management*. Retrieved from https://keydifferences.com/difference-between-strategic-planning-and-strategic-management.html.

The Teal Trust. (1998). *Our Definition of Leadership*. Retrieved from http://www.teal.org.uk/Leadership/definition.htm.

Webster's. (2003). Leadership. *The New International Webster's Vest Pocket Dictionary*. Naples, FL: Trident Press International.

2

THE HISTORY OF LEADERSHIP

History has demonstrated that the most notable winners usually encountered heartbreaking obstacles before they triumphed. They won because they refused to become discouraged by their defeats.

—B. C. Forbes

Bertie Charles Forbes was a Scottish-born American financial journalist and author who founded *Forbes* magazine.

—*Chicago Tribune*

According to Ecoggins (2016), leadership has been a subject of interest since the dawn of humanity; however, leadership and management studies were taken up seriously in the early twentieth century. The core of these studies records myriad evolution in behavior studies of leadership from the traits of effective leaders to follower-centered leadership theories proposed in the late-twentieth century and early twenty-first century. The thought leaders of the core of the leadership studies have been Dr. Peter Northhouse and Dr. Gary Yukl and their respective publications *Leadership: Theory and Practice* and *Leadership in Organizations*.

Here are the pioneer thought leaders of leadership and management, as stated by Ecoggins (2016).

FREDERICK WINSLOW TAYLOR: SCIENTIFIC MANAGEMENT (1911)

In the early twentieth century, Frederick Winslow Taylor who was born in 1856 to a Quaker family in Germantown, Philadelphia, Pennsylvania, began the practice of scientific management. Though this is not a leadership theory as such, it made a change on how leaders and managers interacted with people at the workplace, especially in the production of a given product.

Taylor's work experience and informal education helped him recognize that one could get the most of their workers if labor works are broken into different parts and people trained to specialize in each part of the production process. Taylor then did time studies of each part of the production process in order to improve production to maximum efficiency.

In 1911, in *The Principles of Scientific Management,* Taylor summed up all his efficiency techniques. In 2001, the Fellows of the Academy of Management voted it the most influential management book of the twentieth century. Taylor also assumed there was only one form of leadership and believed that leaders were born, not made.

STOGDILL'S HANDBOOK OF LEADERSHIP: GREAT MAN AND TRAIT THEORY (1948)

In the early part of the twentieth century, leadership studies focused on trait theories, a leadership theory that stipulated that leaders are born, not made, and when crises arise, these leaders are able to step up to take their natural place. In other words, successful leaders have the inborn combination of characteristics that lead them to be effective leaders of organizations.

Ralph Stogdill identified a list of the ten best traits and skills of effective leaders through two meta-analytical surveys and wrote a paper in 1948, *Personal Factors Associated with Leadership: A Survey of the Literature, Journal of Psychology,* that cast doubt on trait theory. He concluded that no consistent set of traits differentiated leaders from non-leaders across a variety of situations. An individual with leadership traits who was a leader in one situation might not be a leader in another situation. Rather than being a quality that individuals possess; leadership is reconceptualized as a relationship between people in a social situation.

This leadership trait approach reinforces the notion that leadership is an art rather than a science, that people are born with those traits and that only great people possess them (Bass and Avolio 1994). According to Northouse (2004), this approach emphasizes certain personality traits that contribute to the leadership process, including intelligence, alertness, insight, responsibility, initiative, persistence, self-confidence, and sociability.

Trait theorists would argue that you can spot a potential leader just by their looks, manner, or education level. Trait theory assumes that leaders share certain physical, psychological, and sociological characteristics that determine their effectiveness.

The leadership trait approach emphasizes certain personality traits that contribute to the leadership process, including intelligence, alertness, insight, responsibility, initiative, persistence, self-confidence, and sociability (Northouse P. G. 2004). This approach further reinforces the notion that leadership is an art rather than a science, that people are born with those traits, and that only great people possess them (Jago 1982; Bass and Avolio 1994).

Use this approach if you have above average height and good looks, intelligence or charisma, and sociological characteristics that include education level or socioeconomic class. According to Darren (2007), John F. Kennedy was a very charismatic leader who, along with his wife, Jacqueline, turned the White House into a fairytale story. As a president, he also energized the nation and made the space program a national affair. With his vision, he set a goal that was reached and for which he will be eternally remembered.

KURT LEWIN: LEWIN'S LEADERSHIP STYLES (1939)

In 1939, Kurt Lewin, a German American psychologist, worked with colleagues Lippett and White to propose three leadership styles:

AUTOCRATIC LEADERSHIP

The leader of the organization makes all the decisions without consulting with members of the organization. Authoritarian leaders, also known as autocratic leaders, provide clear expectations for what needs to be done, when it should be done, and how it should be done. This style of leadership is strongly focused on both command by the leader and control of the followers. There is also a clear division between the leader and the members. Authoritarian leaders make decisions independently, with little or no input from the rest of the group (Lewin, Lippitt, and White 1939).

Researchers found that decision-making was less creative under authoritarian leadership. Lewin also concluded that it is harder to move from an authoritarian style to a democratic style than vice versa. Abuse of this method is usually viewed as controlling, bossy, and dictatorial (Lewin, Lippitt, and White 1939).

Authoritarian leadership is best applied to situations where there is little time for group decision-making or where the leader is the most knowledgeable member of the group. The autocratic approach can be a good one when the situation calls for rapid decisions and decisive actions. However, it tends to create dysfunctional and even hostile environments, often pitting followers against the domineering leader (Lewin, Lippitt, and White 1939).

PARTICIPATIVE LEADERSHIP

Also known as democratic leadership, the leader consults with members of the organization in the decision-making process. Lewin's study found that participative leadership, also known as democratic leadership, is typically the most effective leadership style (Lewin, Lippitt, and White 1939). Democratic leaders offer guidance to group members, but they also participate in the group and allow input from other group members. In Lewin's study, children in this group were less productive than the members of the authoritarian group, but their contributions were of a higher quality (Bass and Bass 2008).

Participative leaders encourage group members to participate, but they retain the final say in the decision-making process. Group members feel engaged in the process and are more motivated and creative. Democratic leaders tend to make followers feel like they are an important part of the team, which helps foster commitment to the goals of the group.

LAISSEZ-FAIRE LEADERSHIP

The leader plays little or no role in the decision-making process. Lewin found that children under delegative leadership, also known as laissez-faire leadership, were the least productive of all three groups (Lewin, Lippitt, and White 1939). The children in this group also made more demands on the leader, showed little cooperation, and were unable to work independently.

Delegative leaders offer little or no guidance to group members and leave the decision-making up to group members. While this style can be useful in situations involving highly qualified experts, it often leads to poorly defined roles and a lack of motivation.

Lewin noted that laissez-faire leadership tended to result in groups that lacked direction and members who blamed each other for mistakes, refused to accept personal responsibility, made less progress, and produced less work (Lewin, Lippitt, and White 1939).

In *The Bass Handbook of Leadership: Theory, Research, and Managerial Applications*, Bass and Bass note that authoritarian leadership is often presented solely in negative, often disapproving, terms (Bass and Bass 2008). Authoritarian leaders are often described as controlling and close-minded, yet this overlooks the potential positives of stressing rules, expecting obedience, and taking responsibility.

While authoritarian leadership certainly is not the best choice for every situation, it can be effective and beneficial in cases where followers need a great deal of direction and where rules and standards must be followed to the letter. Another often overlooked benefit of the authoritarian style is the ability to maintain a sense of order.

Bass and Bass note that democratic leadership tends to be centered on the followers and is an effective approach when trying to maintain relationships with others (Bass and Bass 2008). People who work under such leaders tend to get along well, support one another, and consult other members of the group when making decisions.

MAX WEBER: CHARISMATIC AUTHORITY (1930)

A German sociologist, Max Weber, was first to propose and describe Charismatic authority—the precursor to charismatic leadership theory—in *The Protestant Ethic and the Spirit of Capitalism*, which was originally published in 1930 (2012). Weber described charismatic leadership as comprising of a special personality characteristic that gives a person extraordinary powers that result in the person being treated as a leader from the very onset. Peter Northouse (2013) stated that "the personality characteristics of a charismatic leader include being dominant, having a strong desire to influence others, being self-confident, and having a strong sense of one's own moral values" (188).

The word *charisma* was first used to describe a special gift that certain individuals possess that gives them the capacity to do extraordinary things. Weber (1947) stated the most well-known definition of charisma as a special personality characteristic that gives the person superhuman or exceptional powers and is reserved for a few, is of divine origin, and results in the person being treated as a leader.

House (2019), in his theory of charismatic leadership, suggested that charismatic leaders act in unique ways that have specific charismatic effects on their follower, see table 2.1. For House, the personality characteristics of a charismatic leader include being dominant, having a strong desire to influence others, being self-confident, and having a strong sense of one's own moral values. In addition to displaying certain personality characteristics, charismatic leaders demonstrate specific types of behaviors. First, they are strong role models for the beliefs and values that want their followers to adopt. Second, charismatic leaders appear competent to followers. Third, they articulate ideological goals that have moral overtones. Martin Luther King Jr.'s famous "I Have a Dream" speech is an example of this type of charismatic behavior.

Fourth, charismatic leaders communicate high expectations for followers, and they exhibit confidence in followers' abilities to meet these expectations. According to Avolio and Gibbons, (1988), the impact of this behavior is to increase followers' sense of competence and self-efficacy, which in turn improves their performance. Fifth, charismatic leaders express confidence in themselves, and sixth, arouse motives by being driven to perform actions in order to maintain an optimum level of physiological arousal.

According to House's charismatic theory, several effects are the direct result of charismatic leadership. They include follower trust in the leader's ideology, similarity between the followers' beliefs and the leaders' beliefs, unquestioning acceptance of the leader, expression of affection toward the leader, follower obedience, identification with the leader, emotional involvement in the leader's goal, heightened goals for followers, and increased follower confidence in goal achievement. Consistent with Weber, House contends that these charismatic effects are more likely to occur in context in which followers feel distress because in stressful situations, followers look to leaders to deliver then from their difficulties (House R. 2019).

Table 2.1
Personality Characteristics, Behaviors, and Effects
on Followers of Charismatic Leadership

Personality Characteristics	Behaviors	Effects on Followers
Dominant	Is strong role model	Trust in leader's ideology
Desire to influence	Shows competence	Belief similarity between leader and follower
Self-confident	Articulates goals	Unquestioning acceptance
Strong moral values	Communicates high expectations	Affection toward leader
	Expresses confidence	Obedience
	Arouses motives	Identification with leader
		Emotional Involvement
		Heightened goals
		Increased confidence

MAX WEBER AND BERNARD BASS: TRANSACTIONAL LEADERSHIP (1947; 1981)

The transactional leadership theory was first developed by Max Weber and Bass later became part of a three-style model: transformational, transactional, and laissez-faire. Bass believed each leader exhibited a style along a continuum, and he later developed the Multifactor Leadership Questionnaire, or MLQ, to determine where leaders fell on this continuum (Management Study Guide (2020).

Oftentimes used by managers, transactional leadership involves motivating through a system of rewards and punishments. If a follower does what is desired, a reward follows, and if not, a punishment follows. Here, the exchange between leader and follower takes place to achieve routine performance goals.

ASSUMPTIONS OF TRANSACTIONAL THEORY

1. Employees are motivated by reward and punishment.
2. The followers have to obey the orders of the leader.
3. The followers are not self-motivated. They have to be closely monitored and controlled to get the work done from them.

For example, in the classroom, teachers are being transactional when they give students a grade for work completed. The exchange dimension of transactional leadership is very common and can be observed at many levels throughout all types of organizations. It is noteworthy to mention that while exchanges or transactions between leader and member are a natural component of employment contracts, research suggests that employees do not necessarily perceive transactional leaders as those most capable of creating trusting, mutually beneficial leader-member relationships (Notgrass 2014).

LeaderLite leaders can use this transactional leadership approach when you find you followers are not self-motivated and have to be closely monitored and controlled to get the work done. In addition, this approach works well when you want your followers obey your orders and when the only way to motivate them is by reward and punishment.

VICTOR VROOM: EXPECTANCY THEORY OF MOTIVATION (1968)

First proposed by Victor Vroom, (1964), the expectancy theory is a motivation theory says that individuals have different sets of goals and can be motivated if they have certain expectations. The expectancy theory of motivation explains why an individual chooses to act out a specific behavior as opposed to another.

According to Leadership-central.com (n.d.), this cognitive process evaluates the motivational force (MF) of the different behavioral options based on the individual's own perception of the probability of attaining his desired outcome. Thus, the motivational force can be summarized by the following equation:

MF = Expectancy X Instrumentality X $\sum$ (Valence(s))

Expectancy I. Expectancy refers to the "effort-performance" relation.

Instrumentality (I). Instrumentality refers to the "performance-reward" relation.

Valance (V). Valance is the value that the individual associates with the outcome (reward).

It is noteworthy to mention that since the motivational force is the multiplication of the expectancy by the instrumentality, it is then by the valence that any of the perception having a value of zero or the individual's feeling that "it's not going to happen" will result in a motivational force of zero (Tarver 2020).

As a LeaderLite leader, when applying the expectancy theory to your life, make sure you have the following three things: a goal you want, a plan that will grow your skill set and knowledge base, and the belief that if you execute your plan, you will achieve your desired outcome. A lot of people fail at motivating themselves before they even start because, oftentimes, the goal they are going after is not one they actually want. It is easy to get caught up in the trappings of life and setting goals that surround money and material things rather than experiences and fulfillment. If this is the case, and if you find you are often demotivated, it is time to go back to square one and figure out a goal or outcome that will invigorate you and get you to jump out of bed in the morning (Tarver 2020).

FRED FIEDLER: CONTINGENCY THEORY OF LEADERSHIP (1967)

The Taylorists' style of leadership, making your followers work as hard as they can, is not as efficient as optimizing the way the work is performed. This philosophy focused on the belief there was one best style of leadership—and that style fit all situations. On the other hand, Fred Fiedler in various works came to realize that the best leadership style was the one that best fit a given situation. This led Fiedler (1967) to propose the Contingency Theory of Leadership and the Least Preferred Coworker Scale to establish whether a particular manager-supervisor was a good match for their leadership assignment.

A contingency theory is an organizational theory that claims that there is no best way to organize a corporation, to lead a company, or to make decisions. Instead, the optimal course of action is contingent (dependent) upon the internal and external situation. A contingent leader effectively applies their own style of leadership to the right situation (Morgan 2006).

In *Images of Organization,* Gareth Morgan (Morgan 2006) summarized the main ideas underlying contingency:

- Organizations are open systems that need careful management to satisfy and balance internal needs and to adapt to environmental circumstances.
- There is not one best way of organizing. The appropriate form depends on the kind of task or environment one is dealing with.
- Management must be concerned, above all else, with achieving alignments and good fits.

- Different types or species of organizations are needed in different types of environments.

The Contingency Model (Autuum 1978) reports Fred Fiedler's contingency model focused on a contingency model of leadership in organizations. This model contains the relationship between leadership style and the favorableness of the situation. Fielder developed a metric to measure a leader's style called the Least Preferred Coworker. The test consists of sixteen to twenty-two items they are to rate on a scale of one to eight as they think of a coworker they had the most difficulty working with. A high score indicates the test taker is relational in style, and a low score indicates the test taker is more task orientated in style. Situational favorableness was described by Fiedler in terms of three empirically derived dimensions:

- Leader-member relationship—high if the leader is generally accepted and respected by followers.
- Degree of task structure—high if the task is very structured.
- Leader's position power—high if a great deal of authority and power are formally attributed to the leader's position.

Situations are favorable to the leader if all three of these dimensions are high.

William Richard Scott describes contingency theory in the following manner: "The best way to organize depends on the nature of the environment to which the organization must relate" (Scott 1981). The work of other researchers, including Paul R. Lawrence, Jay Lorsch, and James D. Thompson, complements this statement. They are more interested in the impact of contingency factors on organizational structure. Their structural contingency theory was the dominant paradigm of organizational structural theories for most of the 1970s. A major empirical test was furnished by Johannes M. Pennings who examined the interaction between environmental uncertainty, organization structure, and various aspects of performance. Pennings carried out an empirical study on a sample of retail brokerage offices in which aspects of their market environment such as competitiveness, change, and munificence versus organizational arrangements such as decision-making templates and power distribution were juxtaposed for possible implications for performance. While structural attributes of offices strongly impacted performance, the evidence for "contingency" was less pronounced (Pennings 1975).

It can be concluded that there is "no one best way" or approach in management or doing things; different situations call for different approaches to handle, manage, and solve the arising issue concerned (Friedberg 1997). Management and organization is an "open system" that embraces anomalies and challenges every now and then, which requires "adaptable" and "situational" solutions in order to overcome or solve the problems or issues concerned (Hai and Nawi 2012). Other situational or contingency factors are changes in customer demand for goods and services, change in government policy or law, change in environment or climate change, and so forth.

RENSIS LIKERT: PARTICIPATIVE LEADERSHIP (1967)

Rensis Likert (1967) and Gary Yukl (1971) were among the several scholars who proposed and highlighted the participative leadership approach. Likert invented the measurement device called the Likert scale, which is used to measure degrees of acceptance of a given premise. His theory of leadership styles included the following:

LIKERT LEADERSHIP STYLES

1. Exploitative authoritative. The leader shows little or no concern for the followers or their problems. This leader communicates in a demeaning, accusatory manner and makes all decisions without consultation with the followers.
2. Benevolent authoritative. The leader is more concerned with the followers and their problems. This leader rewards the followers for their quality performance but also makes all decisions alone.

3. Consultative. The leader makes a genuine effort to listen to the ideas of the followers, but decision-making processes are still centralized in the leader.
4. Participative. The leader also shows great concern for the followers, listens carefully to their ideas, and often includes their ideas into the decision-making process.

Rensis Likert was the director of the Institute of Social Sciences in Michigan. He conducted extensive research for three decades with the help of forty researchers to understand leadership behavior. His famous writings included *New Patterns of Management* (1961) and *Human Organization* (1967).

He was of the opinion that traditional job-oriented supervision was the cause of low productivity and low morale. He emphasized participative management in the field of decision-making. He has given a continuum of four systems of management (in his management system). Likert has taken seven variables of different management systems. These variables include (1) leadership, (2) motivation, (3) communication, (4) interaction influence, (5) decision-making process, (6) setting goals, and (7) the control process (Likert 1967). See table 2.1.

Table 2.1
Likert's Systems of Management Leadership

Leadership variable	System 1	System 2	System 3	System 4
Trust and confidence of subordinates.	Has no trust and confidence in subordinates.	Has condescending confidence and trust in subordinates, such as master has to a servant.	Substantial but not complete confidence and trust; still wishes to keep control of decisions.	Complete confidence and trust in all matters.
Subordinates' feelings of freedom.	Subordinates do not feel at all free to discuss things about the job with their superior.	Subordinates do not feel very free to discuss things about job with their superior.	Subordinates feel rather free to discuss things about the job with their superior.	Subordinates feel completely free to discuss things about the job with their superior.
Superior seeking involvement with Subordinates.	Seldom gets ideas and opinions of subordinates in solving job problems.	Sometimes gets ideas and opinions of subordinates in solving job problems.	Usually gets ideas and opinions and usually tries to make constructive use of them.	Always gets ideas and opinions and always tries to make constructive use of them.

GARY YUKL: PARTICIPATIVE LEADERSHIP (1971)

Gary Yukl (1971) described a participative leadership style to Rensis Likert, but he used different labels:

1. Autocratic. The leader makes all the decisions alone without any concern for or consultation with followers.
2. Consultation. The leader oftentimes asks for opinions and ideas from followers but makes all the decisions alone.
3. Joint Decision. The leader would ask for ideas from followers and oftentimes include them in the decision-making process.

4. Delegation. The leader oftentimes would give the followers the authority to make decisions on their own.

GEORGE GRAEN: LEADER-MEMBER EXCHANGE THEORY (1975)

In 1975 and 1976, several organizational behavioral scientists, including Dansereau, Graen, and Haga (1975); Graen and Cashman (1975); and Graen (1976) discussed the leader-member exchange theory (LMX). This theory is based on social exchange theory and focuses the quality of relationships and interactions between leaders and followers. These organizational researchers showed through those years that leaders tend to develop separate exchange relationships with each follower. They changed the idea that followers are a group and looked at followers as individuals. According to Graen and Uhl-Bien (1995), higher-quality exchanges between leaders and followers result in the following:

- less turnover
- more positive performance evaluations
- higher frequency of promotions
- greater organizational commitment
- more desirable work assignments
- better job attitudes
- more attention and support from the leader
- greater workplace participation
- faster career progress

PAUL HERSEY AND KEN BLANCHARD: SITUATIONAL LEADERSHIP (1969)

The situational leadership theory was first created in 1969 by Paul Hersey and Ken Blanchard as the "life cycle theory of leadership" and in the mid-1970s, it was renamed "situational leadership theory." This theory proposes that no single leadership style is good enough; instead, it all depends on the situation at hand and which type of leadership and strategies are best suited to the task (Hersey and Blanchard 1969).

It is the belief of the proponents of this theory that the most effective leaders are those who adapt their leadership styles to the situation and look at cues such as the type of task, the nature of the group, and other factors that might contribute to getting the job done in the workplace. The theory generated a four-quadrant configuration based upon the relevant amounts of directive and/or support needed to motivate a follower to accomplish a given task.

These four quadrants labeled according to the corresponding leadership style relate to each of the four sections of the model, a two-by-two matrix, using the highs and lows of two criteria, thereby giving four types of follower groups (Hersey and Blanchard 1969).

Furthermore, there are three notable features of the situational leadership model:

1. It focuses on followers rather than wider workplace circumstances.
2. It emphasizes that leaders should change their behaviors according to the type of followers.
3. Finally, it suggests a "continuum" or progression of leadership adaptation in response to the development of followers.

These points are explained in greater detail in the table below.

Table 2.2.
Interpretation of Hershey and Blanchard Basic Structure

Follower Situation	Leadership Style Emphasis	H and B Terminology	Quick Description	Continuum
Unable and Unwilling	High task-low relationship	Telling	Instruction, direction, autocratic	M1
Unable but Willing	High task-high relationship	Selling	Persuasion, encouragement, incentive	M2
Able but Unwilling	Low task-high relationship	Participating	Involvement, consultation, teamwork	M3
Able and Willing	Low task-low relationship	Delegating	Trust, empowerment, responsibility	M4

- Telling. This is used when the follower is at the least mature whereby the leader uses only directive words and no supportive behaviors to motivate the followers.
- Selling. This is when the leader uses both high-directive and high-supportive words and behaviors in their interactions with followers.
- Supporting. This is when the leader refrains from directive behaviors and focuses on supportive behaviors only. These followers work well on their own but lack self-confidence and may be overwhelmed with new tasks.
- Delegating. This is when the leader no longer needs to offer directives or supportive words and behaviors. These followers have matured to the place where they are competent and confident in the task and do not need anyone to look over their shoulders.

MARTIN EVANS AND ROBERT HOUSE: PATH-GOAL THEORY OF LEADERSHIP (1970, 1971)

Martin G. Evans (1970) and Robert J. House (1971) developed the path-goal leadership theory based on Victor Vroom's expectancy theory. The basic principles of path-goal theory are derived from expectancy theory, which suggests that employees will be motivated if they feel competent, if they think their efforts will be rewarded, and if they find the payoff for their work is valuable. A leader can help subordinates by selecting a style of leadership (directive, supportive, participative, or achievement-oriented) that provides what is missing for them in a particular work setting (Northouse 2004).

In other words, Path-goal theory emphasizes on the relationship between:

- leader's style
- follower's personality characteristics
- work environment or setting

Leaders can take a strong or limited approach in these. In clarifying the path, they may be directive or give vague hints. In removing roadblocks, they may scour the path or help the follower move the bigger blocks. In increasing rewards, they may give occasional encouragement or pave the way with gold, so to speak. This variation in approach will depend on the situation, including the follower's capability and motivation, the difficulty of the job, and other contextual factors.

House and Mitchell (1974) describe four styles of the path-goal leadership:

SUPPORTIVE LEADERSHIP

This style considers the needs of the follower, shows concern for their welfare, and creates a friendly working environment. This includes increasing the follower's self-esteem and making the job more interesting. This approach is best when the work is stressful, boring, or hazardous.

DIRECTIVE LEADERSHIP

Leaders who exhibit this style tell followers what needs to be done and give appropriate guidance. This includes giving them schedules of specific work to be done at specific times. Rewards may also be increased as needed and role ambiguity decreased by providing instructions. This method is appropriate when the task is unstructured and complex and the follower is inexperienced, increasing the follower's sense of security and control.

PARTICIPATIVE LEADERSHIP

This style involves consulting with followers and taking their ideas into account when making decisions and taking particular actions. This approach is best when the followers are expert, their advice is needed, and they expect to be able to give it.

ACHIEVEMENT-ORIENTED LEADERSHIP

These leaders set challenging goals, in work and in self-improvement, and often both together. High standards are demonstrated and expected. The leader shows faith in the capabilities of the follower to succeed. This approach is best when the task is complex.

ROBERT GREENLEAF, LARRY SPEARS: SERVANT LEADERSHIP (1970, 1995)

A set of essays published by Robert Greenleaf (1970; 1977) proposed a new type of leadership, *servant leadership,* which is focused on the follower instead of the leader. However, it was not until the middle of the 1990s that Greenleaf's ideas truly caught on when Larry Spears dissected Greenleaf's ideas. Spears picked after Greenleaf's writings ten proposed characteristics of servant leaders:

- listening
- empathy
- healing
- awareness
- persuasion
- conceptualization
- foresight
- stewardship
- commitment to the growth of the people
- building community

Since Spears outlined these characteristics in 1995, a host of leadership researchers suggested conceptual models that are similar to the servant leadership model. More ethical forms of leadership were discovered and promoted in the aftermath of repeated ethical failures within large brand-name organizations in the United States, including the Enron scandal in 2001, in the first decade of the twenty-first century.

JAMES MCGREGOR BURNS AND BERNARD BASS: TRANSFORMATIONAL LEADERSHIP (1978, 1985)

Transformational leadership was first described by James McGregor Burns (1978) in his important work *Leadership* in which he contrasts the characteristics of transformational leadership with transactional leadership. In *Leadership,* he contrasts the characteristics of transformational leadership with transactional leadership.

Transformational leadership is a leadership style in which the leader (a) identifies a needed change, (b) creates a vision to guide change through inspiration, and (c) executes the change with the commitment of the followers of the group. This leadership style was centered in the followers and motivates the followers to do more than was expected.

Bernard Bass (1985), in his publication *Leadership and Performance beyond Expectation*, expanded the work of James Burns (1978) and broke down the transformational leadership into four concepts:

1. Idealized Influence. This is when the leader acts like a role model of ethical behavior to gain the respect and the trust of the followers.
2. Inspirational Motivation. This is when the leader communicates high expectations and inspires the followers to reach higher than expected.
3. Intellectual Stimulation. This is when the followers are stimulated and encouraged to think outside the box and be creative and innovative in the work they do.
4. Individualized Consideration. This is when the followers are provided a helpful and supportive environment and the leader cares about the needs and desires of each follower.

BILL GEORGE: AUTHENTIC LEADERSHIP (2003)

The idea of authentic leadership has been around since the ancient Greek aphorism "know thyself" first appeared. However, it was not until 2003 that it became a popular leadership concept after Bill George described it as a leadership style that is consistent with a leader's personality and core values, and that is honest, ethical, and practical (2003; 2007).

In 2016, Bill George wrote that authentic leadership was intended as a wake-up call to the new generation to learn from negative examples like Enron, WorldCom, and Tyco, which led to the passage of the Sarbanes-Oxley Act of 2002. In it, authentic leaders are being called to be genuine, moral, and character-based leaders.

Authentic leadership is also defined as a pattern of leadership behavior that draws upon and promotes both positive psychological capacities and a positive ethical climate to foster greater self-awareness, an internalized moral perspective, balanced processing of information, and relational transparency on the part of leaders working with followers, fostering positive self-development (Walumbwa, Avolio, Gardner, Wernsing, and Peterson 2008).

George's model focuses on the different qualities an authentic leader has (or can develop). If a leader demonstrates these qualities or characteristics, they will be a more authentic leader and their followers will respond positively and the organization will benefit. There are five dimensions described by George, and each are associated with an observable characteristic: purpose and passion, values and behavior, relationships and connectedness, self-discipline and consistency, and heart and compassion (Penn State 2017). See figure 2.1.

Figure 2. Authentic leadership. Adapted from The
Secrets to Creating Lasting Value by Bill George.

Authentic leaders have a sense of purpose, and they know what they are about and where they are headed. Purpose manifests itself as passion. Passionate people are interested in what they are doing, are inspired and intrinsically motivated, and care about the work they are doing (Northouse P. G. 2019).

Secondly, authentic leaders have values, know what they are, and don't compromise on those values. This quality manifests itself through the leader's behavior, authentic leaders acting in accordance with their values (Northouse P. G. 2019).

Thirdly, authentic leaders build relationships with others and have connectedness with their followers. They are willing to share their experiences, listen to others' experiences, and are communicative with their followers (Northouse P. G. 2019).

The fourth dimension of authentic leadership is self-discipline, which gives leaders focus, determination, and the ability to focus on a goal and move forward toward that goal even in the face of setbacks (Northouse

2017). This is consistency. Self-disciplined leaders remain cool, calm, and consistent during stressful situations (Northouse P. G. 2019).

Finally, authentic leaders have heart, which shows in their compassion. They are sensitive to others' needs and are willing to help them (Northouse P. G. 2019).

Overall, as an authentic leader, your passion, behaviors, ability to connect, consistency, and compassion are all inspiring. Through these actions, authentic leaders are able to show that they do care about their jobs, the work, how to accomplish it, and how to keep their followers happy, productive, and focused. No matter how stressful or complicated the workplace situation, authentic leaders always cover the back of their followers, find the best approach to get the work done, and help their followers genuinely.

IMPLICIT LEADERSHIP THEORIES: DOV EDEN AND URI LEVIATAN (1975)

Eden and Leviatan (1975) were the first to propose the implicit leadership theories, ILT, and it was based on the notion of implicit theories of personality that describe the specific patterns and biases an individual uses when forming impressions based on a limited amount of initial information about an unfamiliar person.

Eden and Leviatan asked students to rate leadership behaviors in a hypothetical situation. After conducting a factor analysis, the four resulting factors—support, work facilitation, interaction facilitation, and goal emphasis—were the same as those found in prior studies by Halpin and Winer (1957) in which individuals rated their actual organizations' leaders. This finding indicated that a connection among leadership attributes was already in the participants' minds, independently of whom they were evaluating.

Epitropaki et al. (2013) later defined ILT as the cognitive structures or prototypes constituted by individuals' conceptions of the traits and behaviors that characterize a leader. ILT's relevance to leadership, according to Junker and van Dick (2014) relies on the premise that followers use these prototypes as a benchmark to categorize others as leaders. Epitropaki and Martin(2005) found that this categorization process influences followers' attitudes and behaviors toward leaders. Accordingly, individuals are categorized as leaders when their characteristics match with those of the perceiver's leadership prototype. Foti et al. (2017) summed up ILT as when a leader is closer to a follower's idealized image of a leader (i.e., the higher a leader's prototypicality), that leader will be evaluated more positively.

On other hand, Hanges, Braverman, and Rentsch (1991) believe that there are informal theories about leadership that reside within the thoughts of each and every individual. They are pet theories people devise based on their respective beliefs and assumptions about the characteristics of effective leadership. These implicit beliefs, convictions, and assumptions concerning attributes and behaviors help individuals distinguish between

- leaders and followers
- effective leaders and ineffective leaders
- moral leaders and evil leaders

House, Javidan, Hanges, and Dorfman (2002) and Gary Yukl (2010) explained that implicit theories are developed and refined over time as a result of the following:

- actual experience
- exposure to literature (books and other publications)
- other social-cultural influences

Moreover, they explain that these pet theories are influenced by

- individual beliefs, values, and personality traits
- shared beliefs and values about leaders in an organizational culture and a national or local culture

Finally, these implicit theories act to:

- constrain
- moderate
- guide the exercise of leadership

LEADERSHIP SKILLS APPROACH: ROBERT KATZ (1955)

The skills theory of leadership emerged as a prominent theory in 1955 when Robert Katz published his paper "Skills of an Effective Administrator" in the *Harvard Business Review*. Katz (1955) observed executives and identified three skill areas that the executives had in common and used on a regular basis: technical, human, and conceptual. Katz's approach was an attempt to address leadership as a set of developable skills by addressing leadership as a set of developable skills.

More recently, a revitalized interest in the skills approach has emerged. Beginning in the early 1990s, a multitude of studies have been published that contend that a leader's effectiveness depends on the leader's ability to solve complex organizational problems. This research has resulted in a comprehensive skill-based model of leadership that was advanced by Mumford and his colleagues (Mumford, Zaccaro, Harding, Jacobs, and Fleishman 2000; Yammarino 2000).

Our discussion of the skills approach is divided into two parts. First, we discuss the general ideas set forth by Katz regarding three basic administrative skills: technical, human, and conceptual. Second, we discuss the recent work of Mumford and colleagues that has resulted in a new skills-based model of organizational leadership.

THREE-SKILL APPROACH

Based on field research in administration and his own firsthand observations of executives in the workplace, Katz (1955, 34) suggested that effective administration (i.e., leadership) depends on three basic personal skills: technical, human, and conceptual. Katz argued that these skills are quite different from traits or qualities of leaders. Skills are what leaders can accomplish, whereas traits are who leaders are (i.e., their innate characteristics). Leadership skills are defined in this chapter as the ability to use one's knowledge and competencies to accomplish a set of goals or objectives. These leadership skills can be acquired, and leaders can be trained to develop them.

TECHNICAL SKILL

Technical skill is knowledge about and proficiency in a specific type of work or activity. It includes competencies in a specialized area, analytical ability, and the ability to use appropriate tools and techniques (Katz 1955). For example, in a computer software company, technical skill might include knowing software language and programming, the company's software products, and how to make these products function for clients. Similarly, in an accounting firm, technical skill might include understanding and having the ability to apply generally accepted accounting principles to a client's audit. In both these examples, technical skills involve a hands-on activity with a basic product or process within an organization.

Technical skills play an essential role in producing the actual products a company is designed to produce. As illustrated in Figure 3.1, technical skill is most important at lower and middle levels of management and less important in upper management. For leaders at the highest level, such as chief executive officers (CEOs), presidents, and senior officers, technical competencies are not as essential. Individuals at the top level depend on skilled subordinates to handle technical issues of the physical operation.

HUMAN SKILL

Human skill is knowledge about and the ability to work with people. It is quite different from technical skill, which has to do with working with things (Katz 1955). Human skills are "people skills." They are the abilities that help a leader work effectively with subordinates, peers, and superiors to accomplish the organization's goals. Human skills allow a leader to assist group members in working cooperatively as a group to achieve common goals. For Katz, it means being aware of one's own perspective on issues and, at the same time, being aware of the perspective of others. Leaders with human skills adapt their own ideas to those of others.

Furthermore, they create an atmosphere of trust where employees can feel comfortable and secure and where they can feel encouraged to become involved in the planning of things that will affect them. Being a leader with human skills means being sensitive to the needs and motivations of others and taking into account others' needs in one's decision-making. In short, human skill is the capacity to get along with others as you go about your work. In figure 3.1, human skills are important in all three levels of management. Although managers at lower levels may communicate with a far greater number of employees, human skills are equally important at middle and upper levels.

Figure 3.1 Management Skills Necessary at
Various Levels of an Organization

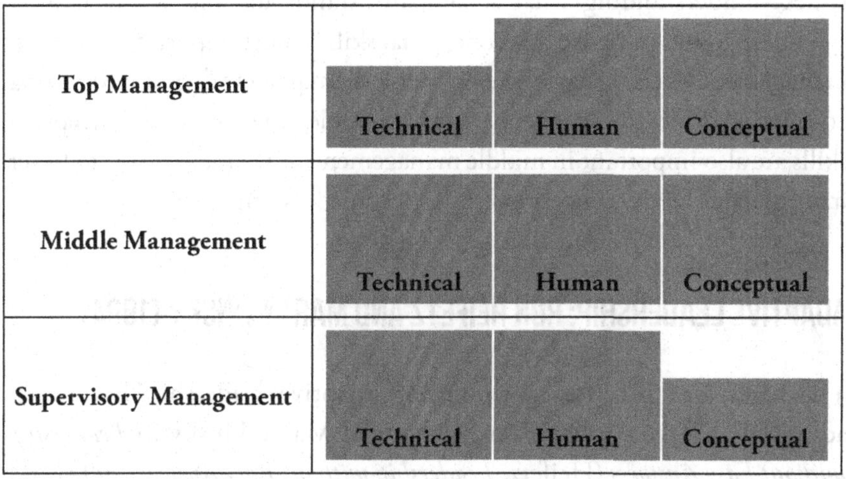

Top Management	Technical	Human	Conceptual
Middle Management	Technical	Human	Conceptual
Supervisory Management	Technical	Human	Conceptual

Source: Adapted from "Skills of an Effective Administrator," by R. L. Katz, 1955, *Harvard Business Review*, 33 (1), 33–42.

CONCEPTUAL SKILL

Broadly speaking, conceptual skills are the ability to work with ideas and concepts. Whereas technical skills deal with things and human skills deal with people, conceptual skills involve the ability to work with ideas. A leader with conceptual skills is comfortable talking about the ideas that shape an organization and the intricacies involved. He or she is good at putting the company's goals into words and can understand and express the economic principles that affect the company.

A leader with conceptual skills works easily with abstractions and hypothetical notions. Conceptual skills are central to creating a vision and strategic plan for an organization. For example, it would take conceptual skills for a CEO in a struggling manufacturing company to articulate a vision for a line of new products that would steer the company into profitability. Similarly, it would take conceptual skill for the director of a nonprofit health organization to create a strategic plan that could compete successfully with for-profit health organizations in a market with scarce resources.

The point of these examples is that conceptual skill has to do with the mental work of shaping the meaning of organizational or policy issues—understanding what a company stands for and where it is or should be going. In figure 3.1, conceptual skill is most important at the top management levels. In fact, when upper-level managers do not have strong conceptual skills, they can jeopardize the whole organization. Conceptual skills are also important in middle management; as we move down to lower management levels, conceptual skills become less important.

ADAPTIVE LEADERSHIP: RON HEIFETZ AND MARTY LINSKY (1994)

The ideas and practices surrounding adaptive leadership have been advanced in large part by Ron Heifetz and Marty Linsky in *Leadership without Easy Answers* (Heifetz, *Leadership without Easy Answers* 1994) and *Leadership on the Line* (Heifetz and Linsky 2017) and more recently with the help of Alexander Grashow in *The Practice of Adaptive Leadership*. These researchers, Heifetz et al. believe that leadership is, at its core, about influencing change that builds and enables the capacity of individuals and organizations to thrive. Specifically, that leadership is the practice of *mobilizing groups of people to tackle tough challenges and thrive.* The bottom line is that leaders need to understand the importance of *adaptation* and are able to employ the relevant processes and tools to build the adaptive capacity of organizations.

In other words, an adaptive leader will understand alternative perspectives and ideas and be able to share them with others by looking at the organization through the eyes of others. They have the ability to respond with empathy, allowing them to influence coworkers, competitors, and other stakeholders. According to Cru Leader Development, (2018) there are three signs that a leader might benefit from employing the adaptive leadership: (a) when there is a gap between your organization's aspirations and its current capabilities, (b) what worked before is not working any longer, (c) when it feels like the goal posts have moved and keep moving. The workplace can be a complex and uncertain environment, and it is the adaptive leadership that can offer very relevant, practical, and powerful tools and principles for leaders who are caught in such an environment.

FOUR MAIN PRINCIPLES OF ADAPTIVE LEADERSHIP

1. The Corporate Finance Institute (2020) states that there are the four main tenets tied to adaptive leadership.
2. Emotional intelligence is the ability to recognize your own feelings and those of other people. With this awareness, an adaptive leader is able to build trust with other participants and foster quality relationships.
3. Another fundamental principle of adaptive leadership is fostering a culture of honesty. Adaptive leaders know the best policies to introduce for the good of the organization. They also know the best ways to introduce these changes so that people embrace them. Adaptive leaders are willing to accommodate other people's views, hence, assuring them that they are valued and respected.
4. Adaptive leadership entails learning new things. If one technique is not yielding desired results, an adaptive leader goes out of his or her way to discover new strategies that can work. With new techniques, both the employees and the company at large will experience growth and development.

Adaptive leadership is about having a deep sense of character and being transparent and creative. Adaptive leaders may not always be right, but they earn the respect of those they work with and practice what they recommend.

Figure 3. Adaptive Leadership Model
Followership: Robert Kelley (1988)

Followers are people who will readily act when told what to do, but they depend heavily on leaders for guidance. They do not tend to be proactive. We often forget that people are neither leaders nor followers; they are leaders for the only reason that they have been followers before. In other words, every great leader was once a great follower (Hambrick 2020).

However, followership is not about the classic view of a "follower" as someone who mindlessly and blindly follows. Rather, followership is complementary to leadership, involving an equally important set of skills. According to a model developed by Dr. Robert Kelley (1988) of Carnegie Mellon University, "effective followers" are employees who not only engage in their work but who also use independent, critical thinking in their work roles. These employees are self-managed, committed to organizational goals, competent, brave, honest, and reliable.

Wigston (2019) argues that effective leadership in an organization is essential, but if teams are unable to carry out the vision, even the best leaders will not be able to meet their goals. This is why followership is a critical role that is often overlooked in an organization. While there are numerous resources dedicated to identifying potential leaders and grooming them to ascend in the organization, there is little written about followers. Organizations typically succeed or fail in part on the actions and behaviors of their followers. On the other hand, not all employees have the skills to be effective followers and for the same reason an individual in a position of leadership is not necessarily a good leader.

According to Wigston (2019), understanding the traits of a good follower will help all individuals play that role when necessary, and it will also help leaders cultivate good followership. The role of a follower is not a simple one. It doesn't just mean following directions or blindly accepting everything a leader says. Good followership is characterized by active participation in the pursuit of organizational goals. In many cases, this means working independently, being accountable for your actions, and taking ownership of necessary tasks. Regardless of the motivation, a good follower sees that their role is indeed essential, and good leaders should gain a clear understanding of the role of followers as well.

In order to understand the types of followers, a researcher, Kelley (1988) at *Harvard Business Review* developed a system for categorizing followers using two metrics, see figure 4: 1) active versus passive, and 2) independent critical thinking versus dependent uncritical thinking. Based on where an individual falls on each spectrum, there are five categories of followers: (a) *survivors* are the people right in the middle of the scale who are adept at surviving change, (b) *sheep* are passive people who do not think critically and do not have a strong sense of responsibility, (c) *yes people* are those who will readily act when told what to do but depend heavily on leaders for guidance, (d) *alienated followers* are the independent critical thinkers who are not proactive and are capable of effectively carrying out their roles, but there is often an undertone of dissatisfaction that prevents them from fully embracing their work and contributing to their fullest potential, and (e) *effective followers* are the independent critical thinkers who follow through enthusiastically and can succeed with or without leadership.

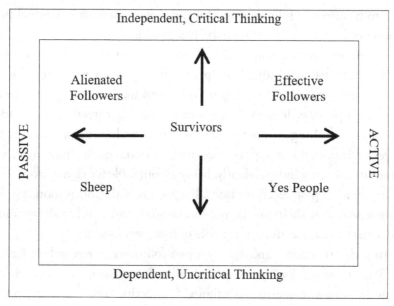

Figure 2.4. Robert Kelley Followership Model

Wigston (2019) believes that an organization with effective followers often performs well because employees are driven self-starters who are motivated to support organizational goals and have the critical thinking skills to do so. To develop effective followers, an organization must:

1. Understand leader and follower roles. Recognize that leaders need followers to carry out organizational initiatives and ensure that leaders understand that the role of a follower is just as important as their own. These roles can be conveyed through training and modeling behavior when leaders are acting in the role of follower.

2. Teach followership skills. Don't assume that people inherently know how to effectively follow. Teach them the necessary skills, such as accountability, self-management, and analytical thinking. This type of training can be done through coaching, mentoring, and experiential learning.

3. Include followership in performance evaluations. Employees need feedback to improve their followership skills, and evaluating these skills during performance reviews highlights the importance of the role. Most reviews focus on leadership, but if you also shine

a spotlight on followership, this will prompt employees to think about how they can also improve as followers.

4. Create a structure that supports followership. When creating teams, think about how you can incorporate the concept of followership. This might include creating small committees with no clear leader, rotating leadership positions on a team, delegating tasks to lower-level employees, or rewarding followers who take on an active role in a project and are vital to its success.

It is important to recognize that a follower is a role and not necessarily an individual. It is often the case that an employee who excels at followership is also an excellent leader. Identifying and cultivating followers is just as important as developing strong leaders and can even be the early stages of leadership development.

ETHICAL LEADERSHIP: GEORGES ENDERLE (1987)

Enderle (1987) started developing the ethical leadership concept by discussing several aspects of ethical leadership, including the specific tasks associated with being an ethical leader and being responsible for the effects of one's decisions on the people while seeking to implement corporate goals.

We cannot really discuss ethical leadership without looking first at ethics. Ask one hundred people—or one hundred philosophers, for that matter—what they mean by ethics, and you might get one hundred different answers. The struggle to define ethical behavior probably goes back to prehistory, and it serves as a cornerstone of both ancient Greek philosophy and most major world religions (Rabinowitz n.d.).

Ethical behavior, in its simplest terms, is knowing and doing what is right. The difficulty is in defining "right." Different individuals, different cultures, and different religions define it in different ways. The accepted treatment of women and attitudes toward slavery in different cultures and at different times in history provide prime examples of how what's "right" can vary (Rabinowitz n.d.).

Many people would define ethics and morality as identical, but it is helpful to view them somewhat differently. Ethics are based on a set of social norms and/or logically coherent philosophical principles; morality is based on a (usually broader) set of beliefs, religious and cultural values, and other principles that may or may not be logically coherent. Morality can, however, form the basis for an ethical system (Rabinowitz n.d.).

John Rawls (Rawls 1971), one of the most important ethical philosophers of the twentieth century, makes a distinction between comprehensive moral systems, such as religions, which cover not only behavior, but such issues as humanity's place in the universe, and less comprehensive systems, which cover the political, social, and/or economic spheres. Ethical leadership, at least for the purposes of this section, falls into the second category (Rabinowitz, n.d.).

Ethical leadership really has two elements. First, ethical leaders must act and make decisions ethically—as must ethical people in general. But, secondly, ethical leaders must also *lead* ethically in the ways they treat people in everyday interaction, in their attitudes, in the ways they encourage, and in the directions in which they steer their organizations or institutions or initiatives (Rabinowitz, n.d.).

Ethical leadership is both visible and invisible. The visible part is in the way the leader works with and treats others, in their behavior in public, and in their statements and actions. The invisible aspects of ethical leadership lie in the leader's character, decision-making processes, mindsets, values and principles, and courage to make ethical decisions in tough situations (Rabinowitz, n.d.).

Ethical leaders are ethical *all* the time—not just when someone's looking—and they're ethical *over* time, proving again and again that ethics are an integral part of the intellectual and philosophical framework they use to understand and relate to the world (Rabinowitz, n.d.).

Rabinowitz (n.d.) shows a few ways to practice ethical leadership:

- The ability to put aside your ego and personal interests for the sake of the cause you support, the organization you lead, the needs of the people you serve, and/or the greater good of the community or the world.
- The willingness to encourage and take seriously feedback, opinions different from your own, and challenges to your ideas and proposed actions.
- The encouragement of leadership in others.
- Making the consideration and discussion of ethics and ethical questions and issues part of the culture of the group, organization, or initiative.
- Maintaining and expanding the competence that you owe those who trust you to lead the organization in the right direction and by the best and most effective methods.
- Accepting responsibility and being accountable.
- Perhaps most important, understanding the power of leadership and using it well—sharing it as much as possible, never abusing it, and exercising it only when it will benefit the individuals or organization you work with, the community, or the society.

Rabinowitz (n.d) names three necessary characteristics of a useful ethical framework:

- Internal consistency. Each of its principles should fit with all the others rather than contradicting any of them.
- Proactivity. It should tell you what to do—not what not to do.
- Dynamism. It should be constantly reexamined and readjusted as your ethical thinking evolves.

Having such a foundation does not necessarily make you an ethical leader, but it helps your development as an ethical person, a necessary characteristic for an ethical leader. Your ethical framework should agree with that of the ethical framework, vision, and mission of the organization or initiative (Rabinowitz, n.d.).

If you do not buy into the ethical stance of the organization, you shouldn't take the job in the first place. An organization that is dedicated to collaborative decision-making and equal status as an ethical principle, for instance, can't be ethically led by someone who truly believes her ethical duty is to make decisions for everyone (Rabinowitz, n.d.).

An exception here is when you've been hired to change the ethical framework and/or the culture of the organization. This might happen if a previous director proved to be highly unethical—misusing funds, treating staff members abusively or with disrespect—and a major shift in the organizational climate is called for. In that case, you're expected to model and import a different set of ethical standards and assumptions in order to restore the integrity of the organization (Rabinowitz, n.d.).

An implication for ethical leadership here is that the vision and mission of the organization must be uppermost in any decision-making. An ethical leader does nothing to compromise the philosophy or the vision and mission of the organization. You should not, for example, accept funding that would require the organization to do something contrary to its best interests or ethical standards (e.g., use methods that it believes are ineffective or harmful) (Rabinowitz, n.d.).

An interesting ethical question arises when an organization is offered money by a funder whose philosophy or worldview is contrary to that of the organization (a corporate foundation whose parent corporation has an antigay stance, for instance, or mistreats its workers in some way). One way of looking at this situation is that it's simply unethical to take money from such a source. Another is that, as long as the funder doesn't require you to endorse or act on its unethical stance or behavior, it's better that the money goes to your organization than to one that does in fact support the funder's philosophy. Some would see this as taking money under false pretenses, others as using it well. The "right" answer here really depends on the ethical standards of the organization (Rabinowitz n.d.).

SPECIFIC COMPONENTS OF ETHICAL LEADERSHIP

Rabinowitz (n.d.) lists specific components of ethical leadership as follows:

1. Put the good of the organization and the general good before your own interests and ego.
2. Encourage the discussion of ethics in general and of the ethical choices involved in specific situations and decisions as an ongoing feature of the organizational culture.
3. Institutionalize ways for people to question your authority.
4. Don't take yourself too seriously.
5. Consider the consequences to others of your decisions—and look for ways to minimize harm.
6. Treat everyone with fairness, honesty, and respect all the time.
7. Treat other organizations in the same way you treat other people— with fairness, honesty, and respect.
8. Collaborate inside and outside the organization.
9. Communicate.
10. Work to become increasingly interpersonally competent.
11. Try to become culturally sensitive and culturally competent.
12. Work to be inclusive.
13. Take your leadership responsibility seriously—and be accountable for fulfilling it.
14. Constantly strive to increase your competence
15. Do not outstay your usefulness.
16. Never stop reexamining your ethics and your leadership

Leadership is a privilege and a responsibility that demands a good deal from those who practice it, whether formally or informally. High on that list of demands is the need to be ethical in both personal life and in leadership. Because leaders are role models whether they choose to be or not, they set the tone for the ethical stance of their individual followers, of the organization or group they lead, and, to some extent, of the larger community (Rabinowitz n.d.).

Ethical leadership requires from the leader a coherent ethical framework that will guide their decisions and actions all the time, not only in specific situations. Among the most important of the characteristics that define an ethical leader are openness and honesty; the willingness to make the discussion of ethical issues and decisions a regular part of the organizational or group conversation and culture; the urge to mentor others to lead; the drive to maintain and increase competence; the capacity to accept and seriously consider feedback, both positive and negative; the ability to put aside personal interest and ego in the interest of the cause or organization; the appropriate use of power, which is never abused or turned toward the leader's own ends; and consciousness of the human beings behind the labels of "opponent," "ally," "staff member," "participant," etc. (Rabinowitz n.d.).

Finally, and perhaps most important, an ethical leader never stops reexamining their own ethical assumptions and what it means to be an ethical leader. Like so many other important tasks, maintaining ethical leadership is ongoing; like only a few others, it can last a lifetime (Rabinowitz n.d.).

TEAM LEADERSHIP: FRANK M. J. LAFASTO AND CARL E. LARSON (1989)

Rather than focusing on ineffective teams, Larson and LaFasto (1989) looked in the opposite direction by interviewing excellent teams to gain insights as to what enables them to function to a high degree. They came away with the following conclusions:

- A clear elevating goal—they have a vision
- Results-driven structure—visions have a business goal
- Competent team members—with right number and mix of diversity
- Unified commitment—they are a team, not a group
- A collaborative climate—aligned toward a common purpose
- High standards of excellence—they have group norms
- Principled leadership—the central driver of excellence
- External support—they have adequate resources

In definition, team leadership refers to the leadership practices and values exhibited by leaders, governing a specific group of individuals who are working toward achieving a particular goal or objective. A team leader is someone who provides direction, instructions, and guidance to a group of individuals, who can also be known as a team, for the purpose of achieving a certain goal. An effective leader will know her team members' strengths, weaknesses, and motivations. Team leaders serve various roles in an organization. Their job is to get tasks done by using all of the resources available to them, including other employees or team members (Gigli 2014).

A team leader is someone who provides guidance, instruction, direction, and leadership to a group of individuals (the team) for the purpose of achieving a key result or group of aligned results. The team leader monitors the quantitative and qualitative achievements of the team and reports results to a manager (a manager may oversee multiple teams). The leader often works within the team, as a member, carrying out the same roles but with the additional "leader" responsibilities—as opposed to higher-level management, which often has a separate job role altogether (Thompson 2011).

In order for a team to function successfully, the team leader must also motivate the team to "use their knowledge and skills to achieve the shared goals." When a team leader motivates a team, group members can function in a goal-oriented manner. A "team leader" is also someone who has the capability to drive performance within a group of people. Team leaders utilize their expertise, their peers, influence, and/or creativeness to formulate an effective team (Thompson 2011).

While there are several team leadership models, Hill's team model is perhaps one of the best-known ones as it provides the leader or a designated team member with a mental road map to help diagnose team problems—and then take appropriate action to correct team problems (Northouse P. G. 2019). This team leadership model is built on a number of research projects:

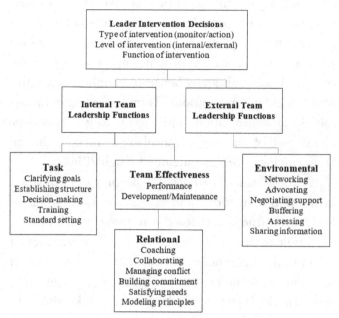

Figure 5. Hill's team leadership model: The four layers or steps in the team leadership model.

THE FOUR LAYERS OR STEPS IN THE TEAM LEADERSHIP MODEL

1. Top layer: Effective team performance begins with leader's mental model of the situation and then determining if the situation requires action or monitoring?
2. Second Layer: Is it at an internal or external leadership level?
3. Third layer: Is it a task, a relational, or an environmental intervention? Select a function depending on the type of intervention.
4. Bottom layer: Correctly performing the above three steps create high performance through development and maintenance functions.

BEHAVIORAL APPROACH: OHIO STATE UNIVERSITY STUDIES (1945)

House (2019) states that the behavioral approach leadership theory focuses exclusively on (a) what leaders do and (b) how they act. Thus, the behavioral approach in shifting the study of leadership to leader behaviors expanded the research of leadership to include the actions of leaders toward followers in various contexts. This distinguishes it from the trait approach, which emphasizes the personality characteristics of the leader, and the skills approach, which emphasizes the leaders' capabilities.

After Stogdill's (1948) findings pointing to the importance of considering more than leaders' traits in leadership research, a group of researchers at the Ohio State University who believed that the results of studying leadership as a personality trait seemed fruitless and decided to analyze how individuals acted when they were leading a group or an organization. In a nutshell, a new approach was needed, and the behavioral theory of leadership was born.

This analysis was conducted by having followers complete questionnaires about their leaders. On this questionnaire, followers had to identify the number of times their leaders engaged in certain types of behaviors. The original questionnaire used in these studies was constructed from a list of more than 1,800 items describing different aspects of leader behavior. Then a questionnaire of 150 questions was formulated from this long list of items, which then was called the Leader Behavior Description Questionnaire or LBDQ (Hemphill and Coons 1957). The LBDQ was given to hundreds of people in educational, military, and industrial settings, and the results showed that certain clusters of behaviors were typical of leaders. Six years later, Stogdill (1963) published a shortened version of the LBDQ, LBDQ-XII, which became the most widely used instrument in leadership research.

Mulholland (2019) writes that the Leaders Behavior Description Questionnaire (LBDQ) was the result of a study by Ohio State University in the 1940s. They gave the questionnaire to groups ranging from college students to administrators and private companies to military personnel. The goal is to find the common leadership behaviors. They found that two behavioral groups, in particular, were commonly related to effective leadership, these being *task-oriented* leaders and *people-oriented* leaders.

TASK-ORIENTED LEADERS

Task-oriented leaders are primarily concerned with the systems and structures that let their teams carry out their work. This includes everything from task descriptions to standard operating procedures, organizational and team structure, communication lines, and so on.

The key to remember here, according to Mulholland (2019), is that task-oriented leaders do not ignore their employees as humans. They're still concerned with motivating their team despite their primary focus being on systems. Task-oriented leaders exhibit the following behaviors: (a) initiating, (b) organizing, (c) clarifying, and (d) information gathering.

PEOPLE-ORIENTED LEADERS

The other group identified as a result of the LBDQ was people-oriented leaders. Unlike task-oriented leaders, this group puts more effort into seeing to the human needs of their team and motivating them through that. It is not that they do not focus on the task or system, but they put more time and behavioral focus on their teams as people with wants and needs (Mulholland 2019).

For example, let us say that your team is having a problem. Someone has not managed to get their work done on time. A *task-oriented* leader would dive into your processes to see if the problem could be prevented in the future or whether a standard operating procedure, SOP, was not followed properly. A *people-oriented* leader would behave differently, going straight to the employee and asking if there was any way they could help and what caused the problem (Mulholland 2019).

According to Mulholland (2019), people-oriented leaders exhibit the following behaviors: (a) encouraging, (b) observing, (c) listening, and (d) coaching and mentoring.

REFERENCES

Avolio, B. J., and Gibbons, T. C. (1988). Developing transformational leaders: A life span approach. In J. A. Conger, R. N. Kanungo, and Associates, *Charismatic leadership: The elusive factor in organizational effectiveness* (276–308). San Francisco, CA: Jossey-Bass.

Avolio, B. J., and Luthans, F. (2006). *The high impact leader: Authentic, resilient leadership that gets results and sustains growth.* New York, NY: McGraw-Hill.

Avolio, B. J., Gardner, W. L., and Walumbwa, F. O. (2007). *Authentic Leadership Questionnaire, ALQ.* Menlo Park, CA: Mind Garden.

Bass, B. M. (1985). *Leadership and performance beyond expectations.* New York, NY: The Free Press.

Bass, B. M., and Avolio, B. J. (1994). *Improving organizational effectiveness through transformational leadership.* Thousand Oaks, CA: Sage Publications.

Bass, B., and Bass, R. (2008). *The Bass handbook of leadership: Theory, research, and managerial applications* (4th ed.). New York, NY: Free Press.

Burns, J. M. (1978). *Leadership.* New York, NY: Harper and Row.

Cambridge Leadership Associates. (n.d.). *Adaptive Leadership.* Retrieved from Cambridge-Leadership.com: https://cambridge-leadership.com/adaptive-leadership/#:~:text=Adaptive%20Leadership%20is%20purposeful%20evolution%20in%20real%20time.,defining%twentiethe%20frontier%20of%20leadership%20training%20and%20development.

Clark, D. (2019). *What is path-goal theory?* Retrieved July 7, 2019, from Pathgoal.com: https://pathgoal.com/path-goal-theory/

Corporate Finance Institute. (2020). *Adaptive Leadership: The act of mobilizing a group of individuals to handle difficult challenges.* Retrieved from Corporatefinanceinstitute.com: https://corporatefinanceinstitute.com/resources/careers/soft-skills/adaptive-leadership/

Cru Leader Development. (2018). *Three signs that you might benefit from adaptive leadership.* Retrieved from Cruleaderdevelopment.com: https://www.cruleader-development.com/adaptive-leadership/

Dansereau, F., Graen, G., and Haga, W. (1975). A Vertical Dyad Linkage Approach to Leadership within Formal Organizations: A Longitudinal Investigation of the Role-Making Process. *Organizational Behavior and Human Performance, 13*, 46–78. doi:10.1016/0030-5073(75)90005-7

Darren, W. (2007). *A number of famous leaders and their different leadership styles.* Retrieved July 6 201, from Ezinearticles.com: https://ezinearticles.com/?A-Number-Of-Famous-Leaders-And-Their-Different-Leadership-Styles&id=815747

ecoggins. (2016, June 14). *Toughnickel.com.* Retrieved December 24, 2016, from The History of Leadership Studies and Evolution of Leadership Theories: https://toughnickel.com/business/The-History-of-Leadership-Studies-and-Evolution-of-Leadership-Theories

Eden, D., and Leviatan, U. (1975). Implicit leadership theory as a determinant of the factor structure underlying supervisory behavior scales. *Journal of Applied Psychology, 60,* 736–741. doi:10.1037/0021-9010.60.6.736

Enderle, G. (1987). Some Perspectives of Managerial Ethical Leadership. *Journal of Business Ethics, 6*(8), 657–663.

Epitropaki, O., and Martin, R. (2005). From ideal to real: a longitudinal study of the role of implicit leadership theories on leader-member exchanges and employee outcomes. *Journal of Applied Psychology, 90,* 659–676. doi:10.1037/0021-9010.90.4.659

Epitropaki, O., Sy, T., Martin, R., Tram-Quon, S., and Topakas, A. (2013). Implicit leadership and followership theories "in the wild": Taking stock of information-processing approaches to leadership and followership in organizational settings. *Leadership Quarterly, 24,* 858–881. doi:10.1016/j.leaqua.2013.10.005

Evans, M. G. (1970). The effects of supervisory behavior on the path-goal relationship. *Organizational Behavior and Human Performance, 5,* 277–298.

Fiedler, F. E. (1967). *A Theory of Leadership Effectiveness.* New York, NY: McGraw-Hill.

Foti, R. J., Hansbrough, T. K., Epitropaki, O., and Coyle, P. T. (2017). Dynamic viewpoints on implicit leadership and followership theories: approaches, findings, and future directions. *Leadership Quarterly, 28,* 261–267. doi:10.1016/j.leaqua.2017.02.004

Friedberg, E. (1997). *Local Orders. The Dynamics of Organized Action.* Greenwich, CT: JAI Press.

GAMA International Canada. (2004). *Coaching and leadership.* Retrieved from Mafac.org: http://www.mafac.org/CMP_Course_Outlines_Coaching_Leadership.html

George, B. (2003). *Authentic Leadership: Rediscovering the secrets to creating lasting value.* San Francisco, CA: Jossey-Bass.

George, B. (2007). *True north: Discover your Authentic Leadership.* San Francisco, CA: Jossey-Bass.

George, B. (2016, November 17). *What Does Authentic Leadership Really Mean?* Re trieved January 28 2020, from Huffpost.com: https://www.huffpost.com/ entry/what-does-authentic-leade_b_8581814?guccounter=1&guce_refer- rer=aHR0cHM6Ly93d3cuYmluuZy5jb20vc2VhcmNmNoP3E9d2hhdCtp- cythdXRoZW50aWMrbGVhZGVyc2hpcCUzRiZmb3JtPUVWER0VBUiZx- cz1QRiZjdmlkPTQ0MGU4OTdkZmE5ZjQxMDU5MDUwwZjMzMzMxN- mQ4MTAzJmNjP

Gigli, M. (2014, September 21). *What Is a Team Le–der? - Description, Role and Responsibilities.* Retrieved from Study.com: https://study.com/academy/lesson/ what-is-a-team-leader-description-role-responsibilities.html

Graen, G. (1976). Role making processes within complex organizations. In M. D. Dunnette, *Handbook in industrial and organizational psychology* (1201–1245). Chicago, IL: Rand McNally.

Graen, G., and Cashman, J. (1975). A role making model of leadership in formal organizations: A developmental approach. In J. G. Hunt, and L. L. Larson, *Leadership Frontiers.* Kent, OH: Kent State University Press.

Graen, G., and Uhl-Bien, M. (1995). *6*, 219–247.

Greenleaf, R. K. (1970). *The servant as leader.* South Orange, NJ: Robert K. Green- leaf Publishing Center.

Greenleaf, R. K. (1977). *Servant Leadership: A Journey Into the Nature of Legitimate Power and Greatness.* Mahwah, NJ: Paulist Press.

Hai, J. C., and Nawi, N. F. (2012). *Principles of Public Administration: Malaysian Perspectives.* Kuala Lumpur, Malaysia: Pearson Publishers.

Halpin, A. W., and Winer, B. J. (1957). A factorial study of the leader behavior de- scriptions. In R. M. Stogdill, and A. E. Coons, *Leader Behavior: Its Description and Measurement* (39–51). Columbus, OH: Ohio State University.

Hambrick, R. (2020, July 21). *The Side Of Leadership We Don't Talk About: Follow- ership.* Retrieved from Pinsight.com: https://www.pinsight.com/blog/the-side- of-leadershIe-dont-talk-about-followership/

Hanges, P. J., Braverman, E. P., and Rentsch, J. R. (1991). Changes in raters' per- ceptions of subordinates: A catastrophe model. *Journal of Applied Psychology, 76*, 878–888.

Heifetz, R. A. (1994). *Leadership without easy answers.* Boston, MA: Harvard Uni- versity Press.

Heifetz, R. A., and Linsky, M. (2017). *Leadership on the line, with a new preface: Staying alive through the dangers of change.* Boston, MA: Harvard Business Review Press.

Heifetz, R. A., Linsky, M., and Grashow, A. (2009). *The practice of Adaptive Leadership: Tools and tactics for changing your organization and the world.* Boston, MA: Harvard University Press.

Hersey, P., and Blanchard, K. H. (1969). *Management of organizational behavior— Utilizing human resources.* Upper Saddle River, New Jersey: Prentice Hall.

Hersey, P., and Blanchard, K. H. (1988). *Management of organizational behavior: Utilizing human resources* (5th ed.). Englewood Cliffs, NJ: Prentice Hall.

House, R. (2019). *Leadership: Theory and practice.* Thousand Oaks, CA: SAGE Publishing.

House, R. J. (1971). A path-goal theory of leader effectiveness. *Administrative Science Quarterly, 16,* 321–328.

House, R. J. (1971). A path-goal theory of leader effectiveness. *Administrative Science Quarterly, 16,* 321–328.

House, R. J., and Mitchell, R. R. (1974). Path-goal theory of leadership. *Journal of Contemporary business, 3,* 81–97.

House, R., Javidan, M., Hanges, P., and Dorfman, P. (2002). Understanding cultures and implicit leadership theories across the globe: an introduction to project GLOBE. *Journal of World Business, 37*(1), 3–10. doi:10.1016/S1090-9516(01)00069-4

Jago, A. G. (1982). Leadership: Perspectives in theory and research. *Management Science, 28*(3), 315–336.

Junker, N. M., and van Dick, R. (2014). Implicit theories in organizational settings: a systematic review and research agenda of implicit leadership and followership theories. *Leadership Quarterly, 25,* 1154–1173. doi:10.1016/j.leaqua.2014.09.002

Katz, R. L. (1955). Skills of an effective administrator. *Harvard Business Review.*

Katz, R. L. (1974). Skills of an effective administrator. *Harvard Business Review* (September-October 1974), 90–101.

Kelley, R. (1988, November). In Praise of Followers. *Harvard Business Review.* Retrieved from https://hbr.org/1988/11/in-praise-of-followers

Larson, C. E., and LaFasto, F. M. (1989). *Teamwork: What must go right/What can go wrong* (1st ed.). Thousand Oaks, CA: SAGE Publications.

Leadership-central.com. (n.d.). *Expectancy Theory of Motivation - Victor Vroom.* Retrieved from Leadership-central.com: https://www.leadership-central.com/expectancy-theory-of-motivation.html

Lewin, K., Lippitt, R., and White, K. (1939). Patterns of aggressive behavior in experimentally created "social climates." *Journal of Social Psychology, 10*(2), 271–301.

Likert, R. (1967). *The Human Organization* (1ˢᵗ ed.). Columbus, OH: McGraw-Hill Book. Retrieved from Yourarticlelibrary.com.

Likert, R. (1967). *The human organization: Its management and value.* New York, NY: McGraw-Hill Book.

Lombardo, C. (2019). *9 Bill Gates leadership style traits, skills, and qualities.* Retrieved from FutureofWorking: https://futureofworking.com/9-bill-gates-leadership-style-traits-skills-and-qualities/

Lord, R. G., and Maher, K. J. (1991). *Leadership and Information Processing: Linking Perceptions and Performance.* London, UK: Routledge.

Lord, R. G., Foti, R. J., and De Vader, C. L. (1984). A test of leadership categorization theory: internal structure, information processing, and leadership perceptions. *Organizational Behavior and Human Performance, 34,* 343–378. doi:10.1016/0030-5073(84)90043-6

Management Study Guide. (2020). *Transactional Leadership Theory.* Retrieved from Managementstudyguide.com: https://www.managementstudyguide.com/transactional-leadership.htm

Martin, J. (1995). On the quest to become a leader. Tribune Business Weekly, 6(31), 1. *Tribune Business Weekly, 6*(31), 1.

Morgan, G. (2006). *Images of organization* (Updated ed.). Thousand Oaks, CA: SAGE.

Mumford, M. D., Zaccaro, S., Harding, F. D., Jacobs, T., and Fleishman, E. A. (2000). Leadership skills for a changing world: Solving complex social problems. *Leadership Quarterly, 11*(1), 11–35.

Northouse, P. G. (2004). *Leadership theories and practice* (3ʳᵈ ed.). Thousand Oaks, CA: Sage Publications, Inc.

Northouse, P. G. (2004). *Leadership theories and practice* (3ʳᵈ ed.). Thousand Oaks, CA: Sage Publications, Inc.

Northouse, P. G. (2013). *Leadership: Theory and practice.* Thousand Oaks, CA: SAGE Publications.

Northouse, P. G. (2016). *Leadership: Theory and Practice* (7ᵗʰ ed.). Thousand Oaks, CA: SAGE Publications, Inc., CA: SAGE Publications, Inc.

Northouse, P. G. (2019). *Leadership: Theory and practice.* Thousand Oaks, CA: SAGE.

Notgrass, D. (2014). The relationship between followers perceived quality of relationship and preferred leadership style. *Leadership and Organization Development Journal, 35*(7), 605–621.

Penn State University. (2013). *Mark Zuckerberg and skills approach leadership theory*. Retrieved July 6, 2019, from Psu.edu: https://sites.psu.edu/leadership/2013/05/26/mark-zuckerberg-and-skills-approach-leadership-theory/

Pennings, J. M. (September 1975). The Relevance of the Structural-Contingency Model for Organizational Effectiveness. *Administrative Science Quarterly 20*(3), 393–410.

Penn State. (2013). *Steve Jobs and the Path-Goal mentality*. Retrieved July 7, 2019, from Penn State Leadership: https://sites.psu.edu/leadership/2013/05/29/steve-jobs-and-the-path-goal-mentality/

Rabinowitz, P. (n.d.). *Ethical Leadership*. Retrieved from Community Toolbox: https://ctb.ku.edu/en/table-of-contents/leadership/leadership-ideas/ethical-leadership/main

Rawls, J. (1971). *A Theory of Justice*. Cambridge, MA: Belknap Press of Harvard University Press.

Scott, W. R. (1981). *Organizations: Rational, Natural, and Open Systems*. Englewood, NJ: Prentice Hall Inc.

Spahr, P. (2014). What is transformational leadership? How new ideas produce impressive results. *Leadership Is Learned*. Retrieved November 16 2017, from https://online.stu.edu/transformational-leadership/

Spears, L. C. (2004). Practicing servant-leadership. *Leader To Leader 2004*(34), 7–11.

Tarver, E. (2020, February 28). *Vroom's Expectancy Theory of Motivation: Definition, Principles and Uses*. Retrieved from Evantarver.com: https://www.evantarver.com/expectancy-theory-of-motivation/

The Contingency Model. (Autuum 1978, Autuum). New Directions for Leadership Utilization. *Journal of Contemporary Business, 3*(4), 65–80.

Thompson, L. (2011). Making the team, Performance and Productivity: Team Performance Criteria and Threats to Productivity.

Vroom, V. H. (1964). *Work and motivation*. New York, NY: Wiley.

Walumbwa, F. O., Avolio, B. J., Gardner, W. L., Wernsing, T. S., and Peterson, S. J. (2008). Authentic Leadership: Development and Validation of a Theory-Based Measure. *Journal of Management, 34*(1), 89–126.

Weber, M. (1947). *The theory of social and economic organizations*. New York, NY: Free Press.

Weber, M. (2012). *The protestant ethic and the spirit of capitalism*. Scotts Valley, CA: CreateSpace Publishers.

Wigston, S. (2019). *Followership in Leadership: The role it plays*. Retrieved from Eaglesflight.com: https://www.eaglesflight.com/blog/the-critical-role-of-followership-in-leadership

Williams, D. K. (2017, January 3). 10 Influential American business leaders today. *Forbes*. Retrieved from https://www.forbes.com/sites/davidkwilliams/2017/01/03/top-10-list-americas-most-influential-business-leaders-today/#6e6338976e67

Yammarino, F. J. (2000). Leadership skills: Introduction and review. *Leadership Quarterly, 11*(1). doi:10.1016/S1048-9843(99)00040-5

Yukl, G. (1971). Organizational Behavior and Human Performance. *Volume 6, Issue 4, July 1971, 414–440, 6*(4), 414–440. doi:10.1016/0030-5073(71)90026-2

Yukl, G. (2010). *Leadership in organizations* (7th ed.). Upper Saddle River, NJ: Pearson.

CROSS-CULTURAL MODELS

The most important single ingredient in the formula of
success is knowing how to get along with people.
> —Theodore Roosevelt

Theodore Roosevelt Jr. was an American statesman,
politician, conservationist, naturalist, and writer who
served as the twenty-sixth president of the United States
from 1901 to 1909. He served as the twenty-fifth vice
president from March to September 1901 and as the
thirty-third governor of New York from 1899 to 1900.
> —Murray, Robert K; Blessing, Tim H (2004).

THE IMPORTANCE OF CROSS-CULTURAL LEADERSHIP THEORIES

In the wake of globalization of industrial organizations and increase
interdependencies among nations across the world, there is a loud
cry for better understanding of cultural influences on leadership and
organizational practices. Today, situations in the global workplace are
highly complex, constantly changing, and difficult to understand let alone
interpret. Moreover, leaders and managers of multinational organizations
are facing fierce and rapidly changing international competition (House R.
et al. 1991). Furthermore, McFarland, Senen, and Childress (1993) believe
the trend toward the global market is crystal clear—and the twenty-first
century may very well become known as the century of the "global world."

So far Geert Hofstede Cultural Model, and the GLOBE (Global Leadership and Organizational Behavior Effectiveness) are the topmost research studies that address the concept of national culture. Gunnell (2016) states that the GLOBE study extended Hofstede's study by adding new dimensions: (a) assertiveness, (b) human orientation, and (c) performance orientation. The GLOBE study also divided individualism versus collectivism into two variables: (a) in-group collectivism, and (b) institutional collectivism. GLOBE defined assertiveness as the "beliefs as to whether people are or should be encouraged to be assertive, aggressive, and tough, or nonassertive, nonaggressive, and tender in social relationships" (House et al. 2004, 395).

The GLOBE goals are both *etic* (investigating aspects of leadership and organizational practices that are comparable across cultures) and *emic* (examining and describing culture-specific differences in leadership and organizational practices and their effectiveness).

The success of international operations is contingent upon the effectiveness of the organizational leadership. However, the globalization of industrial organizations presents numerous organizational and leadership challenges. For example, the cultural diversity of employees found in worldwide multinational organizations presents a substantial challenge with respect to the design of multinational organizations and their leadership (Gunnell 2016).

It is thereby clear that cross-cultural research and the development of cross-cultural theory are needed to fill this knowledge gap. In other words, there are inherent limitations in transferring theories across cultures because what works in one culture may not necessarily work in another culture (House R. et al. 1991). The best that leadership researchers can do currently according to Triandis (1993) is to "fine-tune" theories by investigating cross-cultural issues in order to uncover new relationships by forcing investigators to include a much broader range of variables such as the importance of religion, language, ethnic background, history, or political systems often not considered in contemporary theories.

Table 1
Comparing GLOBE and Hofstede Models,
Shi and Wang (2011, 98) updated.

No.	Area	Hofstede	GLOBE
1.	Time Period	1967–1973	1994–present
2.	Number of primary researchers involved	1	170
3.	Type of respondents	Non managers, managers	Managers
4.	Number of organizations surveyed	1	951
5.	Types of Organizations	IBM and subsidiaries	Non-multinational
6.	Type of industries surveyed	Information technology	Food processing, financial, and telecommunication services
7.	Number of societies surveyed	72	62
8.	Analysis	Single effort	Team effort
9.	Project Design	Dutch-based	US-based
10.	Number of cultural dimensions	6	9

GEERT HOFSTEDE'S NATIONAL CULTURE

Geert Hofstede defines culture as the collective programming of the mind that distinguishes members of one group or category of people from others. He further wrote that national culture must be understood and respected because it cannot be changed (Hofstede's Insights n.d.).

DIMENSIONS OF NATIONAL CULTURE

From 1967 to 1973, while working at IBM as a psychologist, Geert Hofstede collected and analyzed data from more than 100,000 individuals from forty countries. From those results and later additions, Hofstede developed a model that identifies six primary dimensions to differentiate cultures.

According to Hofstede's Insights (n.d.), these six cultural dimensions only represent independent preferences for one state of affairs over the other, which distinguishes countries (rather than individuals) from each other. As humans and simultaneously unique, the country scores on the dimensions are relative and as such culture can only be used meaningfully by comparison. Here are the following six cultural dimensions of the Geert Hofstede Cultural Model:

POWER DISTANCE INDEX (PDI)

The Power Distance Index (PDI) focuses on the degree of equality, or inequality, between people in the country's society (Hofstede 2001). PDI conveys the extent to which the less powerful members of a society accept and expect that power is distributed unequally. When people in societies exhibit a large degree of PDI, it shows that these people do accept a hierarchical order in which there is a place for everyone, and no further justification is needed.

On the other hand, in societies with low PDI, people strive to equalize the distribution of power and demand justification for inequalities of power (Hofstede's Insights n.d.). See table 3.1.

Table 3.2
Basic Traits of High/Low Power Distance

High power distance	Low power distance
Power and authority are facts of life	Minimize social and class structures
Everyone has a specific place	No set hierarchy
Those in power emphasize position	Those in power minimize position
Respect for authority	Respect for individuality
Centralized authority	Decentralized authority

INDIVIDUALISM VERSUS COLLECTIVISM (IDV)

This is the degree to which the society reinforces individual or collective achievement and interpersonal relationships. Individualism is the high side of this dimension, and it is defined as a preference for a loosely knit social framework in which individuals are expected to take care of only themselves and their immediate families (Hofstede's Insights n.d.).

Collectivism, in contrast, portrays a preference for a tightly knit framework in society whereby individuals can expect their relatives or members of a particular ingroup to take care of them in exchange for unquestioning loyalty. People's self-image is defined in terms of "I" for individualism and "we" for collectivism (Hofstede's Insights n.d.).

MASCULINITY VERSUS FEMININITY (MAS)

The degree to which a society reinforces, or does not reinforce, the traditional masculine work role model of male achievement, control, and power is referred to as *masculinity versus femininity (MAS)*. The masculinity side of this dimension portrays a society that is more competitive at large, where the society emphasizes a preference for achievement, heroism, assertiveness, and material rewards for success.

On the other hand, the femininity side of this dimension portrays a society that is more consensus oriented at large, in which the society emphasizes a preference for cooperation, modesty, caring for the weak, and quality of life. Masculinity versus femininity in the business context is sometimes related to "tough versus tender" cultures (Hofstede's Insights n.d.).

UNCERTAINTY AVOIDANCE INDEX (UAI)

The degree to which the members of a society feel uncomfortable with uncertainty and ambiguity is referred to as the *uncertainty avoidance index (UAI)* dimension. The primary concern here is how a society deals with the fact that the future can never be known. Questions that arise include: Should we try to control the future or just let it happen?

Countries that exhibit strong UAI maintain rigid codes of belief and behavior and are intolerant of unorthodox behavior and ideas. On the other hand, countries with weak UAI societies maintain a more relaxed attitude in which practice counts more than principles (Hofstede's Insights n.d.).

LONG-TERM ORIENTATION VERSUS SHORT-TERM NORMATIVE ORIENTATION (LTO)

The degree the society maintains some links with its own past while dealing with the challenges of the present and the future is referred to as the *long-term orientation versus short-term normative orientation (LTO)* dimension. Different societies prioritize these two existential goals in various ways.

Societies that maintain time-honored traditions and norms while viewing societal change with suspicion are low on this dimension. On the other hand, societies that score high on this dimension take a more pragmatic approach. For example, they encourage thrift and efforts in modern education as a way to prepare for the future.

INDULGENCE VERSUS RESTRAINT (IVR)

A society that is referred to as *indulgent* allows relatively free gratification of basic and natural human drives related to enjoying life and having fun. On the other hand, a society that suppresses gratification of needs and regulates it by means of strict social norms are referred to as *restrained*.

THE GLOBE PROJECT

According to House et al. (1991), the GLOBE project is perhaps the most large-scale international management research project that has ever been undertaken, involving some 170 coinvestigators from sixty-two participating countries. Although Chhokar, Brodbeck, and House (2007) state there is no universally agreed-upon definition of culture among social scientists, House and Javidan (2014, 5) define culture as "shared motives, values, beliefs, identities, and interpretations or meanings of significant events that result from common experiences of members of collectives and are transmitted across age generations."

There are three major constructs of interest in GLOBE: (a) culture, (b) organizational practices and values, and (c) leadership (Chhokar, Brodbeck, and House 2007).

GLOBE is a research program comprising of a network of about 170 social scientists and management scholars from about sixty-one cultures across the world. Its primary goal is to study the interrelationships between societal culture, organizational culture and practices, and organizational leadership. Its ultimate or long-term goal is to develop an empirically based theory to describe, understand, and predict the impact of cultural differences on leadership and organizational styles and the effectiveness of these styles (House R. et al. 1991).

One difference between GLOBE and Hofstede's cultural model is while the former is a combination of quantitative and qualitative data, the latter is solely of quantitative data. In addition, GLOBE has proven that leadership is culturally contingent to a large extent and demonstrated that what is expected of leaders, what leaders may and may not do, and the status and influence bestowed on leaders vary considerably as a result of the cultural forces in the countries or regions in which the leaders function. For example, while the Americans, Arabs, Asians, English, Eastern Europeans, French, Germans, Latin Americans, and Russians tend to glorify the concept of leadership and consider it reasonable to discuss leadership in the context of both the political and the organizational arenas, the people of the Netherlands and Scandinavia often have distinctly different views of leadership (House R. et al. 1991).

Interviews with managers from different countries across the globe conducted by House et al (1991) show that Americans appreciate two kinds of leaders. There are some who seek empowerment from leaders who grant autonomy and delegate authority to subordinates. There are others who respect the bold, forceful, confident, and risk-taking leaders, as personified by John Wayne. On the other hand, the Dutch place emphasis on egalitarianism and are skeptical about the value of leadership. For the Dutch people, terms like *leader* and *manager* carry a stigma. For example, if a father is employed as a manager, the children will not admit it to their schoolmates.

House, et al. (1991) also found that Arabs do worship their leaders—as long as they are in power—and the Iranians seek power and strength in their leaders. They also found out that while the Malaysians expect their leaders to behave in a manner that is humble, modest, and dignified, the French appreciate two kinds of leaders: the de Gaulle, strong, charismatic leader and Mitterrand, the consensus builder, coalition former, and effective negotiator.

REFERENCES

Chhokar, J., Brodbeck, F. C., and House, R. J. (2007). Culture. In J. Chhokar, F. C. Brodbeck, and R. J. House, *Culture and leadership across the world: The GLOBE book on in-depth studies of 25 societies* (3). Mahwah, NJ: Lawrence Erlbaum Associates, Publishers.

Hofstede, G. (2001). *Culture's consequences, comparing values, behaviors, institutions, and organizations across nations.* Thousand Oaks, CA: SAGE.

Hofstede's Insights. (n.d.). *National Culture.* Retrieved from Hofstede's Insights: https://www.hofstede-insights.com/models/national-culture/

House, R. J., Hanges, P. J., Javidan, M., Dorfman, P. W., and Gupta, V. (2004). In R. J. House, P. J. Hanges, M. Javidan, P. W. Dorfman, and V. Gupta, *Culture, leadership, and organizations: The GLOBE study of 62 societies.* Thousand Oaks, CA: Sage Publications.

House, R., Hanges, P., Ruiz-Quintanilla, S., Dorfman, P., Falkus, S., and Ashkanasy, N. (1991). Cultural influences on leadership and organizations: Project GLOBE. *Advances in Global Leadership.*

McFarland, L. J., Senen, S., and Childress, J. R. (1993). *Twenty-first-century leadership.* New York, NY: Leadership Press.

Triandis, H. C. (1993). The contingency model in cross-cultural perspective. In R. Ayman, and M. M. Chemers, *Leadership theory and research: Perspectives and directions* (167–188). San Diego, CA: Academic Press.

GLOBALIZATION: WHAT IT IS—CRITICISM, COMPLIMENTS, AND ITS IMPACT ON LEADERSHIP

> We need to promote greater tolerance and understanding among the peoples of the world. Nothing can be more dangerous to our efforts to build peace and development than a world divided along religious, ethnic, or cultural lines.
>
> —Kofi Annan

> Kofi Atta Annan was a Ghanaian diplomat who served as the seventh secretary-general of the United Nations from January 1997 to December 2006. Annan and the UN were the corecipients of the 2001 Nobel Peace Prize.
>
> —NobelPeace.org

We need to promote greater tolerance and understanding among the peoples of the world. Nothing can be more dangerous to our efforts to build peace and development than a world divided along religious, ethnic, or cultural lines. In each nation, and among all nations, we must work to promote unity based on our shared humanity.

Globalization for all that we know has come to stay. We may like it or not, but there is nothing we can do about it. We have three choices of attitude toward globalization. First, we can choose to embrace it, and it will take us globally to places where all can live as one with one global economy whereby, we will learn to love one another, and be helpful and supportive of each other. Second, we can reject it and fight it, and at some point in time, we will become exhausted and give up because globalization is a force for good that we cannot interfere with. Lastly, we can choose to do nothing, and it will come crushing down on us ruthlessly.

WHAT IS GLOBALIZATION?

To begin, let us look at what globalization really is, what critics say, and how it impacts society today. The Levin Institute (2016) defines globalization as a process of interaction and integration among the people, companies, and governments of different nations. This process is driven by international trade and investment and aided by information technology, and it has effects on the environment, on culture, on political systems, on economic development and prosperity, and on human physical well-being in societies around the world.

Steve Jones (2019) defines globalization as the removal of barriers to trade, communication, and cultural exchange. The major intent behind globalization is that such worldwide openness will promote the inherent wealth of all nations, something that is still debatable today. It is noteworthy to mention that the United States has been a leader in globalization since World War II, but it was not until the North American Free Trade Agreement (NAFTA) debates in 1993 that most Americans began paying attention to globalization (Jones 2019).

For all that we might believe, globalization is not new, according to The Levin Institute (2016). For thousands of years, people and later corporations have been buying from and selling to each other in lands at great distances, such as through the famed Silk Road across Central Asia that connected China and Europe during the Middle Ages. Likewise, for centuries, people and corporations have invested in enterprises in other countries. In fact, many of the features of the current wave of globalization are similar to those prevailing before the outbreak of the First World War in 1914.

CRITICISM OF GLOBALIZATION

Moisés Naím (2019) states that critics of globalization believe that globalization is the cause of today's financial collapse, growing inequality, unfair trade, and insecurity. Other opponents of globalization, according to the Levin Institute (2016) claim that globalization has created an unconstrained international free market that is benefiting multinational corporations in the Western world at the expense of local enterprises, local cultures, and common people in developing countries.

This is so true, Lisa Smith (2018) states, because cheaper labor overseas enables multinational corporations to build production facilities in locations where labor and health care costs are low and then sell the finished goods in locations where wages are high—benefiting the business leaders and members of the economic elite. In addition, net profits soar due to the greatly reduced wages for workers, and Wall Street rewards the big-profit gains with higher stock prices.

The CEOs of global companies are not left out; they also get credit for the profits, and they are rewarded with generous compensation packages in which company stock and stock options figure prominently. Institutional investors and wealthy individuals also take home the big gains when stock prices increase, leaving the poor and disadvantaged with little or nothing to gain.

Similarly, Lisa Smith (2018) argues that globalization is weakening national sovereignty and allows rich nations to ship domestic jobs overseas, where labor is much cheaper, leaving the workers of the rich nations having to compete for jobs that stretch far beyond the immediate area in a global marketplace. Workers in these rich nations must compete with job applicants from around the world, and most times, they are left at the mercy of cheap labor from technology call centers in India to automobile manufacturing plants in China.

Finally, for other critics, globalization means Americanization. It is an American project aimed at expanding American economic, military, and cultural dominance across the globe (Naím 2019).

COMPLIMENTS OF GLOBALIZATION

The Levin Institute (2016) found in their research that technology has been one principal driver of globalization, transforming economic life dramatically and globally, giving consumers, investors, and businesses valuable new tools for identifying and pursuing economic opportunities. In addition, policy developments among nations of the past few decades have incited increases in cross-border trade, investment, and migration so large that many observers believe the global world will become economically developed soon. For example, since 1950, the volume of world trade has increased by twenty times—and from just 1997 to 1999, flows of foreign investment nearly doubled, from $468 billion to $827 billion.

Naím (2019) who agrees with the impact of technology, wrote that the internet access has reached the most remote corners of the globe, transforming the lives of more people, in more places, more cheaply than ever before, accelerating the pace of change faster than we can hope to account for it.

Certainly, globalization has resulted in loss of jobs in the developed countries, but it has brought employment and technology to developing countries, helping those populations move toward industrialization and the possibility of increased standards of living. In fact, it has helped provide solutions to today's financial collapse, growing inequality, unfair trade, and insecurity (Naím 2019). In other words, globalization allows poor countries and their citizens to have access to employment, to raise their standards of living, and to develop economically.

Retailers in developed countries, where shopping has become an ingrained part of the culture, are now able to sell clothing, cars, and other goods at reduced rates because these commodities are made in foreign countries with low wages. Net-profit margins of these companies have increased substantially as a result. In addition, shoppers who buy these goods save money due to lower prices. Not only do the CEOs and the multinational corporations gain from the stock market due to globalization, the lower-income workers also enjoy some of the benefits of stock price appreciation. Workers, especially in developed countries, who have mutual funds holdings, particularly in their 401(k) plans get rewarded with rising share prices, mutual funds because those shares also increase in value (Smith 2018).

All in all, globalization is a double-edged sword, and it comes with both gains and losses—depending on which side you look at it from. What is not debatable is that though it is such a diverse, broad-based, and potent force for good or bad, globalization is here to stay. What you do about it to make it work for you is the question for all humankind.

IMPACT OF GLOBALIZATION ON LEADERSHIP

A new kind of corporate leader has been created as a result of globalization—a leader who can deal with complex intellectual and technical issues on one hand, while also being sensitive to cultural differences and local needs on the other (Greiner and Poulfelt 2010). Global leadership—LeaderLite—is necessary to provide this new type of leadership. According to Annan (2008), "Globalization is affecting every entity in the world in many ways" (92) and thus, leaders must to adapt to this environment quickly. There is no longer such a thing as leaders. Now, we have what are called global leaders, which Mendenhall (2008) defined as:

> individuals who effect significant positive change in organizations by building communities through the development of trust and the arrangement of organizational structures and processes in a context involving multiple cross-boundary stakeholders, multiple sources of external cross-boundary authority, and multiple cultures under conditions of temporal, geographical and cultural complexity (17).

Meanwhile, von Emmel (2013) argues global leaders as individuals with "competencies and skills necessary to facilitate change in a demanding, rapidly moving, complex system" (1).

Today, the workplace in this global world is hungry and thirsty for this new kind of leadership because organizations cannot get very far in accomplishing their goals without them. People who work as employees are the most important puzzle piece in the organization. Knowing how to motivate them to perform the best work they can do to help the organization reach its objectives becomes a significant part of leading and managing them. Knowing when to motivate them is even more significant. There is a delicate balance of knowing how to motivate them and knowing when to intervene to keep them motivated and when to let them fly on their own (Daviault and Campbell 2017).

However, motivating people to perform their best in the workplace is not an easy task because people are different and unique in nature—even within same culture. In addition, in the wake of globalization, this act of motivating people in the workplace has become even more complex due to the several dimensions involved, including the psychological, physiological, geographical, geopolitical, anthropological, and sociological effects of globalization (Daviault and Campbell 2017).

To date, no research shows whether globalization has or has not helped women, people of color, or foreign-born leaders to rise to the top executive role of Fortune 500 companies. There is very little movement of women and other minorities making up these high-ranking positions as company leaders. Research shows that leadership roles can be even more challenging for women, people of color, and foreign-born leaders and managers because traditional notions of leading and managing are largely derived from a White, usually urban, male context.

Dhiraj (2019) states that out of the five hundred companies that make up the 2019 Fortune 500 list, thirty-three have female CEOs, a remarkable increase from twenty-four women CEOs on the 2018 list, but the bad news is there are no Latina or African American women in charge of Fortune 500 companies. For some reason, Black CEOs in Fortune 500 companies are now down from four in 2017 to three, continuing a downward trend among the Fortune 500 (Donnelly 2018).

On the other hand, there are currently eleven Fortune 500 Latino CEOs (Reiss 2018) and only five Asian CEOs leading Fortune 500 companies (Reiss 2018). Surprisingly, 45 percent of Fortune 500 companies were founded by immigrants or their children, including tech heavy hitters like Amazon, Apple, Tesla, and Google's parent company Alphabet (Luce 2019).

REFERENCES

Annan, B. (2008). *Immigrants in US: Insights, Views, and Approaches.* Los Angeles, CA: Sharp Image.

Daviault, C., and Campbell, C. (2017). *Leading and managing people.* Retrieved November 5 2017, from https://oeru.org/oeru-partners/oer-foundation/leading-and-managing-people/

Dhiraj, A. B. (2019, July 26). Women CEOs In The Fortune 500 Are At A Record High. Retrieved from https://ceoworld.biz/2019/07/26/women-ceos-in-the-fortune-500-are-at-a-record-high/

Diversity Best Practices. (2019). 5 Asian CEOs to Know. Retrieved from https://www.diversitybestpractices.com/5-asian-ceos-to-know

Donnelly, G. (2018, February 28). The Number of Black CEOs at Fortune 500 Companies Is at Its Lowest Since 2002. *Fortune.* Retrieved from https://fortune.com/2018/02/28/black-history-month-black-ceos-fortune-500/

Greiner, L., and Poulfelt, F. (Eds.). (2010). *Management consulting today and tomorrow.* New York, NY: Routledge.

Jones, S. (2019, July 3). *What Is Globalization? The U.S. has supported globalization for decades.* Retrieved from ThoughtCo: https://www.thoughtco.com/what-is-globalization-3310370

Luce, I. D. (2019, August 5). There's a record number of immigrant-founded companies on the Fortune 500, despite Trump-era policies. Retrieved from https://www.businessinsider.com/immigrants-have-a-huge-role-in-founding-american-startups-2019-8

Mendenhall, M. E. (2008). Leadership and the birth of global leadership. In M. E. Mendenhall, J. S. Osland, A. Bird, G. R. Oddou, and M. L. Maznevski, *Global leadership 2e: Research, practice, and development* (1–17). New York, NY: Routledge.

Naím, M. (2019). Think Again: Globalization. *Foreign Policy* (March/April).

Pixel, H. (2019). *Organizational behavior.* Retrieved from howlingpixel.com: https://howlingpixel.com/i-en/Organizational_behavior

Reiss, R. (2018, February 27). Latino CEOs Share Insights On Business Success. Retrieved from https://www.forbes.com/sites/robertreiss/2018/02/27/latino-ceos-share-insights-on-business-success/#5dfaf3d62264

Smith, L. (2018, November 2). Globalization: Progress Or Profiteering? Retrieved from https://www.investopedia.com/articles/07/globalization.asp

The Levin Institute. (2016). *Globalization 101.* New York: State University of New York. Retrieved June 26 2019, from http://www.globalization101.org/what-is-globalization/

von Emmel, T. (2013). *Leading across cultures and differences.* Retrieved from vonemmel.com: http://vonemmel.com/global-leadership-development/

5

LITE LEADERSHIP: THEORY AND PRACTICE

I believe that any leadership system that is short in
attending to these three components—body, mind, and
spirit—will be inadequate and will be unable to provide
good service to mankind.

—Bennett Annan

Bennett Annan is the founder and president of the
Institute of African Leadership, IoFAL. He is a mechanical
engineer, manufacturing and quality engineer, business
manager, counselor, professor, professional consultant,
author, and researcher.

— iofal.org (n.d.)

A new kind of global leader—one who is holistic (body, mind, and spirit)
in nature—has been created as a result of globalization—a leader who can
deal with multifaceted intellectual and cultural issues while also being
sensitive to the ethical needs of the people they serve. The concept of Lite
leadership is necessary to provide this new type of leadership. According
to Annan (2008), "Globalization is affecting every entity in the world in
many ways" (92); thus, Lite leadership will help lead and manage people
so that they can quickly adapt to this environment.

In the wake of globalization, it is not that the globalization philosophy
should be Americanized, but rather that the American leadership philosophy
must be globalized for multinational corporations and organizations in
the global world to be successful. There is no longer such a thing as

American leadership philosophy. Now, we have what I call "Lite leadership philosophy."

DEFINITION OF LITE LEADERSHIP

It is a well-known fact that human beings are comprised of three components: (a) the body, (b) the mind, and (c) the spirit. I believe that any leadership system that is short in attending to these three components will be inadequate and will be unable to provide good service to humankind. Lite leadership attends to all three of these components of the human being along with two more, forming the personal leadership, emotional stability, physical health, spiritual resilience, and environmental culture (PEPSE) system. Thus, Lite leadership insists that leadership no longer settle for anything less than the best for humankind. Currently, few if any, leadership theories consist of the application of all three components of the human being. Lite leadership theory, as you will notice, truly incorporates all aspects of human beings into its system.

The meaning of the term Lite leadership is threefold. The primary meaning is that it is holistic in nature, encompassing the whole human being, not just parts—or the problematic parts—of an individual, group, or organization.

The secondary meaning of Lite leadership is that it is low in matter (i.e., lite) and removes all the undesirable and unnecessary features of the typical conventional and traditional leadership approaches. Though it is grounded in American leadership styles, it does not demand that one practice these styles in their fullest, ignoring one's holistic self to be considered a typical leader. Rightfully so, it allows one to consider an array of demands—from the physical self, emotional self, and spiritual self—to provide the right flavor of the rich and diverse skills across numerous cultural domains. Lite leadership extends beyond typical and conventional leadership skills learned in most classroom encounters. It aims to remove undesirable skills from conventional models so that leadership can be successful in any particular situation, with any group of people, and in any geographical location, at any time. A trained Lite leader also knows which ingredients and aspects from various cultural domains to add to conventional or traditional skills in order to be successful at any given time. The model provides the basic structure and skeleton for American leadership skills with added ingredients for an array of cultural domains.

The third meaning of Lite leadership is that it is a candle that burns without a flicker—a perfect flame with five rays of light: personal leadership, emotional stability, physical health, spiritual resilience, and environmental exposure (the PEPSE system); it has a bright and resourceful core. Each of the rays comprises a component of the Lite leadership model; together, these components form the quintet of Lite leadership (see figure 5.1).

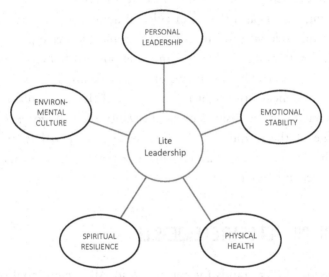

Figure 5.1. PEPSE system: The quintet of Lite leadership.

In other words, a Lite leader is a leader with global instincts who possesses the "fire" (energy) that lights the darkness (problematic situations) of the environment within which it operates and makes it bright (solution) for all humankind. It gives people who are stuck or being crushed the hope to carry on. It inspires people to live their lives to their fullest potential. This model is devised to be agnostic with respect to race, ethnicity, religion, etc.

The application of Lite leadership enhances the chances of success in many leadership and management endeavors. Several multinational organizations send their employees to the United States for leadership training. When such personnel go back to their respective countries, they try really hard to practice the leadership skills learned in the United States, often with little or no success. They then become frustrated, give up using the skills they learned, and revert to the old system of leadership practice, which they often know very well does not work. Little do they know it is not that the global leadership philosophy should be Americanized, but rather that the American leadership style should be globalized to make multinational organizations and corporations in the global world successful.

A typically trained Lite leader stands and watches situations as they arise, applying the finest combination of the various conventional and traditional leadership styles. As stated by Northouse (2004), they look for the right ingredients and flavors of cultural domains to add to the basic structure and skeleton (Hofstede 2001) of typical leadership models. As spelled out by Grayson (n.d.), they mix components homogenously and apply them bigheartedly—with love and compassion. This is a dynamic process, which means the right ingredients and flavors should be added and subtracted continuously as deemed fit until the situation is resolved. Knowledge of the quintet of the Lite leadership model is needed to provide the right ingredients and flavors to make this process unique, less cumbersome, and dynamic.

PEPSE: THE QUINTET OF LITE LEADERSHIP

As discussed, PEPSE stands for personal leadership, emotional stability, physical health, spiritual resilience, and environmental exposure (see figure 5.1). These principles together form the quintet of Lite leadership. The quintet can be used as a tool to help understand these five principles and rebuild leaders with this new philosophy.

PERSONAL LEADERSHIP

Personal leadership is the first component of the quintet. It refers to the ability to form one's own thoughts and beliefs based on knowledge and cultural experiences. If one works with this knowledge, it will lead and motivate them in a direction that alleviates the obstacles in their path and helps them reach their ultimate goal.

Leadership is a burning fire inside with so much energy that it constantly wants to be let out, and if let out, it will work for an individual because it is a force of good. To become a Lite leader, one needs this principle because it will help them tread and trample on the obstacles, difficulties, and challenges in the way. It will take them to places they never imagined.

EMOTIONAL STABILITY

Emotional stability is the second component of the quintet of the PEPSE system. Emotional stability is the ability to keep one's thoughts and beliefs about any event, incident, or situation positive no matter what happens in life.

To become a Lite leader, people need this principle because it will help them strive toward perfection. This means that emotional stability not only helps one become successful, but it also helps one achieve a higher level of success—a never-ending pattern of continuous improvement. This is especially true if one wants to move forward and not get stuck in a negative state.

A Lite leader must be conscious of negative thoughts and beliefs because they always clip-clop into the mind; dwelling on these thoughts can drag a person down and stop them from moving toward higher ground or changing their negative thoughts. According to Bradberry and Greaves (2009), it is critical to recognize not only one's own emotional state, but also those of followers. This information can be used to guide thinking and actions.

PHYSICAL HEALTH

Physical health is the third component of the PEPSE system. According to the Center for Creative Leadership (2019), leading and managing people comes with positive and negative demands. Establishing and maintaining interpersonal relationships is very important for the Lite leader; however, dealing with difficult personalities, political maneuvering, and managing conflict can increase stress levels.

To be a Lite leader, one must be able to handle difficult people and tense situations with diplomacy and tact. One must be able to spot difficult conflict, bring disagreements into the open, and help de-escalate issues. Leaders should also be able to encourage debate and open discussion in order to orchestrate win-win solutions.

According to the Center for Creative Leadership (2019), regular physical activity can relieve stress, anxiety, frustration, and anger that results from interpersonal relationships. Lack of physical activity or exercise can impair one's health and increase risk for developing diseases such as type 2 diabetes, cancer, and cardiovascular disease. In other words, physical activity can have immediate and long-term health benefits.

SPIRITUAL RESILIENCE

Spiritual resilience is the fourth component of the quintet. Bodner (2010) defined spiritual resiliency as the strengthening of a set of beliefs, principles, or values that sustain a person beyond family, institutional, and societal sources of strength. In other words, because so much is demanded of a Lite leader, spiritual resilience is needed to keep going—even when one does not feel like it.

Spiritual resilience can be learned through teachers, trainers, and counselors. Like physical resilience, spiritual resilience has to be practiced on a daily basis. For those who are believers, meeting in fellowship and praying together daily helps build spiritual resilience.

Colonel Mike Lembke, a chaplain of the US Forces in Iraq (as cited in Bodner 2010) once said that it is important to build spiritual resilience by exercising one's faith on a daily basis. This will help understand and integrate the joys and sorrows of each day into one's life. As Lite leaders, the philosophy of life is not waiting for something to happen; it is preparing to be well grounded when it does.

For many, spiritual resilience is all about being religious. That is not true. Delgado (2014) argued that religion is not the only way of exercising spiritual resilience. According to Aaliyah Negley (as cited in Delgado 2014), it is a lot more than religion.

For Lite leaders to be successful, they need to have a solid, spiritual foundation because this enables them to have everything under control—something that they can lean on during the tough times, which are inevitable, instead of relying on themselves to make it through those times.

ENVIRONMENTAL CULTURE

Environmental culture is the fifth and the last component of the quintet. The culture of the environment typically has little to do with ecology, landscape, plants, or animals. Instead, it has to do with the environment within the organization and why workers do things the way they do. Heathfield (2019) described this as a set of beliefs, practices, customs, and behaviors common to everyone within the organization.

The environmental culture is abstract and cannot actually be seen, except through its physical manifestations like language, decision-making, symbols and objects, stories and legends, level of empowerment, celebrations, the interactions of employees in meetings, and daily work practices in the workplace. It is crucial for Lite leaders to know that environmental culture creates social and organizational forces in the workplace that are very powerful because they operate outside of one's awareness (Schein 2010).

To become a Lite leader, one needs to understand these forces so that they do not become a victim to them. Besides explaining puzzling and frustrating experiences in social and organizational life in the workplace, understanding these forces helps one understand oneself even better (Schein 2010).

As a Lite leader, it is good to know that the environment in which you will be operating is comprised of three types of environmental cultures: (a) constructive, (b) aggressive/defensive, and (c) passive/defensive (Cooke and Lafferty 2019).The constructive type of environmental culture is a force for good that promotes effective goal-setting and achievement, growth and learning, and teamwork and collaboration. The aggressive/defensive type is a force that leads to internal competition, management by exception, and short-term emphasis as opposed to long-term effectiveness. Finally, the passive/defensive type of environmental culture leads to conformity, rigidity, and lack of team member accountability and initiative (Cooke and Lafferty 2019).

THE MOONIC ELEMENTS OF PEPSE

Moonic elements are the components surrounding the quintet (see figure 5.2). There are thirty-eight moonic elements in all in the PEPSE system: ten for personal leadership, seven for emotional stability, five for physical health, seven for spiritual resilience, and eight for environmental culture. Each of the moonic elements will be described in greater detail along with how they help shape each component of the quintet.

Like the solar system, the PEPSE system is the imaginary gravitationally bound system of Lite leadership. The objects that orbit Lite leadership directly are personal leadership, emotional stability, physical health, spiritual resilience, and environmental culture. The objects that orbit the Lite leadership indirectly are the moonic elements. There is a total of thirty-eight moonic elements. The personal leadership quintet has the largest number of moonic elements, ten in total. The Lite leadership object is the largest in the PEPSE system. The five objects of the quintet objects are the second largest objects, each of equal size; the moonic elements are the smallest objects, also of equal size.

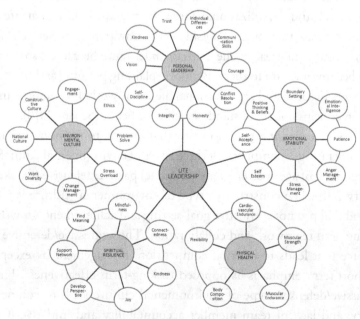

Figure 5.2. PEPSE system: The quintet of Lite leadership with its moonic elements.

REFERENCES

Annan, B. (2008). *Immigrants in US: Insights, views and approaches.* Los Angeles, CA: Sharp Image.

Bodner, B. (2010, May 11). *Spiritual resiliency leads to strength.* Retrieved from https://www.army.mil/article/38907/spiritual_resiliency_leads_to_strength

Bradberry, T., and Greaves, J. (2009). *Emotional intelligence 2.0.* San Diego, CA: TalentSmart.

Center for Creative Leadership. (2019). *The most common causes of stressed-out leaders.* Retrieved from https://www.ccl.org/multimedia/podcast/causing-stress-demands-on-leaders/

Cooke, R. A., and Lafferty, J. C. (2019). *Organizational Culture Inventory.* Mount Prospect, IL: Human Synergistics International.

Delgado, A. D. (2014, December 22). *Pillars of resiliency: Spiritual resilience.* Retrieved from https://www.aetc.af.mil/News/Article-Display/Article/559208/pillars-of-resiliency-spiritual-resilience/

Grayson, L. (n.d.). The top 10 leadership skills. *Small Business Chronicle.* Retrieved from http://smallbusiness.chron.com

Heathfield, S. M. (2019, February 4). *What is integrity—really?* Retrieved from https://www.thebalancecareers.com/what-is-integrity-really-1917676

Hofstede, G. (2001). *Culture's consequences, comparing values, behaviors, institutions, and organizations across nations.* Thousand Oaks, CA: Sage.

Northouse, P. (2004). *Leadership theories and practice* (3rd ed.). Thousand Oaks, CA: Sage.

Schein, E. H. (2010). *Organizational culture and leadership.* Hoboken, NJ: Wiley.

6

MOONIC ELEMENTS FOR PERSONAL LEADERSHIP

Change will not come if we wait for some other person or some other time. We are the ones we've been waiting for. We are the change that we seek.

—Barack Obama

Barack Obama was the forty-fourth president of the United States and the first African-American commander in chief. He served two terms, in 2008 and 2012. The son of parents from Kenya and Kansas, Obama was born and raised in Hawaii. He graduated from Columbia University and Harvard Law School.

—Biography.com (n.d.)

Personal leadership is the first quintet of the PEPSE framework of LeaderLite. To achieve personal leadership, one needs to acquire and practice its ten moonic elements: (a) individual differences, (b) communication skills, (c) courage, (d) conflict resolution, (e) honesty, (f) integrity, (g) self-discipline, (h) vision, (i) kindness, and (j) trust (see figure 6.1).

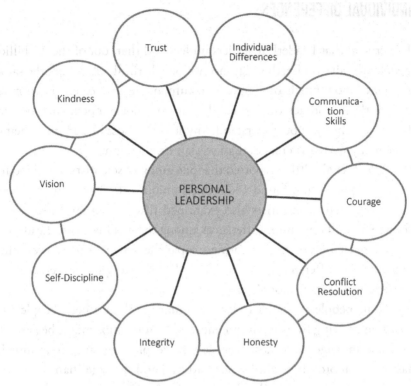

Figure 6.1. The moonic elements for
personal leadership quintet.

Personal leadership has been defined in myriad ways. Covey (1994) defined it as "the process of keeping your vision and values before you and aligning your life to be congruent with them" (140). Leadership Excellence Ltd. (2020), on the other hand, defined personal leadership as "the ability to develop and utilize your positive leadership traits to guide the direction of your life instead of letting time and chance determine your course. Personal leadership can begin when you decide to be your own life coach and live by a personal mission statement that reflects your values and life goals" (para. 1)

Though personal leadership develops internally, its cumulative effects can be felt by everyone around an individual, including friends, family members, and coworkers.

INDIVIDUAL DIFFERENCES

It is crucial that LeaderLite leaders understand that, out of the 7.7 billion people who live on Earth today, no two people think and/or act the same, no matter how much they have in common. Leaders often try to make people think and act the same; when it does not happen, they become frustrated and do not understand why it is not possible. Human beings have many more differences than we can ever imagine.

Telenti et al. (2016) reported that one group of scientists examined ten thousand people and found 146 million unique differences among them. Another group of scientists also examined fifteen thousand people and found 254 million unique differences among them. This means LeaderLite leaders must refrain from treating people the same; instead, they must explore these differences and tweak their LeaderLite appropriately (i.e., use more or less of their moonic elements).

Some people are easier to lead and manage than others. People who focus on creating lively environments and relationships might be easier to lead and manage than those who do not. People who take an optimistic, fast-paced approach might be easier to lead and manage than those who work at a steadier pace. People who are more enthusiastic and easier to relate to might be easier to lead and manage than people who are analytical.

It is important for leaders to understand that not all people will think or act like them. The first step in recognizing individual differences and a good mindset about teamwork is to take the Everything DiSC assessment, a simple tool that helps leaders better understand how to utilize their managerial priorities and preferences to lead and manage the people in an organization. It helps leaders learn how to connect better with people whose priorities and preferences differ from their own. Leaders can improve the quality of their management experience by using DiSC to build more effective relationships (Zigarmi, Fowler, and O'Connor 2017).

TIPS FOR LEARNING ABOUT DISC BEHAVIORAL STYLES

To lead and manage people effectively, leaders may want to know their DiSC behavioral style and understand the DiSC behavior styles of others without having them take the DiSC assessment. The following tips can help leaders improve communications and productivity while reducing stress.

The "D" in DiSC stands for *dominance*. People who possess this behavioral style tend to shape their work environment by overcoming opposition to accomplish results. They are control specialists, and they (a) prioritize tasks and results over anything else, (b) are motivated by challenges, and (c) appear to be direct and self-assured. Being taken advantage of is their greatest fear. In all they do, they want their followers to be efficient.

The "i" stands for *influence*. People who possess this behavioral style tend to shape their work environments by influencing or persuading others. They are communication specialists, and they (a) prioritize people and communication over everything else, (b) are motivated by social recognition, and (c) appear to be persuasive and enthusiastic. Social rejection is their greatest fear. In all they do, they want their followers to be enthusiastic.

The "S" stands for *steadiness*. People who possess this behavioral style tend to cooperate with others within existing circumstances to carry out the task. They are harmonizing specialists, and they (a) prioritize people and collaboration over everything else, (b) are motivated by stability and status quo, and (c) appear to be loyal to the team. Unplanned change is their greatest fear. In all they do, they want their followers to be sincere.

The "C" stands for *conscientiousness*. People who possess this behavioral style tend to work conscientiously within existing circumstances to ensure quality and accuracy. They are information specialists, and they (a) prioritize task and accuracy over everything else, (b) are motivated by order and proper ways, and (c) appear to be detail-oriented. Criticism of work is their greatest fear. In all they do, they want their followers to be correct. See table 1 for a summary of the DiSC behavioral styles.

Table 6.1
DiSC Behavioral Styles

DiSC Styles	Relationship	What This Style Does Best	Specialist Type	Priority	Motivated By	Appears to Be	Fears	This Style Wants You to Be
D	Dominance	Shapes the environment by overcoming opposition to accomplish results	Control	Task and results	Challenges	Direct and self-assured	Being taken advantage of	Efficient
i	influence	Shapes the environment by influencing or persuading others	Communication	People and communication	Social recognition	Persuasive and enthusiastic	Social rejection	Enthusiastic
S	Steadiness	Cooperates with others within existing circumstances to carry out the task	Harmonizing	People and collaboration	Stability and status quo	A loyal team person	Unplanned change	Sincere
C	Conscientiousness	Works conscientiously within existing circumstances to ensure quality and accuracy	Information	Task and accuracy	Order and proper ways	Detail-oriented	Criticism of work	Correct

Rosenberg (2016) came up with a novel way to explain the DiSC styles, introducing an engaging and memorable way to relate the DiSC styles to four birds to make them easier to understand and remember. His intent was to match each dimension with the respective bird that aligns with commonly held perceptions of how those birds typically behave, making it easier to retain the information through associative learning:

- "D" refers to dominance and is represented by an eagle. Eagles are commonly considered to be daring, decisive, direct, and driven.
- "i" refers to influence and is represented by a parrot. Parrots are commonly considered to be imaginative, influential, intuitive, and inspirational.
- "S" refers to steadiness and is represented by a dove. Doves are commonly considered to be sincere, steadfast, sympathetic, and satisfied.
- "C" refers to conscientiousness and is represented by an owl. Owls are commonly considered to be cautious, critical, concise, and consistent.

The next sections will discuss how leaders can interact positively with the people they lead and manage to avoid unnecessary conflicts.

"C" LEADERS AND MANAGERS INTERACTING WITH OTHER STYLES

"C" people approaching a "C" leader or manager. It is important to note that both have styles that are passive, task-oriented, detail-oriented, high quality, and take a much longer time to make decisions. They should be mindful about time and refrain from overutilizing research and information to make decisions so projects are not delayed.

"D" people approaching a "C" leader or manager. It is important to note that both styles are task-oriented and see the big picture, but a "C" leader or manager has a passive style and a "D" person has an active style. Since a "D" person prefers to lead rather than follow, a "C" leader or manager should make suggestions to achieve a goal; instead of talking about why it won't work, the leader or manager must ask "what?"

"i" people approaching a "C" leader or manager. It is important to note that a "C" leader or manager has a passive style and is task-oriented, but an "i" person has an active style and is people-oriented. It should be no wonder, then, that "C" and "i" styles often butt heads. A "C" leader or manager should consider encouraging an "i" person by allowing their natural creative problem-solving abilities and thinking outside the box. This can be accomplished by asking "who?"

"S" people approaching a "C" leader or manager. It is important to note that both styles are passive; however, an "S" person is people-oriented and a "C" leader or manager is task-oriented. They should always try to reconcile conflict and strive for consensus.

"D" LEADERS AND MANAGERS INTERACTING WITH OTHER STYLES

"C" people approaching a "D" leader or manager. It is important to note that both styles are task-oriented and see the big picture; however, a "C" person is passive and a "D" leader or manager is active. They should consider allowing the "C" person to be the anchor of reality in team thought.

"D" people approaching a "D" leader or manager. It is important to note that both have styles that are active, task-oriented, and dominant. The "D" leader or manager should listen more and refrain from being argumentative.

"i" people approaching a "D" leader or manager. It is important to note that both styles are active; however, an "i" person is people-oriented and a "D" leader or manager is task-oriented. They should recognize the 'i' person for their creativity and minimize conflict and arguments.

"S" people approaching a "D" leader or manager. It is important to note that "D" leaders and managers tend to be overly aggressive and task-oriented, while "S" people tend to be more passive and people-oriented. "D" leaders and managers should be aware that their personalities often clash with those of "S" people. They should do try to be less intimidating or impatient, and act as a catalyst for an "S" person to be less indecisive and hesitant to enact change.

"I" LEADERS AND MANAGERS INTERACTING WITH OTHER STYLES

"C" people approaching an "i" leader or manager. It is important to note that, while a "C" person has a passive and task-oriented personality style, an "i" leader or manager has an active and people-oriented style. They should persuade a "C" person to minimize excessive research and information required to reach a decision in order to avoid the delay of projects.

"D" people approaching an "i" leader or manager. It is important to note that both styles are active; however, and a "D" person is task-oriented, and an "i" leader or manager is people-oriented. They should consider relinquishing control and power to a "D" person when appropriate to get things done.

"i" people approaching an "i" leader or manager. It is important to note that both have active and people-oriented styles. The "i" leader or manager should persuade the other "i" person so they both can try harder to be (a) better with details, and (b) less optimistic, talkative, and impulsive.

"S" people approaching an "i" leader or manager. It is important to note that, while both are people-oriented, an "i" leader or manager has an active style and an "S" person has a passive personality style. Since an "S" person usually has a vested interest in maintaining the status quo, an "i" leader or manager should be the catalyst to influence the "S" person to make necessary changes.

"S" LEADERS AND MANAGERS INTERACTING WITH OTHER STYLES

"C" people approaching an "S" leader or manager. It is important to note that both have passive styles; however, "C" people are task-oriented and "S" leaders and managers are people-oriented. They should be patient, listen, and work with "C" people in a harmonious way to achieve very high standards because the "C" person focuses on the details and sees what many people of other styles do not.

"D" people approaching an "S" leader or manager. It is important to note that "D" people are active and task-oriented, while "S" leaders and managers are passive and people-oriented. Predictably, these styles often butt heads. Since "D" people are risk takers and problem solvers, "S" leaders and managers should look to them for decisions and direction.

"i" people approaching an "S" leader or manager. It is important to note that "i" people have an active personality style, but "S" leaders and managers have a passive personality style. Also note that both are people-oriented. "S" leaders and managers should try to motivate "i" people using approval, flattery, and praise and by avoiding conflicts and arguments.

"S" people approaching an "S" leader or manager. It is important to note that both have passive personality styles and are people-oriented. Since both tend to avoid conflict, an "S" leader or manager should try to encourage another "S" person to face frustration and other issues head-on so that neither is resentful of the other.

Table 6.2
DiSC Behavioral Styles Interactions

Person Approaching / Style	Leader or Manager: C	D	i	S
C	Both passive, task oriented, detail-oriented, high-quality. Takes much longer to make decisions. I'll be mindful about time, refrain from plenty of research and information to make decisions so we don't hold up projects.	Both task-oriented, see the big picture. However, D has active style and C has passive style. I might consider allowing C to be the anchor of reality in team thought.	i is active and people-oriented. C is passive and task-oriented. I'll persuade C to minimize excessive research and information to reach a decision, so we don't hold up projects.	Both passive. However, S is people-oriented and C is task-oriented. Because C focuses on the details and sees what many other styles do not, I'll be patient, listen, and work with C in a harmonious way to achieve very high standards for both of us.
D	Both C and D are task-oriented and see the big picture. However, C is passive, and D is active. D's would prefer to lead than follow, so I'll make suggestions to achieve a goal. Instead of talking about why it won't work, I will ask "what?"	Both active and task-oriented. Both want to be dominant. I will refrain from being argumentative and listen more.	Both active. i is people-oriented, and D is task-oriented. I might consider relinquishing control and power when appropriate to get things done.	S is passive and people-oriented. However, D is active and task-oriented. No wonder they often butt heads. Because D's are risk takers and problem solvers, I'll look to them for decisions and direction.
i	C is passive and task-oriented. i is active and people-oriented. No wonder C and i personalities often butt heads.	Both active. However, D is task-oriented, and i is people-oriented.	Both active and people-oriented.	I is passive, and i is active. Both are people-oriented.

Person Approaching

S

I might consider encouraging i by allowing their natural creative problem-solving abilities and thinking outside the box. I will do this by asking "why?"	I'll recognize i for their creativity and minimize conflict and arguments.	I'll persuade the other i so we both try harder to be better with details, and less optimistic, talkative, and impulsive.	I will have to motivate i by using approval, flattery, and praise and avoiding conflicts and arguments.
Both passive. However, C is task-oriented, and S is people-oriented.	D's tend to be overly aggressive and task-oriented, while S's are more passive and people-oriented. No wonder D and S personalities often clash.	Both are people-oriented. However, i is active and S is passive.	Both are passive and people-oriented.
I might try hard to reconcile conflict and strive for consensus.	I'll try to be less intimidating or impatient, and act as a catalyst for S to be less indecisive and hesitant to enact change.	Because S usually has a vested interest in maintaining the status quo, I need to be the catalyst in influencing S to make necessary change.	Because S is passive and avoids conflict, I'll encourage them to face issues head-on, so they don't hold grudges when they experience frustrations and resentments.

COMMUNICATION SKILLS

Having good communication and decision-making skills often helps a LeaderLite leader; however, having the skill of actively listening to other people improves a LeaderLite leader's capability tremendously. Listening involves focusing on what the team is saying and using this information to guide the group toward its objectives. An effective leader should also identify the things left unsaid, as well as the inner voices. To be an active listener, one should not simply focus on the spoken word, but regularly venture among team members and assess the mood in the room; conflicts can often be sensed, and unhappiness felt without someone having to voice it (Spears 2004).

In order to improve active listening skills, a leader should focus on being attentive. Attention skills can be improved by cueing into body language and by improving one's ability to give and receive feedback (Spears 2004).

UNDERSTANDING TYPES OF COMMUNICATION

Avedian (2014) discussed four basic types of communication: (a) passive, (b) aggressive, (c) passive-aggressive, and (d) assertive.

PASSIVE

People who have difficulty expressing their concerns and feelings and tend to hold them inside are regarded as *passive* individuals, ineffectively hoping that situations will improve with time. Since passive individuals have difficulty expressing their thoughts and needs, they often expect others to read and interpret their minds. It is not difficult for the LeaderLite leader to spot such individuals because they are typically shy and reserved. The shortcoming of people with a passive communication style is that their needs will often go unmet, causing them to become bitter and resentful.

AGGRESSIVE

People who express their thoughts and feelings by offending those they communicate with, having little or no regard for the other person's rights or feelings, are regarded as *aggressive* individuals. Aggressive people have a need to control their surroundings and relationships, and they tend to lack boundaries. In the short term, people with an aggressive style of communication might get what they want; however, they tend to get into trouble with others, lose relationships, risk their careers, and offend many others, including family members, friends, and coworkers.

PASSIVE-AGGRESSIVE

Like passive individuals, people who are *passive-aggressive* have difficulty expressing their thoughts and feelings clearly. However, unlike passive individuals, they tend to resort to indirect forms of communication, such as sarcasm and cynicism, to get their points across, rather than speaking directly about their concerns. They may shy away from conflict or tension, even though they want others to know how they feel. They may also show their frustration, but they don't express themselves verbally—and their words don't match their behaviors.

Despite their attempts at communicating their frustrations, people with passive-aggressive communication styles end up feeling unheard or misunderstood. They try to avoid conflict, but their behavior creates tension within relationships, often leading to a toxic environment. As a LeaderLite leader, just imagine the confusion and frustration of being on the receiving end of this style—very stressful.

ASSERTIVE

People who express their thoughts and feelings clearly and directly in a respectful manner are regarded as *assertive* individuals. This communication style is the healthiest and most effective way of communicating. It is a win-win approach because the goal is to understand one another and not to prove the other person wrong. Individuals with an assertive style of communication are direct, and that reduces the likelihood of misunderstandings.

Others may get upset when a LeaderLite leader says what they feel directly, but because it is done in such a respectful and diplomatic manner, their message will be better received. No wonder it is the best of all the communication styles, especially when it has the highest likelihood of achieving your desired outcome. Finally, it has been demonstrated that the assertive communication style also fosters a sense of trust in others since they know they are being communicated with in an honest and direct way.

ASSERTIVE COMMUNICATION SKILLS

The LeaderLite leader's successful use of assertive communication skills depends on the relationship they share with the other person. One has to assume there is no such thing as altruism. The acronym WIIFM (What's In It For Me?) often works well; a leader should identify and convey how they and the other person each will benefit from the other person doing what is asked. A LeaderLite leader's goal is to create a brilliant way of involving—early on—others who can have an impact on the leader's success. The leader should make them feel special, included, and benefited in some way. This results in future favors (or offers) when none have been requested (Sobieck 2010). Assertive communication skills will help achieve this goal.

The following is a step-by-step procedure (Avedian 2014) for the use of the assertive communication style. As a LeaderLite leader, the goal of being assertive is to express thoughts and feelings respectfully. Paying attention to feedback and concerns from the other person is important.

1. Use "I" statements (Gordan 1975). For example, "I feel hurt." Here, there is something in it for the speaker. Refrain from using "you" statements. They represent attacking language, and they tend to make the listener defensive.
2. State the specific behavior of the other person that needs correction. For example, "When you were late to the meeting this morning ..."

Here, there is something in it for both the speaker and the listener. This allows a leader to be direct, honest, and transparent.

3. Relate the perceived reason why the person acted in that particular way and sympathize with them. People like to be heard and understood. This usually reduces the likelihood of getting defensive. For example, "I understand that the traffic is heavy during rush hour." Here, there is something in it for the listener.

4. Say what is desired in a respectful way. Format to follow: "I would like you to_____." For example, "I would like you to get the report in on time."

5. Say why it is important, listing reasons for the desired behavior. For example, "This is important to me because when your report is not in on time, then my report is also delayed, and I don't want to get into trouble. It's also important so I don't stress and worry as much."

6. List some alternatives that can increase the likelihood of a possible change. For example, "If you cannot have the report in on time, please communicate that to me in advance so that I can better prepare myself. I can also potentially help you with the report if I have the time."

7. End by saying, "What do you think?" This will prompt feedback and allow the other person the opportunity to express concerns.

A leader should avoid the following because they tend to lead to defensiveness in others:

- Absolute words such as "always," "never," "everyone," or "no one."
- "I told you so."
- "You should or could have ..."
- Giving advice
- "You" statements
- Asking "why" questions (it's accusatory).
- Bringing other people into the conversation ("_____ thinks the same way about you.")
- "I feel that you are_____."

Practicing the assertive communication skill and self-examination on a regular basis will help leaders create healthy relationships with their followers and enhance their skills in leading and managing people effectively.

ACTIVE LISTENING

LeaderLite leaders are required to actively listen to their people and not just be good at communication and decision-making. Listening involves focusing on what the team is saying and using this information to guide the group toward its objectives. A LeaderLite leader should identify the things left unsaid and the inner voices. To be an active listener, one should focus not just on the spoken word, but regularly venture among team members and assess the mood in the room, as conflicts can often be sensed, and unhappiness felt without someone having to voice it (Spears 2004).

In order to improve listening skills, leaders should focus on being attentive. Attention skills can be improved by cuing into body language and by improving your ability to give and receive feedback (Spears 2004).

COURAGE

Life is full of uncertainty, and according to Beck (2015), uncertainty is an awesome phenomenon of human consciousness; if not controlled, it can lead to worry and distress and shatter the moonic element of courage. Things will happen that make one doubt the outcome of a situation, such as opposition, shame, scandal, discouragement, or even personal loss.

A LeaderLite leader must have the courage to act rightly in the face of these uncertain situations. They must build mental and moral strength to undertake ventures, persevere in difficult times, and withstand danger or fear of the unknown.

Courage is an emotion. There are several ways to acquire, maintain, and build on courage, but the simplest is to persevere in difficult situations despite fear and uncertainty. If a leader never quits, even when things are their worst, they will soon see success. Repeating this act and having successful outcomes will lead to achieving and building courage.

CONFLICT RESOLUTION SKILLS

Thomas and Kilmann (1974) stated that no two individuals have exactly the same expectations and desires; thus, conflict is a natural part of our interactions with others. Additionally, Holt (n.d.) explained that conflict in the workplace often occurs due to a lack of communication, and if not confronted, it can cause major problems for any organization. Many leaders mistake disagreements with conflicts. In contrast to conflict, disagreements are differences in opinion that could, but do not always, lead to conflict. Researchers such as Dana (1996) have found out that 60–80 percent of all conflicts in organizations in the United States come from strained relationships between employees (i.e., relational factors). Ilgaz (2014) also found that a typical manager spends 25–40 percent of their time dealing with workplace conflicts, amounting to between one and two days out of every workweek.

A LeaderLite leader must be able to handle disagreements and other forms of possible conflict rather quickly, and that can be healthy. Ignoring them, however, may be very destructive and result in detrimental outcomes to organizations, including rapid turnover rates, loss of productivity, and absenteeism. The cost of turnover in the workplace is, of course, extraordinary.

Thomas (1976) discussed five conflict management styles: (a) competing, (b) collaborating, (c) avoiding, (d) accommodating, and € compromising. These five styles were plotted on two axes: (a) concern for self and (b) concern for others. LeaderLite leaders should use the *collaborative* style because it constructs solutions to conflict to meet the needs of all parties involved.

HONESTY

Being honest and good to others is the most important moonic element in the PEPSE framework. To be *honest* is to act in the way that one knows within is right. This comes from having good character and morals and from being able to distinguish right from wrong. To be honest also means not hiding the truth—and speaking the truth at all times in any situation, challenging or not.

LeaderLite leaders are obliged to do things that are morally right and not hide actions they know are wrong. In other words, LeaderLite leaders don't lie. Honesty builds and revamps relationships. It makes others feel secure and safe in the relationship. According to Adams (2019), relationships with honesty at their core are the best ones imaginable. Initiating awkward confrontations to deliver the truth is difficult, but in the long run, being honest promotes better relationships with others and with yourself.

LeaderLite leaders shouldn't be tempted to conceal the truth because it will get them in trouble or be hurtful to others. While the truth may be painful, it is usually less so when delivered honestly rather than being wrapped in deception.

TRUST

Trust is defined as a firm belief in the reliability, truth, ability, or strength of someone or something (Dictionary.com n.d.). Grossman (2019) stated that good relationships are built on trust. A LeaderLite leader's ability to inspire and motivate employees is based on trust. When people trust their leader, they have confidence in their decisions. Even in uncertainty, they will be influenced by their leadership because people expect their leaders to do what they say they will do.

A LeaderLite leader must align their words and actions because this is a key pillar for building trust with others and, ultimately, for an organization's success. People often say that what leaders say and do has the most impact on their perception of an organization. When there is a disconnect between a leader's words and actions, people are less likely to become engaged with and committed to the organization (Grossman 2019).

INTEGRITY

Killinger (2010) described *integrity* as the practice of being honest and adhering to strong moral and ethical principles and values on a consistent basis (i.e., being the same regardless of the situation). In another way, Heathfield (2020) looked at integrity in the ethics realm as the honesty and truthfulness or accuracy of one's actions, and it is the underpinning on which people build trust and effective relationships.

It is extremely difficult to have integrity 100 percent of the time; inevitably, situations will arise that challenge a leader's integrity. For example, fear of what others may think can cause a leader to lose their integrity and hurt others. There are other times when it can be difficult to intentionally manage one's behavior and actions because emotions get in the way (Kang 2017). When such situations arise, a leader should relax, learn lessons, and then move on because oftentimes things happen to make us grow.

A LeaderLite leader must strive to keep honesty and trust central to their relationships with others. Integrity is important because it helps draw good people to a leader since they are trustworthy and dependable. All a leader needs to do is demonstrate the two basic tenets in a person with integrity consistently. For LeaderLite leaders, the challenge is never to let any situation overcome their integrity.

PERSUASION

A LeaderLite leader should not always want to rely on authority to get things done. Instead, *persuasion* may be advisable in order to facilitate decision-making. Seeking consensus rather than compliance, which is perhaps the biggest difference to traditional authoritarian models, is the way to go (Spears 2004). Greenleaf (1977) wrote that it is when taking a fresh look at the issues of power and authority that people are able to learn to relate to one another, which creates a less coercive and more creative, supportive environment. In a large part, persuasion in business is highlighted by the organization's need to make its case. Employees should be involved in decision-making, and a leader should explain what the objectives are and why; this can help influence employees to act in a positive manner.

There are a few ways a leader can master the art of persuasion, an important tool: (a) improving body language, (b) improving communication, including the ability to sense the right time to talk and to listen, and (c) aiming to be the expert in their field, as it can guarantee that the team looks up to them and feels inspired by them. Leaders can inspire others by demonstrating enthusiasm and expertise with their actions (Spears 2004).

SELF-DISCIPLINE

Self-discipline is not about doing things right; it is about doing the right thing. *Self-discipline* can be described as the ability to control one's thoughts and beliefs, moods and feelings, and behavior in order to overcome weaknesses. For example, there are times when one pursues doing what is right, but the pressure from others calls them to abandon it, losing their self-discipline.

Self-discipline is one of the most important moonic elements that LeaderLite leaders need in order to be successful in life. According to Jacob (2018), self-discipline can help one achieve their goals, overcome their frustrations and distresses, and help them embrace life the way it comes. However, without it, one is set adrift among these constant uncontrollable changes in life, causing suffering from disappointments and failures.

The effort and focus that self-discipline requires can be draining because it takes a lot of work to stay on top of it. It is noteworthy to mention that no one is born with self-discipline. The good news is that anyone can acquire it because it is a learned behavior. LeaderLite leaders must build and master self-discipline by practicing it repetitively, just like going to the gym (Patel 2019).

VISION

Vision is the mental picture of the destination where one wants to be in the future, normally within a loosely defined time frame. Vision should not be confused with mission. Mission involves the steps required to realize one's vision. Vision begins with imagination or wisdom. In other words, it can also be described as what you want to achieve in the long run. Bechervaise (2013) describes vision as an idea of what the future can hold.

The good news for LeaderLite leaders is that vision is not something that has to be sought out; it is the thing inside of us that guides, guards, comforts, strengthens, teaches, and counsels us. "Your vision will become clear only when you can look into your own heart. Without, everything seems discordant; only within does it coalesce into unity. Who looks outside dreams; who looks inside awakes" (Jung, 1916/1973, 33). According to Bechervaise (2013), vision (a) creates that burning desire to grow and improve, (b) embodies one's hopes and ideals, and (c) gives a sense of purpose.

LeaderLite leaders have to look forward to see where they are headed. Having a vision helps keep them on course during rocky times or unexpected setbacks. It also provides motivation to carry them through to the end, through thick and thin, by providing them with the focus needed to accomplish their goals.

Leaders need to keep the end result in mind. A leader's vision needs to be strong enough to carry them through to the end; otherwise, they may stop short of their goals. Finally, without vision, one loses the meaning and purpose of life.

A LeaderLite leader needs to have the idea and conviction that they can achieve their vision and use this power and energy inside them to accomplish it. They may fail occasionally, but it does not mean they have lost their vision and direction. After all, Walt Disney was once fired from a newspaper and was told he lacked imagination and had no good ideas. Thomas Edison failed some ten thousand times before he was able to create the light bulb. Oprah Winfrey was told she was unfit for TV and got fired from her job as a television reporter at the age of twenty-two. These are very few examples of many who made it because they had vision, despite failure and rejection (Bechervaise 2013).

FORESIGHT

The concept of *foresight* is directly related to conceptualization in many ways. A LeaderLite leader is required to foresee likely outcomes through an understanding of the past. There are three key points to foresight in leadership: the ability to (a) learn from past experiences, (b) identify what is currently happening, and (c) understand the consequences of specific decisions.

For both Spears (2004) and Greenleaf (1977), foresight is tightly related to intuition. It is an area where leadership studies have not yet ventured in great detail. Nonetheless, in order to improve foresight and become better at predicting the future, one should improve one's analytical skills. This can be achieved by focusing on the decision-making process and by following up on decisions previously made; in short, a deeper understanding of the consequences of decisions needs to be developed (Spears 2004).

KINDNESS

The Oxford English Dictionary defines *kindness* as the quality of being friendly, generous, and considerate (Lexico n.d.). Kindness, to a large extent, draws attention to positive and pro-social attitudes that result in a compassionate environment. It is the responsibility of LeaderLite leaders to create the type of kindness culture in the environment in which they operate, one that fosters an atmosphere of affection, gentleness, warmth, concern, and care.

According to Hall (2017), there is a school of thought that likens being kind to being weak or naïve, but that is untrue. Being kind often requires courage and strength. Kindness is an interpersonal skill that is so important for LeaderLite leaders, who need kindness to strengthen their relationships and provide a sense of satisfaction in their lives.

Practicing kindness on a daily basis is the key to LeaderLite leaders being successful in their relationships with others. Examples of kindness include (a) smiling, (b) opening doors for others, (c) helping to carry a heavy load), (d) celebrating others, (e) giving honest compliments, (f) thanking others, (g) telling others how special they are, and (h) helping the elderly with yard work or food. The key point is for LeaderLite leaders to open their eyes to look for people in need and offer help as a way to practice kindness (Price 2012).

STEWARDSHIP

Stewardship means taking responsibility for one's own actions and those of the people they serve. The main assumption is to commit to serve others' needs first. For Greenleaf (1977), this means that not only is the organization holding its trust in the leader, but the whole organization is there to serve the wider community. Stewardship requires openness as well as persuasion. It is not about controlling actions; it is about allowing oneself to be accountable (Spears 2004).

Including stewardship in a leader's style involves the leader understanding (a) their values, (b) how their values guide them in their leadership roles, and (c) how their values align with the values of the organization or the team they are leading. Leaders shouldn't be afraid to point out when values are not aligned (Spears 2004).

TAKEAWAY ARTICLES

To see how personal leadership can be applied in different organizational settings, you may want to understand diversity in organization by reading the following articles. After each reading, ask yourself what you would do if you found yourself in a similar situation.

ARTICLE 1

I have always been a proponent of training and development programs as a vehicle to changing behaviors in the workplace until I encountered a diversity awareness training program in my previous workplace that failed to provide any positive results and rarely resulted in the transfer of immediately useful information to the organization. I have always wondered why the training program did not achieve its goals—even though the training program by itself was superb: The learners demonstrated their knowledge by performing various role-plays.

However, Gebert, Beungeler, and Heinitz's (2017) article "Tolerance: A Neglected Dimension in Diversity Training?" suggests that corporate diversity training programs often are not as effective as people would think, despite organizations investing considerable time and money into these trainings to reduce discrimination. This research delved into the underlying barriers to learning that may cause diversity training to fail. One barrier that makes a lot of sense to me involves trainees' tendency to keep their thoughts to themselves when they are likely to lead to latent conflict, thus hindering learning. This research also showed why the currently dominant diversity-training models are insufficient to overcome these barriers to learning (Gebert et al. 2017).

I am very glad I read this article and now understand that a training model focusing on fostering tolerance and sustained by tolerance-supportive trainer beliefs is key to an effective training program—one that could provide positive results in the transfer of immediately useful information to the organization. After all, organizations that invest considerable time and money into diversity training to reduce discrimination and achieve a sustainable integration of diverse employees must recognize the specific return on investment (ROI) and other organizational impacts of the training.

ARTICLE 2

After reading "Diversity at the Workplace: Whom Does It Benefit?" (Ilmakunnas and Ilmakunnas 2011), I learned that using productivity with workforce characteristics and age diversity is positively related, while educational diversity negatively related to total factor productivity. While I was not surprised that age diversity is positively related, I was shocked about educational diversity negatively related to total factor productivity.

For starters, I had never heard the term *educational diversity*. I have tried to understand what the researchers meant by this term, but to no avail. In the article, I read educational diversity to mean diversity in terms of educational background, but what does educational background have to do with educational diversity? In another section of the article, I believe I understood that educational diversity is equated to skill diversity, which only served to confuse me even more. In the end, I have taken educational diversity to mean people with different educational levels in the same workplace—employees with higher levels of education could discriminate against those with lesser levels of education (e.g., PhD versus high school graduates).

I completely agree with Ilmakunnas and Ilmakunnas (2011) that the effects of diversity can be modeled in several ways, including preferences, strategies, or the production function. Looking through these lenses, I now understand why the authors argue that diversity, to some extent, can have negative consequences on productivity, especially when an employee's effectiveness and work performance depend on the share of employees who are different in terms of ethnicity, age, gender, etc. I can include educational diversity here as well. I experience this kind of situation at Phillips Graduate University, where among employees as well as in the classrooms, people tend to spend time with others who are similar to them in terms of education levels. I have also come to realize that I am a culprit of this form of discrimination.

All through my educational training, I have been made to believe that any form of diversity is of great benefit to any organization because it helps increase cultural awareness, knowledge, and communication in the workplace. However, I now recognize that though educational diversity could be beneficial in the workplace, those with a litigious mentality and lack of any dimension of diversity in the workplace may cite civil rights violations, which could be detrimental to the organization.

ARTICLE 3

In "Unclogging the MENtal Block: Ensuring Greater Gender Diversity at the Workplace," Shirodkar (2013) stressed that women are underrepresented at the top management levels in most organizations and that almost three-quarters of a century has gone by since the women's liberation movement emerged, yet, the situation of the working woman has not really changed much to this day. The author continued, pointing to the fact that with the rise of talent as a dominant business issue, there is a significant potential for women that cannot be ignored. A significant key success factor in transforming the workplace in a global economy thus involves developing, encouraging, and retaining female talent across both the for-profit and nonprofit organizations (Shirodkar 2013).

The part of the article that appealed to me the most is the fact that women's power as consumers has increased tremendously, and it is important to bring women into decision-making positions to help tap this growing market. In fact, women control about $20 trillion in total consumer spending globally and influence up to 80 percent of buying decisions (Shirodkar 2013).

Most importantly, after reading this article, I was stunned and have truly come to know what being a woman means to me today in emerging and developing countries in the world: (a) women still make less money as men for the same jobs; (b) women seldom make it to the top as men do; (c) families too often are unable to get flex-time, child care, medical leave, or paid family leave; (d) the United States is the only major industrialized nation to not provide comprehensive child care and family leave policies; (e) women are often charged more for the exact same health coverage as their male counterparts; (f) tax codes designed when men were the sole breadwinners are still in place in several nations and seek to punish women, especially in single-mother families; (g) sexual harassment is still of great concern in the workplace with one in five women experiencing it in the workplace at some time; (h) women still are excessively impacted by lack of health care services compared men; and (i) older women and lesbian couples are among the poorest segment of most societies today (Shirodkar 2013).

My father died suddenly of massive heart attack in the 1980s when my mother was only forty-nine years old in Ghana, a developing country. While reading this article, I realized the challenges that my mother had to face when she began to work after being a homemaker for several years. These challenges, according to Shirodkar (2013) included: (a) unfriendly policies, (b) inflexible rules, (c) approach of male colleagues, (d) harassment, and (e) roles and growth prospects among others.

I like the author's suggestions as to how to improve women's rights in developing countries and ensure greater gender diversity at the workplace. Among these suggestions, I believe the following are extremely crucial for women (Shirodkar 2013): (a) the need for women to demand and fight for what is theirs, rather than suffering passively; (b) incorporating constitutional changes in policies, rules, and regulations in the organizations to foster greater representation of women at the workplace; and most of all, (c) conducting periodic training and development in changes in psychological mindset among both men and women in the workplace.

Though this research was conducted in India, discrimination against women persists around the globe, and it remains a major obstacle to economic development in emerging and developing countries. Coming from Ghana, in West Africa, I can relate to these gender-based discriminatory sentiments that face women in most emerging and developing countries of the world today. According to Shirodkar (2013), women in such countries are searching for a place to connect, to fill the emotional void created by the increased isolation, invisibility, and constant stress.

ARTICLE 4

Jones, Nelson, King Geller, and Bowes-Sperry's (2013) article, "Beyond the Business Case: An Ethical Perspective of Diversity Training," focuses on diversity training programs that continue to yield little evidence of their overall effectiveness. The authors argue that approaching diversity training from an ethical perspective may bolster the effectiveness of traditional approaches. Furthermore, the article reveals the fact that if the traditional bottom-line justifications are enhanced with social justice arguments, training effectiveness increases (Jones et al. 2013). This is the second article I have read so far for this coursework that argues that there is lack of empirical data supporting the effectiveness of diversity training in the workplace. Nevertheless, trainers should not become complacent, but instead begin to seek new, innovative ways to reinvent and revive diversity training.

One reason why the traditional method of diversity training is ineffective is that focusing on economic justifications alone makes it difficult to achieve an understanding and integration of individuals from a wide range of social identity groups. Though the business case of diversity training (i.e., return on investment) is important, it is also critical to begin strengthening diversity training programs by building not only a "business case," but also a "moral case" for such programs (Jones et al. 2013).

Jones et al. (2013) presented two key reasons why taking an ethical approach to diversity training might enhance the training's effectiveness. One reason is based on the fact that people generally appreciate fairness and justice. I can relate this key reason to the ethics of justice, which I learned from a legal and ethics class a few months ago. As I understood it, the ethics of justice deals with moral choices employees must make to find a solution that damages the fewest people. Thus, in diversity training, trainers who subscribe to this principle of ethics of justice can incorporate it into their programs since an interest in fairness is a distinctive characteristic of humankind that gives rise to intrinsic expectations about the way people should be treated. The second key reason, according to Jones et al. (2013), is that the ideal organization should seek to convey a sincere commitment to multiculturalism in its approach to diversity management rather than simply a diverse numerical representation. What this means to me is creating a cultural pluralism in which various ethnic groups collaborate and dialogue with one another without having to sacrifice their particular identities. I can accept this notion to be true and effective. I was in a typical predominantly White school in Utah years ago, and its Department of Multicultural Services did exactly that, and today, it embraces a larger proportion of diverse groups on its campus.

I am surprised to read that research has shown that economic indicators can create backlash and resistance in managers, and the manner by which these indicators are presented to managers indeed affects their reception of the intended message (Jones et al. 2013). As such, why does almost every organization seek to conduct diversity training in the workplace? After reading this article, I no longer believe that management of organizations do conduct diversity training programs not necessarily to increase the employees' cultural awareness, knowledge, and skills, thereby increasing the inclusion of different identity groups, and by promoting better teamwork, but rather to benefit the organization by protecting against them against civil rights violations.

ARTICLE 5

In "How to Break the Cycle of Low Workforce Diversity: A Model for Change," O'Brien, Scheffer, van Ness, and van der Lee (2015) argued that although social justice concerns and perceived business advantage are behind the widespread drive to increase workplace diversity, dominance in terms of ethnicity, gender, or other aspects of identity have been resistant to change in many sectors. The authors claimed that the different factors that contribute to low diversity are often hotly contested and difficult to untangle (O'Brien et al. 2015).

I have learned in this article about the incentives to increase diversity, including access to a larger talent pool, improvements in team creativity, innovation and problem-solving, return on investment in training, and greater connection to clients and customers. The authors labeled these incentives as the "business case" for diversity, similar to Jones et al.'s (2013) article. This could be the reason why numerous companies, professions, government agencies, and leadership teams worldwide are actively working to increase workforce diversity. Again, it is all about the "business case" and diversity training programs rather than overall effectiveness. No wonder Jones et al. posited that many of the barriers to change arise from self-reinforcing feedback between low group diversity and inclusivity increases.

It has never crossed my mind that even though workforce diversity has increased in many sectors over recent decades, change has been slow or confined to only one area. For example, although African Americans are well represented in police departments in large American cities, they only account for 5–6 percent of the police forces in smaller towns. After reading the previous articles, it is not new to me that despite all the benefits of diversity training programs, social categorization and similarity-attraction theories suggest that diversity can undermine group performance through reducing cohesion, trust, and communication and increasing intergroup bias and conflict. However, this article also explains how different classes and dimensions of diversity (e.g., values, education, personality, gender, and race) affect group dynamics differently and can create "fault lines" that undermine group processes (Jones et al. 2013).

I am mathematically inclined, and when I read that Jones et al. (2013) used mathematical modeling to investigate long-term changes in workforce composition, I was eager to explore how this model was developed and applied to diversity training in the workplace:

$$t = (1/r_{\mathrm{T}}) \ln \left[(d_{\mathrm{Applicant}} - x_{\mathrm{Employee}}(0)) / [(d_{\mathrm{Applicant}} - x_{\mathrm{Employee}}(t)) \right]$$

This mathematical model demonstrates that time t taken to reach target diversity x Employee(t) will depend on turnover rate rT, applicant diversity, as well as applicant and initial employee diversity x Employee (0).

Currently, we have four Asian, one African American, three Caucasian, and three Latino employees. I quickly inserted numbers represented in my workplace into the equation to estimate the time taken to reach target diversity representative of the San Fernando Valley, and it came up with thirty-eight years given a very low turnover rate of 0.01 per year. In my workplace, the initial employee diversity is high enough, and thus the model predicts that workforce composition will slowly approach that of the applicant pool. It is good to know that by using this dynamic model, we can demonstrate how bias in employee appointment and departure can trap organizations in a state with much lower diversity than the applicant pool itself—a workforce diversity "poverty trap."

ARTICLE 6

Carmeli, Reiter-Palmon, and Ziv's (2010) article "Inclusive Leadership and Employee Involvement in Creative Tasks in the Workplace: The Mediating Role of Psychological Safety" examines how inclusive working environments that value individual and group differences within the workforce (manifested by a leader's openness, accessibility, and availability) foster employee creativity in the workplace. The authors used the leader–member exchange (LMX) theory, which posits that leadership outcomes are dependent the amount of interaction between the leader and the members. According to Carmeli et al., inclusive leaders use the LMX leadership style.

The idea that leadership is a particularly important factor that influences workplace creativity and innovation had never dawned on me until I read this article. It truly makes sense now after thinking about visionaries such as Mark Zuckerberg and Bill Gates, who probably use this concept in influencing creativity and innovation in their organizations. In reading Carmeli et al.'s (2010) article, I also learned that leaders who use the LMX leadership style contribute to employee creativity in multiple ways: (a) they serve as role models for creative behaviors; (b) they provide resources including time, funding, and information necessary for the creative endeavor; (c) they invigorate and energize employees to become more creative; (d) they support creative behavior by providing relational support to followers; and (e) they influence employee creativity by shaping the climate of the team or organization—noncontrolling supervision and support of innovation. If these are the factors that help employees be creative and innovative, I believe I am also a proponent of the LMX leadership style.

This research investigated the relationship between inclusive leadership, psychological safety, and employee involvement in creative work. Results from structural equation modeling indicate that inclusive leadership was positively linked to psychological safety, which then enhances employee involvement in creative work, thus suggesting that members' feeling accepted and respected plays a mediating role in the relationship between inclusive leadership and employee creativity increases (Jones et al. 2013). In my master's-level psychology classes, I studied about Carl Rogers's theory of acceptance, empathy, and genuineness, which seems very similar to this concept of LMX leadership style. Rogers's theory has helped me initiate and sustain better and healthier relationships, and it has helped me help clients develop wholesome solutions to their problems. I am, therefore, not surprised how this concept would work in employee creativity and innovation.

ARTICLE 7

In this review of *Managing Diversity: Toward a Globally Inclusive Workplace*, Barzantny (2007) argued that the book is filled with theoretical, conceptual, as well as practical content with numerous case examples on workforce diversity management. It could thus be very useful managers and future managers alike wanting to succeed in the globalizing economy. The author claimed the book could help the reader better understand the challenges of managing diversity in a global context and offers a framework for an inclusive workplace for comprehensively managing diversity, and an analysis to help managers understand the potential of diversity management for resourcefulness and synergy with theoretical and practical considerations. A particular strength of the book is the idea of integration of its inclusive workplace model into the business rationale, a concept which I would like to learn and apply in the workplace (Barzantny 2007).

According to Barzantny (2007), the book has sixteen chapters divided into three major parts. The first part presents the macro-level with the global context of diversity management in four chapters supported by empirical data. The second part, in the next four chapters, addresses the micro-mezzo level with social psychological perspectives of workforce diversity. The third and the last part presents solutions or practical intervention approaches. After reading this book review, I decided to buy it right away because of its theoretical and practical insights into managing a diverse workforce in the global context (Barzantny 2007).

I like the first chapter because it raises the challenge of managing and controlling diversity with all the issues and tensions arising through global workforce trends, including (a) accepting and utilizing a workplace's diversity, (b) being active in the community, (c) helping alleviate the needs of disadvantaged groups in the broader community, and (d) collaborating across cultural and national boundaries with a focus on global mutual interests (Barzantny 2007).

The second chapter presents the legislative aspects of diversity and the impact on equality and fairness in the workplace, which I have learned about in my human resource management class. However, I do like the international framework for managing workforce diversity, rooted in the UN's International Bill of Human Rights; this stimulated my interest in reading the book to better understand the varied antidiscrimination legislation in the world as well as the gaps between laws and practice. The ethical dilemmas presented at the end of this chapter would be of good use to set the challenge for global business practice (Barzantny 2007).

The book arrived today, and I read the entire third chapter, which presents the social policies and affirmative or positive action programs as reactions or actions against discrimination in employment as well as for promoting equality in the workplace. This chapter seems very familiar to materials I learned from the human resource management class. In fact, what I learned in the human resource management class is deeper than what this chapter presents in this book. I find the numerous examples helpful, including various countries' overviews on topics (Barzantny 2007).

Chapter 4 is very factual, addressing the impact of global demographic trends on workforce diversity in developed as well as developing countries. The author argued that population growth, as well as global migration, will result in more diversity in the global workplace; however, the issue of possible conflicts for the developed and developing world will manifest through various attributes of discrimination, which I believe have already began (e.g., United States versus Mexico; Barzantny 2007).

There is not much in Chapters 5 through 10 that is unfamiliar to my knowledge nor excites me about what the author presents except for the detail on occupational diversity and migration. I must admit, I do like the author's suggestion that organizations scrutinize and change their policies and procedures on several levels if they want to change their organization's culture to become truly diverse and inclusive in the workplace (Barzantny 2007). Finally, I learned from the training and development class the importance of *transfer of learning*—learners' effectively and continually applying knowledge they have acquired to other contexts—in this case, their jobs. According to Barzantny (2007), there are numerous case examples, vignettes, and suggestions for transfers and applications of theoretical considerations into business realities, and I believe these make the transfer of learning more successful.

ARTICLE 8

In "See No Evil: Color Blindness and Perceptions of Subtle Racial Discrimination in the Workplace," Offermann, Basford, Graebner, Jaffer, Basu De Graaf, and Kaminsky (2014) argued that workplace discrimination has grown more ambiguous, with interracial interactions often perceived differently by different people. In their research, the authors studied a key individual difference variable in the perception of discrimination at work—individual colorblind attitudes—by examining the relationships between three dimensions of colorblind attitudes: (a) racial privilege, (b) institutional discrimination, and (c) blatant racial issues and racial microaggressions in the workplace enacted by a White supervisor toward a Black employee (Offerman et al. 2014).

In reading this article, I learned that blatant discrimination appears to be declining in American workplaces; however, it is being replaced by more ambiguous manifestations of prejudice. On the other hand, subtle prejudice, often unconscious on the part of the perpetrator, may be no less damaging to the worker or work environment, threatening the mental well-being of the individuals involved. In addition to impacting the target of discrimination, recent work suggests that racial and ethnic harassment can negatively impact the occupational health of those who witness it or are aware of the harassment of coworkers, making it a concern for all employees (Offerman et al. 2014).

I can agree with the authors that organizations must be able to recognize and discourage even subtle forms of discrimination, but identifying such discrimination can be challenging because it may be largely in the eye of the beholder. In ambiguous situations, those subjected to subtle discrimination may be left wondering about the validity of their own perceptions, and hence be less likely to report such incidents to their organizations for possible remediation. Even social acceptance can create causal uncertainty (Offerman et al. 2014). I also learned that individuals who believe that race does not and should not matter are said to hold colorblind racial attitudes. There are three aspects of color blindness in their well-known twenty-item Color-Blind Racial Attitudes Scale: (a) racial privilege, (b) institutional discrimination, and (c) blatant racial issues. Racial privilege assesses one's lack of awareness of the existence of White privilege in the United States, including its role in determining who is successful, who gets opportunities and social services, or who gets sent to prison. Institutional discrimination indicates limited awareness of the implications of institutional forms of racial discrimination, such as affirmative action and immigration and language policies. Blatant racial issues indicate a more general unawareness of racism and racial discrimination as a current problem in United States at large, including in public schools (Barzantny 2007).

I find the results of this research findings very intriguing, as they (a) showed that observer views on institutional discrimination can be fully mediated and demonstrated that (b) blatant racial issues are partially mediated between racial group membership and the perception of workplace microaggressions. White participants were more likely to endorse colorblindness and blatant racial issues as institutional discrimination significantly more than racial or ethnic minorities. In turn, higher levels of colorblind worldviews were associated with decreased likelihood of recognizing microaggressions. Racial group did not significantly affect attitudes on racial privilege or affect microaggression perceptions (Barzantny 2007).

This article is very different from the others I read. From the very beginning, I wanted to keep reading. The more I read, the more things I learned. This article opened up a whole world of knowledge on diversity management, and I am very glad I chose it for my project.

REFERENCES

Adams, T. (2019). TBH: 5 Reasons why honesty is important [Blog post]. Retrieved from http://trudyadams.squarespace.com/blog/tbh-5-reason-why-honesty-is-important.html

Barzantny, C. (2007). Managing diversity: Toward a globally inclusive workplace. *Academy of Management Learning and Education*, 285–286. doi:10.5465/AMLE.2007.25223469

Bechervaise, C. (2013, October 14). 5 reasons why vision is important in leadership [Blog post]. Retrieved from https://takeitpersonelly.com/2013/10/14/5-reasons-why-vision-is-important-in-leadership/

Beck, J. (2015, March 18). How uncertainty fuels anxiety: An inability to live with life's unknowns can lead to worry and distress. *The Atlantic.* Retrieved from https://www.theatlantic.com/health/archive/2015/03/how-uncertainty-fuels-anxiety/388066/

Biography.com. (n.d.). *Barack Obama.* Retrieved April 14, 2020 from https://www.biography.com/us-president/barack-obama

Carmeli, A., Reiter-Palmon, R., and Ziv, E. (2010). Inclusive leadership and employee involvement in creative tasks in the workplace: The mediating role of psychological safety. *Creative research journal, 22,* 250–260. doi:10.1080/10400419.2010.504654

Dana, D. (1996). *Managing differences: How to build better relationships at work and home* (2nd ed.). St. Louis, MO: MTI Publications.

Dictionary.com. (n.d.). Trust. Retrieved from Dictionary.com: https://www.dictionary.com/browse/trust?s=t

Gebert, D., Beungeler, C., and Heinitz, K. (2017). Tolerance: A neglected dimension in diversity training? *Academy of Management Learning and Education, 16,* 415–438. doi:10.5465/amle.2015.0252

Grossman, D. (2019, May 6). Trust in the workplace: 6 steps to building trust with employees [Blog post]. Retrieved from http://www.yourthoughtpartner.com/blog/bid/59619/leaders-follow-these-6-steps-to-build-trust-with-employees-improve-how-you-re-perceived

Hall, K. (2017, December 4). The importance of kindness: Being kind can strengthen your relationships and sense of satisfaction in life. *Psychology Today.* Retrieved from https://www.psychologytoday.com/us/blog/pieces-mind/201712/the-importance-kindness

Heathfield, S. M. (2020, June 22). What is integrity? Definition and examples of integrity [Blog post]. Retrieved from https://www.thebalancecareers.com/what-is-integrity-really-1917676

Holt, M. (n.d.). Risks of not confronting conflict in the workplace. *Houston Chronicle*. Retrieved November 14 2017 from https://smallbusiness.chron.com/risks-not-confronting-conflict-workplace-1205.html

Ilgaz, Z. (2014, May 15). Conflict resolution: When should leaders step in? *Forbes*. Retrieved from https://www.forbes.com/sites/85broads/2014/05/15/conflict-resolution-when-should-leaders-step-in/#e681d0f33576

Ilmakunnas, S., and Ilmakunnas, P. (2011). Diversity at the workplace: Whom does it Benefit? *De Economist, 159*, 223–255. doi:10.1007/s10645-011-9161-x

Jacob, C. (2018, December 19). Why is self-discipline important [Blog post]? Retrieved from https://upjourney.com/why-is-self-discipline-important

Jones, K. P., King, E. B., Nelson, J., Geller, D. S., and Bowes-Sperry, L. (2013). Beyond the business case: An ethical perspective of diversity training. *Human Resource Management, 52*, 55–74.doi:10.1002/hrm.21517

Jung, C. G. (1973). To Fanny Bowditch, 22 October 1916 (R. F. C. Hull, Trans.). In G. Adler and A. Jaffé (Eds.), *C. G. Jung Letters: Vol. 1. 1906–1950* (1st ed., 33). London, United Kingdom: Routledge and Kegan Paul.

Kang, S.-Y. (2017, December 6). The true meaning of integrity. *The Huffington Post*. Retrieved from https://www.huffpost.com/entry/the-true-meaning-of-integ_b_11273420

Killinger, B. (2010). *Integrity: Doing the right thing for the right reason* (2nd ed.). London, United Kingdom: McGill-Queen's University Press.

Lexico. (n.d.). Kindness. Retrieved from https://www.lexico.com/en/definition/kindness

O'Brien, K. R., Scheffer, M., van Ness, E. H., and van der Lee, R. (2015). How to break the cycle of low workforce diversity: A model for change. *PLoS ONE, 10*, 1–15. doi:10.1371/journal.pone.0133208

Offermann, L. R., Basford, T. E., Graebner, R., Jaffer, S., De Graaf, S. B., and Kaminsky, S. E. (2014). See no evil: Color blindness and perceptions of subtle racial discrimination in the workplace. *Cultural Diversity and Ethnic Minority Psychology 20*, 499–507. doi:10.1037/a0037237

Patel, D. (2019, May 14). 10 powerful ways to master self-discipline. *Entrepreneur*. Retrieved from https://www.entrepreneur.com/article/287005

Price, D. (2012). *Well said! Presentations and conversations that get results.* New York, NY: AMACOM.

Shirodkar, P. (2013). Unclogging the MENtal block: Ensuring greater gender diversity at the workplace. *Journal of Commerce and Management Thought, 4,* 339–355. Retrieved from http://www.jcmt.net/

Spears, L. C. (2004). Practicing servant-leadership. *Leader to Leader* 2004(34), 7–11. doi:10.1002/ltl.94

Telenti, A., Pierce, L. C. T., Biggs, W. H., di Iulio, J., Wong, E. H. M., Fabani, M. M., … Venter, J. C. (2016). Deep sequencing of 10,000 human genomes. *Proceedings of the National Academy of Sciences, 113,* 11901–11906. doi:10.1073/pnas.1613365113

Thomas, K. W. (1976). Conflict and conflict management. In M. D. Dunnette, *Handbook of industrial and organizational psychology: Vol. 1* (889–935). Chicago, IL: Rand McNally.

Thomas, K. W., and Kilmann, R. H. (1974). *Thomas-Kilmann conflict mode instrument.* Palo Alto, CA: Consulting Psychologists Press.

APPENDIX 6.1
PERSONAL LEADERSHIP GROWTH INSTRUMENT

In this section, the Personal Leadership Growth Questionnaire (PLGQ) is provided as an example of a measure that can be used to assess personal leadership growth. The PLGQ quantifies the perceptions of the individual leader and selected observers, such as followers or peers. It measures an individual's personal leadership growth and points the individual to the areas in which they may have special strengths or weaknesses.

By taking the PLGQ, one can gain an understanding of how personal growth is used for leadership assessment. One can also assess their own personal growth.

PERSONAL LEADERSHIP GROWTH QUESTIONNAIRE

Instructions. The purpose of this questionnaire is to measure personal leadership growth in leadership. The questionnaire should be completed by the leader and three people who are familiar with the leader.

Make three additional copies of this questionnaire. This questionnaire should be completed by you and three people you know (e.g., family members, friends, coworkers, or relatives). Using the following scale, have each individual indicate the degree to which they agree or disagree with each of the twelve statements below. Do not forget to complete one for yourself.

_____ (leader's name)

Key: 1 = Strongly disagree   2 = Disagree   3 = Neutral   4 = Agree   5 = Strongly agree

1.	Individual differences: accepts people the way they are	1 2 3 4 5
2.	Communication skills: talks directly, honestly, and respectfully	1 2 3 4 5
3.	Active listening skills: attentive to people when they speak	1 2 3 4 5
4.	Courage: perseveres in difficult and uncertain times	1 2 3 4 5
5.	Conflict resolution: is able to handle disagreements rather quickly	1 2 3 4 5
6.	Honesty: acts in a way that they know is the right thing to do	1 2 3 4 5

7.	Integrity: adheres to ethical principles regardless of the situation	1 2 3 4 5
8.	Self-discipline: has the ability to control their moods and feelings	1 2 3 4 5
9.	Vision: has an idea of where they want things to be in the future	1 2 3 4 5
10.	Kindness: is friendly, generous, and considerate	1 2 3 4 5
11.	Trust: does what they say they will do (i.e., walks the talk)	1 2 3 4 5
12.	Persuasion: seeks consensus rather than compliance in decision-making	1 2 3 4 5

SCORING

1. Enter the responses for Rater 1, 2, and 3 in the appropriate columns as shown in example 6.1. The example provides hypothetical ratings to help explain how the questionnaire can be used.
2. For each of the twelve items, compute the average for the three raters and place that number in the "average rating" column.
3. Place your own scores in the "self-rating" column.

Example 6.1 Personal Leadership Growth Questionnaire Ratings

		Rater 1	Rater 2	Rater 3	Average rating	Self-rating
1	Individual differences	3	4	4	3.7	4
2	Communication skills	4	3	3	3.3	4
3	Active listening skills	3	4	3	3.3	4
4	Courage	5	2	4	3.7	5
5	Conflict resolution	5	4	4	4.3	4
6	Honesty	4	3	3	3.3	4
7	Integrity	3	3	4	3.3	5
8	Self-discipline	5	4	4	4.3	5
9	Vision	1	1	2	1.3	3
10	Kindness	3	3	1	2.3	4
11	Trust	4	3	3	3.3	5
12	Persuasion	2	2	3	2.3	4

SCORING INTERPRETATION

The scores you received on the PLGQ provide information about how you see yourself and how others see you as a leader. The chart allows you to see where your perceptions are the same as those of others and where they differ.

The example ratings show how the leader self-rated higher than the observers did on the metric of individual differences. On the fourth metric, courage, the leader self-rated substantially higher than others. On the conflict resolution metric, the leader self-rated quite close to others' rating but lower. There are no ideal ratings on this questionnaire. The purpose of the instrument is to give you a way to assess your strengths and weaknesses and to evaluate areas where your perceptions are congruent with those of others and where there are discrepancies.

7

MOONIC ELEMENTS FOR EMOTIONAL STABILITY

A man watches his pear tree day after day, impatient for the ripening of the fruit. Let him attempt to force the process, and he may spoil both fruit and tree. But let him patiently wait, and the ripe pear at length falls into his lap.

—Abraham Lincoln

Abraham Lincoln was the sixteenth president of the United States and is regarded as one of America's greatest heroes due to his role as savior of the Union and emancipator of slaves. Lincoln was assassinated at a time when his country needed him to complete the great task of reunifying the nation.

—Biography.com (n.d.)

Emotional stability is the second quintet of the PEPSE framework of Lite leadership. To achieve emotional stability, one needs to acquire and practice its eight moonic elements: (a) emotional intelligence, (b) self-esteem, (c) self-acceptance, (d) stress management, (e) anger management, (f) patience, (g) boundary setting, and (h) positive thinking and beliefs (see figure 7.1).

Figure 7.1. The moonic elements for emotional stability quintet.

EMOTIONAL INTELLIGENCE

Daniel Goleman (2000) defined *emotional intelligence* (EQ) as the capacity for effectively recognizing and managing one's own emotions and the emotions of those around them, including groups of people. Having EQ helps a person to be able to build others up, bring them together, and motivate them to do their best. EQ is one of the very important characteristics that differentiates a Lite leader from any other leader.

Lite leaders need to cultivate EQ and use it to (a) respect and relate well to people from varied backgrounds, (b) understand diverse worldviews, and (c) be sensitive to group differences. They see diversity as an opportunity and are able to create an environment where diverse people can thrive (Goleman 2000).

As previously discussed, individuals are very unique and carry different emotions that have the potential to get in the way of important business and personal relationships. EQ helps leaders (a) handle difficult people and tense situations with diplomacy and tact, (b) spot difficult conflict, (c) bring disagreements into open and help de-escalate, (d) encourage debate and open discussion, and (e) orchestrate win-win solutions. Finally, there is convincing evidence that severe lack of EQ could affect your health (Goleman 2000).

Lite leaders must be aware that active listening and the ability to empathize go hand in hand, and the focus is to serve others. In order to do so, leaders must be able to accept and recognize people's individual values and feelings. Even when someone is underperforming at work, a Lite leader should be able to love and understand that person. Empathy is often hard to achieve in a business environment because the focus is on company objectives and performance. Lite leaders, however, must shift this focus to the individual employee and their well-being.

To improve their ability to be empathic, when having a conversation, leaders should try to put their own viewpoints aside and openly listen to what the other person is saying. They need to be inquisitive and learn more about different ways of doing things. Instead of rejecting an idea or thought, learn more about it to understand where the person suggesting it is coming from.

SELF-ESTEEM

Lopez and Snyder (2009) described *self-esteem* as one's subjective evaluation of their own worth. In other words, self-esteem incorporates beliefs about oneself as well as emotional states, such as triumph, despair, pride, and shame. Smith and Mackie (2007) defined self-esteem as positive or negative evaluations of oneself.

A Lite leader's worth should not be based upon others' esteem of them, or else they would seek approval and validation from others, and their perception of their worth would be low until they get it. A person's true self-esteem is not based on what others think; it is based on what they think of themselves. Self-esteem may fluctuate with life's ups and downs (e.g., illness), but a person with good self-esteem will usually return to feeling good about themselves eventually. Lite leaders need good self-esteem so that they don't blame themselves or take other's opinions or what fate throws at them too personally (Lancer 2011).

Learning to accept losses, ill health, mistakes, and rejection will increase one's self-esteem. However, self-esteem can plummet if one's focus shifts to their flaws at the expense of acknowledging their assets. Self-criticism is the biggest obstacle to self-esteem.

SELF-ACCEPTANCE

Henriques (2014) described *self-acceptance* as one's awareness of their strengths, weaknesses, and feelings of self-satisfaction in spite of their deficiencies and regardless of past behaviors and choices. Lite leaders must realize that sometimes they fail, and sometimes they succeed; sometimes they are right, and sometimes they are wrong. They must allow themselves to fully be and accept who they are.

No matter how resilient they are emotionally, one's self-esteem will vary depending on positive and negative external factors that they cannot control. On the contrary, self-acceptance is steady and unaffected by external factors. Lite leaders should accept themselves the way they are despite their flaws, failures, and limitations (Lancer 2011).

Lite leaders must be more self-forgiving and let go of self-judgment. People make mistakes; they do or say things that they may regret in the future. This is when they should depend on their self-acceptance for self-forgiveness and overcoming guilt. They should appreciate their singular individuality and never compare themselves to others, either positively or negatively, because it could make them feel as though they are not good enough (Lancer 2011).

Self-acceptance can work wonders if allowed to do so. For example, one might find themselves gradually ceasing to worry what others think about them and their actions; instead, they will become more spontaneous and natural. One requirement of a Lite leader is to be authentic, and it is self-acceptance that helps make that happen. Practicing self-acceptance often can allow more of one's inner self to emerge. Being in this mode may reduce the shame or fear of revealing one's true self, creating a feeling that one is untouchable. Finally, self-acceptance enables a Lite leader to accept other people the way they are, which creates important, intimate, and spiritual relationships (Lancer 2011). This is a key ingredient to the pursuit of joy.

STRESS MANAGEMENT

Stöppler (2019) defined *stress* as any physical, chemical, or emotional factor that causes bodily or mental disturbance and may be a cause for disease. Examples of stress that are due to physical and chemical factors include trauma, infections, toxins, illnesses, and injuries of any sort. There are numerous and varied types of stress that are due to emotional factors. The term "stress" is often associated with psychological stress; however, scientists and physicians use this term more generally to denote the force that impairs the stability and balance of bodily functions.

Lite leaders need to realize that not all stress is bad; a mild amount of stress and tension can sometimes be beneficial. For example, feeling mildly stressed trying to meet a deadline for a project or assignment often forces people to do a good job, focus better, and work energetically. However, when stress is overwhelming and not properly managed or controlled, its negative effects may appear (Stöppler 2019).

It is noteworthy to mention that Lite leaders often find themselves under stress, and elimination of stress is almost impossible. Stöppler (2019) argued that the goal is to learn methods (e.g., relaxation techniques) to manage the stress and its effects on your physical and mental health.

ANGER MANAGEMENT

Kazdin (2000), described *anger* as a natural human emotion characterized by dislike or hatred toward something or someone one feels has deliberately done them wrong. Anger is a common emotion, and it's safe to say that everyone feels it from time to time. People deal with anger in different ways—some suppress it, and others express it. Anger is a completely normal, usually healthy human emotion. When it is not controlled and managed properly, however, it can get out of control and turn destructive, leading to problems in relationships, at work, and in the overall quality of life. People can do and/or say things they regret when angry (Avedian 2014).

One thing that Lite leaders have to know is that not all anger is bad. In fact, anger can be a good thing. It can provide a way to express negative feelings instead of suppressing them, which is not good. Anger can also motivate people to find solutions to problems. However, excessive anger can cause problems. Increased blood pressure and other physical changes associated with anger make it difficult to think straight and can harm one's physical and mental health (Kazdin 2000).

Anger causes the body to release stress hormones such as adrenaline, noradrenaline, and cortisol. The heart rate, blood pressure, body temperature, and breathing rate all increase. Regular episodes of anger can eventually make people ill. In other words, uncontrolled or unresolved anger can lead to physical health problems, such as backaches, headaches, hypertension (high blood pressure), insomnia, irritable bowel syndrome or other digestive disorders, stroke, heart attack, and weakened immune system, resulting in more infections, colds, and influenza (Avedian 2014).

My best advice to Lite leaders is "control your anger before it controls you." A Lite leader should learn (a) to track the specific triggers in their own life that often cause anger, (b) to see these triggers coming long before they have a chance to erupt into serious problems at home or at work, (c) to identify when anger is useful and when it is not, and (d) utilize practical tools to handle tough situations (Avedian 2014).

Lite leaders should be proactive when it comes to anger. This can be accomplished by learning and practicing effective methods to (a) communicate in a safe environment, (b) express complaints or dissatisfaction, and (c) be clear and assertive. If anger becomes a problem, therapists, psychologists, or psychiatrists may be able to help manage it and bring it under control.

PATIENCE

The Cambridge Dictionary (n.d.) defined *patience* as the ability to wait, to continue doing something despite difficulties, or to suffer without complaining or becoming annoyed. Lite leaders need to have the capacity to accept or tolerate delay, trouble, or suffering without getting angry or upset.

Life is not always smooth. Expectations will be violated, goals will go unmet, and things will go wrong. As Mercury stated (2016), it is when things get uncomfortable that one must revert to patience, a virtue, to help deal with the discomfort in a suitable manner. With patience comes self-control; it shows that a person can handle life when times get tough. In other words, with patience comes the ability to look outside of oneself and withstand judgment when necessary. In a nutshell, having patience is demonstrative of a high moral standard in life (Mercury 2016).

It is noteworthy to mention that being impatient can cause harm. People often get the impression that goals can be achieved very quickly if they push for them. While this may be true on occasion, many great things require time and patience (Mercury 2016).

Lite leaders need to understand that impatience can lead to poor decisions that can (a) affect their health and happiness, (b) waste time, (c) put them under unnecessary stress, (d) affect relationships with others, and even (e) put their lives in danger. Patience can be practiced by adjusting or regulating thoughts and beliefs about events to accept that great things take time, and better decisions are made with patience (Mercury 2016).

Lite leaders should not try to cut corners or do things in an unethical way. Rather, they should make a commitment to patiently work things out, do what needs to be done, and make things happen. This commitment will ensure they always do the right thing, sending a positive message to people around them. This is a good example of the light that shines in the dark—an important characteristic of Lite.

AWARENESS

General awareness and self-awareness are requirements for becoming a Lite leader. *Self-awareness*, in particular, requires one to see their own emotions and behaviors in the context of how they affect the rest of the team. Through self-awareness, a leader becomes better at noticing what the people around them are doing so they can fix problems more quickly. Self-awareness is tightly connected to the feedback culture within the organization. It is important that employees are able to provide feedback, not just on themselves and each other, but also the management and leadership (Spears).

The secret to awareness is taking a closer look inside oneself. Learning one's strengths and weaknesses is crucial for understanding one's inner self and how it affects others. This can be accomplished through personality tests such as the Myers–Briggs Type Indicator, Change Style Indicator, DiSC assessment, EQ, and others. More importantly, however, leaders may want to seek feedback from their team to learn more about how they are perceived and how their actions are influencing others.

BOUNDARY SETTING

Boundary is defined by Oxford's online dictionary (Lexico n.d.) as a line that symbolizes the limits of an area. In any relationship, whether friends, within the workplace, or in a romantic partnership, a boundary is a line that is clearly drawn so that others know not to cross it. Boundaries are necessary to develop and maintain healthy relationships (Katherine 1994).

According to Benedict (2019), establishing clear physical and emotional boundaries makes it possible for people to define themselves in relation to others. These boundaries determine how they interact with others and how they allow others to interact with them. However, to do this, one must be able to identify and respect their own needs, feelings, opinions, and rights. Healthy boundaries are firm yet flexible.

A Lite leader should know when to set healthy boundaries. If a leader finds themselves whining or complaining, or feeling anger, bitterness, or resentment, a boundary probably needs to be set. They should use their self-awareness to assess their feelings and then determine what needs to be said or done. The necessary boundary should be communicated assertively, even if this might upset others. Setting healthy boundaries avoids the need to put up walls (Benedict 2019).

Lite leaders tend to be fixers, wanting to help people feel better and solve their problems. They care about people, and when others are going through struggles, they try to do all they can to make it better for them. It may not be possible to make others' problems go away, and this can be frustrating. In cases like these, one needs to set a boundary for themselves and know they cannot be everything to everyone. Weber (2019) claimed that, as important as it is, setting healthy boundaries requires commitment, courage, and discipline.

Lite leaders need to learn to set healthy boundaries. One way of doing this, according to Weber (2019), is to learn to say "no" to people and situations that are causing them harm. It is natural to think that saying "no" is cruel or selfish, but it is a way of preserving the relationship a leader has with themselves. Being direct is another way of setting healthy boundaries. There may be times when others behave in ways that make a leader feel uncomfortable, and when that happens, it is an indication that their intuition is sending up an alert that their boundaries are being violated. This is when they have to speak up for themselves clearly and directly in a respectful manner.

CREATE A POSITIVE MINDSET

Sasson (2019) defines *positive mindset* as a state of mind that visualizes and expects good results. In other words, it means positive thinking and the belief that everything will turn out well.

Positive mindset helps leaders (a) see the good in people, (b) recognize opportunities, and (c) focus on the bright side of life. Negative mindset, on the other hand, does exactly the opposite. It makes one think about failure, how bad their life is, and unconsciously cause them to make bad choices. Besides the fact that negative mindset perpetuates negative situations, it affects thinking and actions, and a leader may end up not seeking solutions to their problems.

Creating positive mindset is a must for Lite leaders. Adopting it does not mean that everything will always move smoothly and there will be no bumps in the road. However, it ensures against the possibility that any setback will stop a leader or change their state of mind, and that they will go on, try again, and do their best. One good way of getting rid of negative mindset is to substitute negative thoughts with positive thoughts about success and happiness. It is a beginning of forming a new habit, and it can be tedious at the onset, but with determination and persistence, a leader will be able to change what and how they think (Seppälä 2016).

The bad news is that negative thoughts come to mind easily and have the potential to wreak havoc on a leader's self-confidence. Positive thoughts, which make people feel good about themselves, fade away quickly and negative thoughts are pushed to the front. If caught in the act of thinking negatively, a leader should make a conscious effort to correct course by taking a deep breath, then focusing on three things they can be grateful for (e.g., family, job, and/or health; Seppälä 2016).

It is very important for Lite leaders to question overly self-critical or upsetting thoughts and replace them with more helpful and realistic thoughts. If a leader recognizes that they are about to do something that will make them feel worse, they should instead do something more helpful, continuing to practice changing unhelpful thoughts and behaviors and developing these skills at their own pace until it becomes a new habit (Murphy 2012). This is a never-ending process.

BUILDING COMMUNITY

Lite relies on the development of a community and a sense of togetherness within the organization. With this in mind, businesses can foster a sense of community by focusing on team building. By creating effective and caring teams, the organization as a whole will become more caring.

In order to support community building, a leader should ensure that different people within the organization interact with each other. Organizing social events and get-togethers is important. Diversity and the flow of opinions within the organization should be encouraged as much as possible.

REFERENCES

Avedian, A. (2014). *Anger management essentials* (1st ed.). Glendale, CA: Author.

Benedict, C. (2019). Setting healthy boundaries: Allowing the true self to emerge. *Serenity Online Therapy*. Retrieved from http://serenityonlinetherapy.com/healthyboundaries.htm

Biography.com. (n.d.). *Abraham Lincoln*. Retrieved April 14 202erkelehttps://www.biography.com/us-president/abraham-lincoln

Cambridge Dictionary. (n.d.). Patience. In *Cambridge Dictionaries Online*. Retrieved from erkele://dictionary.cambridge.org/dictionary/english/patience

Goleman, D. (2000). *Working with emotional intelligence*. New York, NY: Bantam.

Henriques, G. (2014, May 15). Six domains of psychological well-being. *Psychology Today*. Retrieved from https://www.psychologytoday.com/us/blog/theory-knowledge/201405/six-domains-psychological-well-being

Lexico. (n.d.). Boundary. In *Lexico.com dictionary*. Retrieved from https://www.lexico.com/definition/boundary

Lopez, S. J., and Snyder, C. R. (Eds.). (2009). *The Oxford handbook of positive psychology* (2nd ed.). Oxford, United Kingdom: Oxford University Press.

Katherine, A. (1991). *Boundaries: Where you end and I begin: How to recognize and set healthy boundaries*. New York, NY: Hazelden.

Kazdin, A. E. (Ed.). (2000). *Encyclopedia of psychology: 8 volume set*. Washington D.C.: American Psychological Association.

Lancer, D. (2011). *10 steps to self-esteem: The ultimate guide to stop self-criticism* (1st ed.). Whitehouse, TX: Carousel.

Murphy, E. (2012, March 15). *Cognitive behavioural therapy and solution focused therapy: Differences, discuss* [Blog post]. Retrieved from https://brief-therapy-uk.com/cognitive-behavioural-therapy-solution-focused-therapy-differences-discuss/

Mercury. (2016, February 6). *Here are 9 reasons why patience is a virtue* [Blog post]. Retrieved from http://www.ilanelanzen.com/personaldevelopment/here-are-9-reasons-why-patience-is-a-virtue/

Sasson, R. (2019). *What is the meaning of positive attitude—Definitions* [Blog post]. Retrieved from https://www.successconsciousness.com/blog/positive-attitude/what-is-the-meaning-of-positive-attitude/

Seppälä, E. (2016). *The happiness track: How to apply the science of happiness to accelerate your success*. New York, NY: HarperOne.

Smith, E. R., and Mackie, D. M. (2007). *Social psychology* (3rd ed.). New York, NY: Psychology Press.

Stöppler, M. C. (2019). Stress management. *MedicineNet*. Retrieved from https://www.medicinenet.com/stress_management_techniques/article.htm

Weber, L. (2019, October 25). Setting boundaries in any relationship is an important act of self-care. *Olean Times Herald*. Retrieved from http://www.oleantimesherald.com/health/setting-boundaries-in-any-relationship-is-an-important-act-of/article_7f406748-837e-5fd5-8fa7-983bb1a26011.html

APPENDIX 7.1
EMOTIONAL STABILITY INSTRUMENT

In this section, the Emotional Stability Questionnaire is provided as an example of a measure that can be used to assess emotional stability. The Emotional Stability Questionnaire quantifies the perceptions of the individual leader. It measures an individual's emotional stability and points the individual to the areas in which they may have special strengths or weaknesses. By taking the Emotional Stability Questionnaire, one can gain an understanding of how emotional stability is used for leadership assessment.

EMOTIONAL STABILITY QUESTIONNAIRE

Instructions: The purpose of this questionnaire is to measure emotional stability in leadership. The questionnaire should be completed by the leader. This questionnaire should be completed by using the following scale to indicate the degree to which you agree or disagree with each of the twelve statements below.

_____ (leader's name)

Key: 1 = Never   2 = Seldom   3 = Often   4 = Usually   5 = Always

1. When trying to express my feelings, I take a moment to step out of my shoes and see the other person's perspective 1 2 3 4 5

2. When my expectations are not met, I cool off and work through the issue before taking action 1 2 3 4 5

3. I have positive evaluations of myself, always feeling good and hardly seeking approval and/or validation from others 1 2 3 4 5

4. I am steady and unconditional to whatever happens in and around me, and I accept myself the way I am despite my flaws, failures, and limitations 1 2 3 4 5

5. I use relaxation techniques and other methods to manage my stress and its effects on my physical and mental health 1 2 3 4 5

6. I have the capacity to accept or tolerate delay, trouble, or suffering without easily getting upset 1 2 3 4 5

7. I see my own emotions and behaviors in the context of how they affect others around me 1 2 3 4 5

8. I seek to know my strengths and weaknesses for understanding my inner self and how it affects others around me 1 2 3 4 5

9. Oftentimes, I say no to people and situations that are causing me harm as a way of preserving the relationship I have with myself 1 2 3 4 5

10. I see the good in people, recognize opportunities, and focus on the bright side of life 1 2 3 4 5

11. I focus on a sense of togetherness within the group in order to foster an effective and caring teams 1 2 3 4 5

12. When others offer opinions that don't align with mine, I discount what they say and make them wrong 1 2 3 4 5

SCORING

Add up the scores on all twelve items.

SCORING INTERPRETATION

- *High range:* A score between forty-eight and sixty means you exhibit strong emotional stability.
- *Moderate range:* A score between thirty-six and forty-eight means you tend to exhibit emotional stability in an average way.
- *Low range:* A score between twenty-four and thirty-six means you exhibit this emotional stability below or expected degree.
- *Extremely low range:* A score between twelve and twenty-four means you are not inclined to exhibit emotional stability—and you need to seek help.

8

MOONIC ELEMENTS FOR PHYSICAL HEALTH

Physical fitness is not only one of the most important keys to a healthy body, it is the basis of dynamic and creative intellectual activity.

—John F. Kennedy

John Fitzgerald Kennedy (May 29, 1917—November 22, 1963), often referred to by the initials JFK and Jack, was an American politician who served as the 35th president of the United States from January 1961 until his assassination in November 1963.

—Web.achive.com

Physical health is the third quintet of the PEPSE framework of LeaderLite. To achieve physical health, one needs to acquire and practice its five moonic elements: (1) cardiovascular endurance, (2) muscular strength, (3) muscular endurance, (4) body composition, and (5) flexibility (see figure 8.1). Practice all the five moonic elements to achieve optimal benefits for your body in the long run.

Healthbeat (2019) suggests you need to talk to your medical doctor to advise you if it is safe to start exercising, especially if you are extremely unsteady on your feet, you have dizzy spells or take medicine that makes you feel dizzy or drowsy, or you have a chronic or unstable health condition, such as heart disease, asthma or another respiratory ailment, high blood pressure, osteoporosis, or diabetes.

As LeaderLites, it is important to get fit and then stay in shape, but many of us find it difficult to go to the gym for exercises even just for a fraction of the recommended 2.5 hours per week of physical activity by the US Centers for Disease Control and Prevention (CDC 2019).

Bautista (2017) states that physical activities are beneficial to our body systems—musculoskeletal, cardiovascular, respiratory, and endocrine—a lowered risk of premature death, coronary heart disease, hypertension, colon cancer, and diabetes. In addition, if you move your body regularly, you are at a lower risk of depression and anxiety, and you are more likely to be in a good mood and will be more able to perform daily tasks with ease throughout your life.

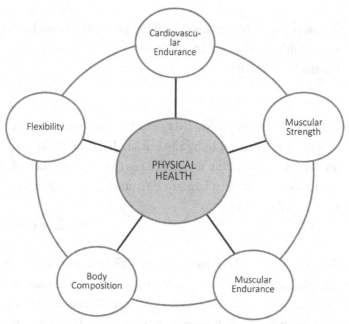

Figure 8.1. The moonic elements for emotional stability quintet.

CARDIOVASCULAR ENDURANCE

Peloquin (2019) describes cardiovascular endurance as the ability of your body to keep up with exercises like running, jogging, swimming, cycling, and anything that forces your cardiovascular system (lungs, heart, blood vessels) to work for extended periods of time. For example, running as far as possible in twelve minutes is a test commonly used to assess your cardiovascular endurance. During this period of time, the heart and lungs together fuel your body with the oxygen needed by your muscles, ensuring that they have the oxygen needed for the work they are doing.

As a LeaderLite, you must practice good cardiovascular endurance exercise, such as walking, jogging, cycling, dancing, running, or bike riding. When you are able to exercise without becoming overly tired, you have achieved good cardiovascular endurance. It is so important to improve your cardiovascular endurance because performing those exercises will boost the capacity of your muscles to extract oxygen from the bloodstream to produce energy that you do need on a constant basis (Sharecare 2019).

LeaderLites must make it a habit to exercise consistently for prolonged periods of time to improve cardiovascular endurance. This will improve your body's ability to bring oxygen from the environment, into the lungs, and diffused into the bloodstream, and into the cells in your body to help your cells work to their full capacity. In addition, as you may already know, the heart is a muscle, and consistent cardiovascular exercise helps the heart become bigger and stronger, allowing more blood to be pumped out with each beat. Because more blood is pumped out with each beat, your heart does not have to beat as fast or work as hard (Sharecare 2019).

MUSCULAR STRENGTH

According to Peloquin (2019), muscular strength is the ability to lift and carry heavy objects in a short period of time. Don't confuse this with simply how strong you are i.e., how much weight you can carry, how many pounds you can lift at the gym, or how many push-ups you can do during a workout. True muscular strength definition is a little bit more complicated than that; it is the ability to generate the maximal amount of muscle force in a particular exercise.

As a LeaderLite, you need to feel strong and build your muscular strength to help you complete daily chores and exercises. Without muscular strength, your body will be weak—and you will not be able to keep up with the demands placed upon it (Scott, Understanding Muscular Strength

2019). Peloquin (2019) suggests the way to increase your muscular strength is to train with weights, working in the four-to-six or twelve-to-fifteen-repetition ranges. The heavier the weight, the fewer repetitions you should perform.

MUSCULAR ENDURANCE

Scott (2019) describes muscular endurance as the ability to produce and sustain muscle force over a sustained period of time—in contrast to muscular strength, which is just lifting or carrying weight for a few seconds. It is important, as LeaderLites, to improve our stamina consistently in order to help us engage in activities both at work and home without becoming too tired too soon. Muscular endurance helps us achieve this goal.

A simple way to increase our muscular endurance is to train with lighter weights, working in the twenty-to-twenty-five-repetitions range. According to Peloquin (2019), lighter weights will train the muscle fibers needed for muscular endurance, and the higher repetition range leads to a longer period of exercise.

FLEXIBILITY

Many of us often overlook the importance of flexibility when it comes to physical health. Peloquin (2019) argues that without flexibility, the muscles and joints would grow stiff, and movement would be limited. As LeaderLites, we need our bodies to be able to move through their entire range of motion without pain or stiffness. Flexibility training ensures that our bodies accomplish this goal.

Flexibility is very important for us LeaderLites because the body was designed to move in a specific way; maintaining the full range of each joint is desirable for optimal physical health and is beneficial to our joints. As LeaderLites, we need better muscle balance, joint stability, proper activation of the working muscles and overall better movement quality to move our bodies in between workstations in the workplace more efficiently. In order to achieve this desirous goal, we need to go through a full range of motion during flexibility exercises (Fetters 2016).

Start your daily flexibility exercises by leaning forward and trying to touch your toes. If you are able to touch your toes, you have good flexibility, but if you are not able to touch your toes, then you have limited flexibility. You may also want to do the sit and reach exercise i.e., sitting on the floor and reaching toward your toes. This is another good way to assess your flexibility. The closer you come to touching your toes and beyond, the more flexible you are (Peloquin 2019).

BODY FAT COMPOSITION

The body composition can be described to contain only two different types of mass, (1) fat-free mass includes bone, water, muscle, organs, and tissues (called lean tissue) and (2) body fat mass. The lean tissues are metabolically active, burning calories for energy, while body fat is not. Body fat percentage is a measurement of body composition telling us how much of the weight of your body is fat (Scott 2019).

Peloquin (2019) describes body fat composition as a measurement of body composition that tells us how much of the weight of our body is just fat. In other words, body fat composition refers to the amount of fat on our bodies. For example, a 150-pound person with a measurement of 30 percent body fat composition will have body fat of forty-five pounds and a lean body mass of 105 pounds.

To be classified as a person who is fit, a man has to have a body fat composition lower than 17 percent, and a woman has to have a body fat composition lower than 24 percent. Though this classification could be more fitting for a professional athletic, it is desirable for LeaderLites to strive to fall within the average man's range of 18–24 percent or the average woman's range of 25–31 percent body fat (Peloquin 2019).

APPENDIX 8.1
PHYSICAL HEALTH INSTRUMENT

In this section, the Physical Health Questionnaire (PHQ) is provided as an example of a measure you can use to assess your physical health. The PHQ quantifies the perceptions of the individual leader. It measures an individual's physical health and points the individual to the areas in which he or she may have special strengths or weaknesses. By taking the PHQ, you can gain an understanding of how physical health is used for leadership assessment.

PHYSICAL HEALTH QUESTIONNAIRE (PHQ)

Instructions: The purpose of this questionnaire is to measure physical health in leadership. The questionnaire should be completed by the leader. This questionnaire should be completed by you using the following scale to indicate the degree to which you agree or disagree with each of the ten statements below.

_____ (leader's name)

Key: 1 = Never   2 = Seldom   3 = Often   4 = Usually   5 = Always

1. I walk, or jog, cycle, dance, run and/or bike ride at least three times per week. 1 2 3 4 5

2. I am able to exercise for prolonged periods of time without becoming overly tired. 1 2 3 4 5

3. I have the ability to lift and carry heavy objects, not too heavy, in a short period of time. 1 2 3 4 5

4. When I exercise, I train with weights, not too heavy, working in the 4—6 or 12–15 repetition ranges. 1 2 3 4 5

5. I am able to produce and sustain muscle force over a sustained period of time. 1 2 3 4 5

6. When I am exercising, I train with lighter weights, working in the 20–25 repetitions range. 1 2 3 4 5

7. I am able to lean forward and touch my toes. 1 2 3 4 5

8.   I am able to do the sit on the floor and reach toward my toes. 1 2 3 4 5

9.   As a man, my body fat is between 18–24 percent, or as a woman
between 25–31 percent. 1 2 3 4 5

10.   My body mass index, BMI, is less than 25. .... 1 2 3 4 5

SCORING

Add up the scores on all ten items.

SCORING INTERPRETATION

- *High range:* A score between forty and fifty means you exhibit strong physical health.
- *Moderate range:* A score between thirty and forty means you tend to exhibit physical health in an average way.
- *Low range:* A score between twenty and thirty means you exhibit this physical health below the expected degree.
- *Extremely low range:* A score between ten and twenty means you are not inclined to exhibit physical health—and you need to seek help.

REFERENCES

Bautista, T. (2017, March 17). *Why do we need to be fit?* Retrieved from Natural-health.ph: https://naturalhealth.ph/why-do-we-need-to-be-fit/

Centers for Disease Control and Prevention. (2019, July 2). *Physical Activity Basics: How much physical activity do you need?* Retrieved from CDC.gov: https://www. cdc.gov/physicalactivity/basics/index.htm

Fetters, K. A. (2016, September 28). *Why range of motion matters for your strength training goals.* Retrieved from Dailyburn.com: https://dailyburn.com/life/fit-ness/strength-training-range-of-motion/

Healthbeat. (2019). *Do you need to see a doctor before starting your exercise program?* Retrieved from Harvard Health Publishing: https://www.health.harvard.edu/ healthbeat/do-you-need-to-see-a-doctor-before-starting-your-exercise-program

Peloquin, A. (2019). *The 5 components of physical fitness.* Retrieved from Fitday.com: https://www.fitday.com/fitness-articles/fitness/body-building/the-5-compo-nents-of-physical-fitness.html

Scott, J. R. (2019, August 24). *Body composition and body fat percentage.* Retrieved from Verywellfit.com: https://www.verywellfit.com/what-is-body-composi-tion-3495614

Scott, J. R. (2019, September 29). *Understanding muscular strength.* Retrieved from Verywellfit.com: https://www.verywellfit.com/how-to-increase-muscular-strength-3496121

Scott, J. R. (2019, September 29). *Understanding muscular strength.* Retrieved from Verywellfit.com: https://www.verywellfit.com/how-to-increase-muscular-strength-3496121

Sharecare. (2019). *What is cardiovascular endurance.* Retrieved from Sharecare.com: https://www.sharecare.com/health/exercise-for-increasing-cardiovascular-en-durance/what-is-cardiovascular-endurance

9

MOONIC ELEMENTS FOR SPIRITUAL RESILIENCE

There are no constraints on the human mind, no walls around the human spirit, no barriers to our progress except those we ourselves erect.

—Ronald Reagan

Ronald Wilson Reagan was an American politician who served as the fortieth president of the United States from 1981 to 1989 and became a highly influential voice of modern conservatism. Prior to his presidency, he was a Hollywood actor and union leader before serving as the thirty-third governor of California from 1967 to 1975.

—ThoughtCo.com

Spiritual resilience is the fourth quintet of the PEPSE framework of Lite. To achieve spiritual resilience, one needs to acquire and practice its seven moonic elements: (a) finding meaning, (b) mindfulness, (c) connectedness, (d) kindness, (e) joy, (f) developing perspective, and (g) support network (see figure 9.1). The Spiritual Resilience Questionnaire (SRQ; see appendix) is a measure that can be used to assess spiritual resilience.

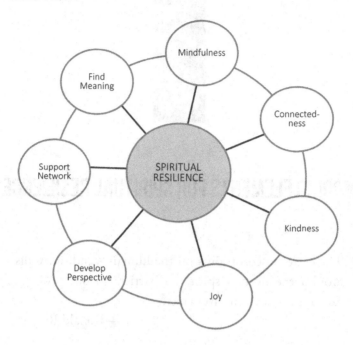

Figure 9.1. The moonic elements for
spiritual stability quintet.

FIND MEANING

Hersh (2018) described *finding meaning* as an idea that one's life has a purpose and is valuable both to oneself and to others. In addition, it is that feeling that life is rewarding and that it matters in many ways. A Lite leader realizes that the majority of their time and energy is spent at their workplace, so turning the workplace into a place where they add meaning and purpose will be beneficial in the long run. Such benefits include being happier, performing better at work, increased productivity, and overall life improvement.

Lite leaders need to know the meaning and purpose of their lives; otherwise, they may feel empty, discontent, and unfulfilled most of the time. Finding meaning in life should not be confused with being happy; they have some similarities, but there are important differences. For example, being a taker rather than a giver brings happiness, whereas being a giver rather than a taker is associated with high meaningfulness.

While integrating the past, present, and future is associated with high meaningfulness, being a present-oriented person is associated with happiness (Baumeister, Vohs, Aaker, and Garbinsky 2013).

A Lite leader may want to find ways to build meaningfulness to their life. One way to do this is to figure out why exactly they are doing what they do at work. Another is to connect and spend more time with people they care about—family, friends, relatives, coworkers—because this can boost the meaning factor in one's life. Leaders may want to note that what is meaningful to others may not necessary be meaningful to them, and that should be fine because meaningfulness comes from examining one's own core values and beliefs to learn things that are important to them and not things that are important to others. Oftentimes, focusing on the meaning of positive moments can help leaders get through the negative ones. Finally, focusing more on giving and helping people without worrying what you will get in return will increase feelings of meaning in life (Baumeister et al. 2013). This is one of the utmost characteristics of the Lite leader.

Hedegaard, Curtin, and Warner (2018) found that, in the period from 1999 through 2017, the suicide rate in the United States increased by 33 percent, from approximately 10.5 to 14 suicides per 100,000 people. Suicide still remains the tenth leading cause of death overall. However, suicide rates have fallen in other countries, including Japan, China, Russia, and most of Western Europe. People who commit suicide tend to feel hopeless; they are hurting so badly at some point in their lives and don't see hope in the future for them. In other words, such people do not find meaning in their lives.

Viktor Frankl (2006) discussed his belief that if humankind can find meaning and purpose in life, they might be able to hold on to hope during periods of pain, loneliness, rejection, abuse, deep depression, guilt, depression, helplessness, and hopelessness. It is my belief that, among these causes, people who feel hopeless are those who live with suicidal ideation.

GoodTherapy (2018) defined "hopelessness" as an emotion characterized by a lack of hope, optimism, and passion. People who have no expectation of future improvement or success typically feel hopeless. Lite leaders may want to watch for people with inhibited motivation, lack of interest, negative thoughts about the future, or a negative view of themselves. People with no hope in the future should be guided to resources to help them regain their hope and achieve lasting mental wellness. They should not be ignored because their feelings may soon become worse—and they may end up committing suicide.

MINDFULNESS

Greater Good Magazine (n.d.) described *mindfulness* as the means of maintaining awareness of one's thoughts, feelings, bodily sensations, and surrounding environment. Mindfulness can also be described as acceptance, meaning that we pay attention to our thoughts and feelings without judging them in a given moment. Lite leaders may want to practice mindfulness to let their thoughts tune into what they are sensing in the present moment rather than ruminating on the past or picturing the future.

Oftentimes, Lite leaders may experience burnout because of the nature of their work, and practicing mindfulness regularly through mind-body exercises can be a way of addressing this issue. More importantly, they can begin enhancing their psychological well-being (Seaward 2018). According to Gupta (2016), mindfulness can help avoid burnout by providing some brain downtime to refresh the spirits. Seaward (2018) argued that practicing mindfulness is beneficial because it helps one create and maintain good rapport and therapeutic relationships with friends, family members, coworkers, and relatives.

There are several mindfulness exercises to choose from; however, using the one that combines diaphragmatic breathing with tranquil natural scenes—an imagery and visualization technique—can be useful for relaxation (Seaward 2018). These can be done within five and no longer than ten minutes, during break times or anytime throughout the day. Lite leaders can even teach these to their friends, family members, relatives, and coworkers.

Mindfulness exercises work on different levels of the physical, mental, emotional, and spiritual self. These techniques are great for Lite leaders because they have benefits such as heart health, reducing sleeplessness, lowering blood pressure, increasing flexibility, and improving muscle strength and tone. Research shows that mindfulness can help relieve neck, back, and other types of pain experienced from working desk jobs. Moreover, it can increase energy, minimize the fatigue experienced at most workplaces, and improve concentration and focus (Seaward 2018).

CONNECTEDNESS

Rath (2007), defined *connectedness* as the belief that humans for some reason are all joined or linked together, not isolated from one another or from the earth and the life on it, as many people may think. The belief that things happen for a reason is very important to Lite leaders—they must be certain about it, that each person is part of something larger. Thus, people are responsible for their own judgments and in possession of their own free will.

It is noteworthy to mention that this feeling of connectedness comes with certain responsibilities. For example, harming others would mean harming oneself, and exploiting others would mean exploiting oneself as well. The awareness of these responsibilities eventually creates a value system that a Lite leader can call their own. Being considerate, caring, and accepting will go a long way to building connectedness (Rath 2007).

To build and sustain connectedness, a leader may want to practice being a bridge builder for people of different cultures, sensitive to the invisible hand, comforting to others who are afflicted, and, as much as possible without surrender, being on good terms with all persons. In addition, they should not be afraid of listening and counseling periodically because they are adept at helping other people see connection and purpose in everyday occurrences. Leaders may seriously consider scheduling time for meditation or contemplation, reflecting upon how their spiritual beliefs encourage their sense of connection to others, and how their connectedness gives them stability through their faith in people, the role of coincidences in their lives. They may also want to explore certain ways to expand their connectedness by starting a book club, attending a retreat, or joining an organization that puts connectedness into practice. Within their place of work, they may also want to help their colleagues understand how their efforts fit into the larger picture. Leading team building and helping people feel important can also help build the connectedness moonic element (Rath 2007).

Finally, helping others cope with unpredictable and unexplainable events, especially helping them find meaning in even sickness and death, will build and boost connectedness and bring comfort to one's perspective. The caveat here is to avoid loud, annoying, aggressive people—do not spend too much time trying to persuade them to see the world as a linked web. Knowing very well that one's sense of connection is intuitive, if others do not share this intuition, it is not worth engaging in rational argument because that will not persuade them anyway (Rath 2007).

COMMITMENT TO OTHERS' GROWTH

Commitment to others' growth simply requires that the Lite leader help people realize their potential beyond just the ability to do the job well. Greenleaf (1977) stated, "The secret of institution building is to be able to weld a team of such people by lifting them up to grow taller than they would otherwise be" (XX).

To demonstrate their commitment to others' growth, a leader can set an example by investing in their own personal and professional development. If they are constantly seeking to grow, they provide motivation to the team around them to do the same. In addition, they may also discuss personal and professional goals with their team. By understanding how others would like to develop, a leader can help provide the tools and routes for them to achieve these objectives. Leaders should learn more about how to grow their people and the benefits associated with this growth.

KINDNESS

Hall (2017) defined *kindness* as the quality of being friendly, generous, and considerate. The act of kindness is important to a Lite leader because being kind helps strengthen relationships and a sense of satisfaction in life. According to Khazan (2018), some people believe that kindness means you are weak or naïve, but that is not the case here. In contrast, being kind often requires courage and strength, and it has been proven to be an interpersonal skill. Research has shown that offering resources to others, rather than having more and more for oneself, brings about lasting well-being.

A good example of being kind is illustrated by Graham (2019), who wrote about how photos of Ellen DeGeneres, an American comedian, actress, writer, producer, and host of her own syndicated TV talk show, *The Ellen DeGeneres Show*, having a grand old time with former President George W. Bush, sharing nachos at a Dallas Cowboys game in Texas, was improper because these two individuals do not share same ideology. President Bush is a Republican, and Ellen is a Democrat. When questioned, she said on her show, "When I say, 'Be kind to one another,' I don't mean only the people that think the same way I do. I mean be kind to everyone" (Gelles, Leman, and Patrick 2019).

Lite leaders have to find different ways to practice kindness. One way is to open their eyes and be active to help those who are in need. They may also see others who are suffering, who need a helping hand; leaders should reach out to them and provide help or assistance. Sometimes all that is needed to practice kindness is to say a kind word to uphold someone who is stumbling. A smile can lift a person's mood, but it can also elevate the mood of those around them. Other acts of kindness include (a) opening the door, especially for the physically burdened, (b) helping to carry a heavy load, (c) celebrating loved ones, (d) giving honest compliments to those who deserve them, (e) sending thank-you emails, (f) telling people how special they are, (g) helping the elderly neighbor with yard work, or (h) sharing food with others (Khazan 2018).

Above all things, Leader Lite leaders should be kind to themselves, speak gently and kindly to themselves, and take good care of themselves. They should be aware of their inner critic—that little voice inside the mind that is quick to judge and is always ready to put them down. They should lean more toward their inner advocate—the other little voice in their mind that is there to defend them. There will be moments when a leader's inner critic comes at them with ridicule and scorn, but they shouldn't listen to it; instead, they should allow their inner advocate to jump in and present arguments on their behalf. A leader should trust that their inner advocate is there for them and learn to shut down their inner critic (Fabrega, n.d.).

Finally, leaders should remember they are not perfect beings and that there are times when they mess up. Perhaps they did something in the past that they are not proud of, they missed a great opportunity, or they failed to follow through on an important goal—these things happen to most people at one point or another. My advice to leaders is to stop blaming themselves, forgive themselves, and resolve to do better from now on. They should make sure to get enough sleep, eat enough fruits and vegetables, and get some form of exercise on a regular basis. In addition, they should conduct stress-relief exercises, be well groomed, and look after their appearance very well. On a tough day, when all seems downhill, a leader should soothe themselves; they could soak in a hot tub with scented bath oil or get a scalp and foot massage. After all, they know how to soothe themselves better than anyone else does.

JOY

Dictionary.com (n.d.) defines *joy* as "a feeling of great pleasure and happiness," and *happiness* as "a state of well-being characterized by emotions ranging from contentment to intense joy" (Dictionary.com, n.d.). These two definitions may make it seem like joy and happiness are one and the same, but according to Alcorn (2015), though there may be some similarities between joy and happiness, joy is a permanent feeling and happiness is short-lived.

Lite leaders must be able to distinguish between joy and happiness (a bubbly, superficial, and circumstantial feeling that comes and goes) and joy (a deep-seated and enduring affection that endures in spite of the circumstances around them). In other words, according to Brown (2012), joy is based on what is happening inside oneself, but happiness is based on what is happening outside and around them.

Lite leaders' joy comes from deeply held spiritual beliefs, but it can also come from a place even beyond that. They can practice joy when they try to make lasting peace with who they are, where they are, why they are, and who they are not with. Leaders should seek this joy frequently because happiness (on the other hand) is only external—based on situations, events, people, places, things, and thoughts—and is future-oriented, putting all one's eggs in someone else's basket.

DEVELOPING PERSPECTIVE

Merriam-Webster (2019) defined *perspective* as a mental view or prospect— the way you "see" things as a result of who you are and what you do. Hereford (n.d.) defined perspective as an attitude or view related to a subject or thing. In life, everything that happens is for a reason, but how people perceive it makes the difference; for example, an event could be catastrophic to one person and a challenge and opportunity for growth to another.

According to McGraw (2014), there are two sides to a pancake, no matter how thin or flat it may be. This is the core to understanding what perspective looks like—there are two sides to a pancake—and being able to see both sides is the beginning of developing one's perspective.

Human beings have the greatest limitations, and that is the danger of looking at the world from their own subjective perspective, especially in situations that directly involve them. Lite leaders have to understand that each person has a built-in, one-sided bias. The good news is they can develop the ability to see through the other person's eyes; if they are able to develop this skill, they will be tapping into an incredibly powerful tool for managing their lives. It is a skill that can be cultivated, and it comes with practice—just like flipping a pancake (McGraw 2014).

Lite leaders often find themselves negotiating with others in order to achieve a goal. One thing they do not want to do is to try to get what they want. A leader's priority is to give the other person as much of what they want as possible, which is only achievable when the leader uncovers what makes the other person tick, what their beliefs are, what they fear, and what they value. If a leader does not go through this process patiently, nothing they say will resonate. In other words, knowing where the other person is coming from is a knowledge that is powerful because without it, the leader will never get to the real issue. To get there, it requires the leader to flip the pancake (McGraw 2014).

SUPPORT NETWORK

Cambridge Dictionary (n.d.) defined *support network* as a group of people who provide emotional and practical help to someone in times of hardship. Lite leaders often find themselves pursuing major life changes or big audacious goals. These may be difficult at times, especially when the leader goes it alone. However, having the support of people with similar interests and passions greatly enhances their chances of success. Such a group support network can provide them with a place that they can bounce ideas off of, and the feedback they get back from this network can be beneficial (Coaching Positive Performance, n.d.).

Lite leaders need to have a good support network. If they do not have one, they should begin to build one gradually, selecting only people they deem to be trustworthy and supportive in times of hardship. There are many places where they might find suitable people to build their support network. They may want to look for family members, especially ones who have the desire to see them succeed and can be willing to offer any support they can. Leaders should be careful who they pick because family members can be the harshest critics (Coaching Positive Performance, n.d.).

Leaders may also look for good friends who have shown a high level of support to them over a prolonged period of time—they may be strong candidates for their support network. Again, they should be selective in choosing the friends who truly care and have been supportive through the years. A mastermind group, where a group of people come together to offer mutual support in a specific area of life or business, can also be beneficial because it can provide an excellent opportunity to learn from the knowledge, experience, and expertise of others (Coaching Positive Performance, n.d.).

Last but not the least, leaders may look for online communities. The internet provides plenty of opportunity for support, regardless of your area of interest. A group, community, or forum can offer support that may include the knowledge of experienced people who love to share their wisdom with other individuals and help solve problems in a matter of minutes (Coaching Positive Performance, n.d.).

HEALING

A Lite leader will serve the people much better if they emphasize emotional health, together with mental and physical well-being, of the people they serve. It is also important to focus on their potential to heal themselves and others. In a business context, healing would be achieved by ensuring that employees have enough support options available. This could mean access to counseling and proper health care facilities, a strong health and safety culture, or focus on self-development through courses and training.

In order to improve their healing abilities, leaders should make the above resources a priority, but they can also help people achieve success by utilizing the approach most optimal to the situation. They should ensure that they do not focus on just work-related things in their conversations with people; they also get to know how the person is doing. Leaders should make sure they (a) read self-development guides, (b) attend seminars, workshops, and conferences on employee engagement, and (c) provide tips on what they have learned to your team. They should ensure they are doing well mentally and physically to ensure they have the strength to help others.

REFERENCES

Alcorn, R. (2015, November 11). *Is there a difference between happiness and joy?* Retrieved from https://www.epm.org/blog/2015/Nov/11/difference-happiness-joy

Baumeister, R. F., Vohs, K. D., Aaker, J. L., and Garbinsky, E. N. (2013). Some key differences between a happy life and a meaningful life. *The Journal of Positive Psychology*, 8, 505–516. doi:10.1080/17439760.2013.830764

Brown, S. L. (2012, December 18). Joy versus happiness. *Psychology Today*. Retrieved from https://www.psychologytoday.com/us/blog/pathological-relationships/201212/joy-vs-happiness

Cambridge Dictionary. (n.d.). Support network. In *Cambridge Dictionary*. Retrieved from erkeletps://dictionary.cambridge.org/us/dictionary/english/support-network

Coaching Positive Performance. (n.d.). *Building a support network*. Retrieved from https://www.coachingpositiveperformance.com/building-a-support-network/

Dictionary.com. (n.d.-a). Happiness. In *Dictionary.com*. Retrieved from https://www.dictionary.com/browse/trust?s=t

Dictionary.com. (n.d.-b). Joy. In *Dictionary.com*. Retrieved from https://www.dictionary.com/browse/trust?s=t

Fabrega, M. (n.d.). *17 ways to be kind to yourself.* Retrieved from https://daringtolivefully.com/how-to-be-kind-to-yourself

Frankl, V. E. (2006). *Man's search for meaning*. Boston, MA: Beacon Press.

Gelles, J. (Head Writer), Leman, K. (Head Writer), and Patrick, L. (Director). (2019, October 8). Jonas Brothers/Kieran Culkin (Season 17, Episode 22) [TV series episode]. In M. Connelly, E. DeGeneres, E. Glavin, A. Lassner, K. Leman, and D. Westervelt (Executive Producers), *The Ellen DeGeneres Show*. A Very Good Production; Telepictures Productions; WAD Productions.

GoodTherapy. (2018, June 19). *Hopelessness*. Retrieved from https://www.goodtherapy.org/blog/psychpedia/hopelessness

Graham, R. (2019, October 12). Ellen DeGeneres is killing us with her kindness. *Boston Globe*. Retrieved from https://www.bostonglobe.com/opinion/2019/10/12/degeneres-killing-with-her-kindness/XdKK562OPOkPOePuhiTiNI/story.html

Greater Good Magazine. (n.d.). *What is mindfulness?* Retrieved from https://greatergood.berkeley.edu/topic/mindfulness/definition

Gupta, S. (2016, May 6). Why America's nurses are burning out. *Everyday Health*. Retrieved from https://www.everydayhealth.com/news/why-americas-nurses-are-burning-out/

Hall, K. (2017, December 4). The importance of kindness. *Psychology Today*. Retrieved from https://www.psychologytoday.com/us/blog/pieces-mind/201712/the-importance-kindness

Hedegaard, H., Curtin, S. C., and Warner, M. (2018). *Suicide mortality in the United States, 1999–2017* (Data Brief No. 330). National Center for Health Statistics, Centers for Disease Control and Prevention, U.S. Department of Health and Human Services. Retrieved from https://www.cdc.gov/nchs/data/databriefs/db330-h.pdf

Hereford, Z. (n.d.). *Perspective*. Retrieved from https://www.essentiallifeskills.net/perspective.html

Hersh, E. (2018, September 4). *Why is finding meaning in life and work so important?* Retrieved from https://positiveroutines.com/finding-meaning/

Khazan, O. (2018, August 16). It pays to be nice. *The Atlantic*. Retrieved from https://www.theatlantic.com/business/archive/2015/06/it-pays-to-be-nice/396512/

McGraw, P. C. (2014, April). Dr. Phil: The powerful ability that will help you manage your life. *O, The Oprah Magazine*. Retrieved from http://www.oprah.com/spirit/develop-perspective-how-to-see-someone-elses-point-of-view

Merriam-Webster. (n.d.). Perspective. In *Merriam-Webster.com*. from https://www.merriam-webster.com/dictionary/perspective

Rath, T. (2007). *StrengthsFinder 2.0*. New York, NY: Gallup Press.

Seaward, B. L. (2018). *Managing stress: Principles and strategies for health and well-being* (9th ed.). Burlington, MA: Jones and Bartlett Learning.

APPENDIX 9.1
SPIRITUAL RESILIENCE QUESTIONNAIRE

In this section, the Spiritual Resilience Questionnaire (SRQ) is provided as an example of a measure that can be used to assess spiritual resilience. The SRQ quantifies the perceptions of the individual leader. It measures an individual's spiritual resilience and points the individual to the areas in which they may have special strengths or weaknesses. By taking the SRQ, a leader can gain an understanding of how spiritual resilience is used for leadership assessment.

SPIRITUAL RESILIENCE QUESTIONNAIRE

Instructions

The purpose of this questionnaire is to measure spiritual resilience in leadership. The questionnaire should be completed by the leader. Below, you will find a list of twenty statements about feelings. If a statement describes how you usually feel, put an X in the column "Yes." If the statement does not describe how you usually feel, put an X in the column "No." There are no right or wrong answers.

1. I know the meaning and purpose of my life. .... ☐ Yes ☐ No

2. I believe my life has a purpose and is valuable, to both myself and others. .... ☐ Yes ☐ No

3. I connect and spend more time with people I care about—family, friends, relatives, and coworkers. .... ☐ Yes ☐ No

4. I have figured out why exactly I am doing what I do at work. .... ☐ Yes ☐ No

5. I watch for people with inhibited motivation, negative thoughts about the future, or a negative view of the self. .... ☐ Yes ☐ No

6. I help people with no hope in the future by finding resources to help them regain their hope and achieve lasting mental wellness. .... ☐ Yes ☐ No

7. I pay attention to my thoughts and feelings without judging them in a given moment. .... ☐ Yes ☐ No

8. The belief that things happen for a reason is very important to me. .... ☐ Yes ☐ No

9. I help people realize their potential beyond just the ability to do the job well. .... ☐ Yes ☐ No

10. I give and help people without worrying what I will get in return. .... ☐ Yes ☐ No

11. I am constantly seeking to grow by investing in my own personal and professional development, and I provide motivation to others around me to do the same. .... ☐ Yes ☐ No

12. I am friendly, generous, and considerate as a means to strengthen relationships and sense of satisfaction in life ...... ☐ Yes ☐ No

13. I strive to make peace with myself in spite of the circumstances around me. .... ☐ Yes ☐ No

14. I am able to see through the other person's eyes. .... ☐ Yes ☐ No

15. I have a good support network with people who are trustworthy and supportive in times of hardship. .... ☐ Yes ☐ No

16. I know my core values, and I pay attention to them. .... ☐ Yes ☐ No

17. I constantly use my core values to make consistent decisions and take committed action. .... ☐ Yes ☐ No

18. I tend to focus on my potential to heal myself and others. ☐ Yes ☐ No

19. I make sure I am doing well mentally and physically to ensure I have the strength to help others. .... ☐ Yes ☐ No

20. I always listen to my inner voice—gut/intuition/universal guidance—as my insanely powerful GPS to guide the decisions I make. .... ☐ Yes ☐ No

SCORING

Count the number of "Yes" responses and multiply by five.

SCORING INTERPRETATION

- *High range:* A score between ninety and one hundred means you exhibit strong spiritual resilience. These scores are much higher than average and indicate a noteworthy strength. These strengths probably come naturally to you or exist because you have worked hard to develop them. Seize every opportunity to use these spiritual resilience behaviors to maximize your leadership success. You are highly competent in this spiritual resilience, so work to capitalize on it and achieve your potential.

- *Moderate range:* A score between eighty and ninety means you tend to exhibit spiritual resilience in an above average way, and it is a strength to build on. Though this score is above average, there are a few situations where you don't demonstrate spiritual resilience behavior. There are many things you've done well to receive this score and a few that could be better with some practice. Study the behaviors for which you received this score and consider how you can polish your skills.

- *Mild range:* A score between seventy and seventy-nine means you exhibit this spiritual resilience below the expected level for a leader, but with a little improvement, this could be a strength. You are aware of some of the behaviors for which you received this score, and you are doing well with them. Other spiritual resilience behaviors in this group are holding you back. Lots of people start here and see a big improvement in their spiritual resilience once it's brought to their attention. Use this opportunity to discover the difference and improve in the areas where you don't do as well.

- *Low range:* A score between sixty and sixty-nine means you are not inclined to exhibit spiritual resilience, and it is something you should work on. This is an area where you sometimes demonstrate spiritual resilience but not usually. You may be starting to let people down. Perhaps this is a skill area that doesn't always come naturally for you or that you don't make use of. With a little improvement in this skill, your spiritual resilience will go way up.

- *Extremely low range:* A score of fifty-nine or below means you are not inclined to exhibit spiritual resilience, and it is a concern you must address. Spiritual resilience is either a problem for you, you don't value it, or you didn't know it was important. The bad news is your skills in this area are limiting your effectiveness as a Lite leader. The good news is that discovering this and choosing to do something about it will go a long way toward improving your spiritual resilience behavior.

10

MOONIC ELEMENTS FOR ENVIRONMENTAL CULTURE

No company, small or large, can win over the long run without energized employees who believe in the mission and understand how to achieve it.

—Jack Welch

John Francis "Jack" Welch Jr. is an American business executive, author, and chemical engineer. He was chairman and CEO of General Electric between 1981 and 2001. During his tenure at GE, the company's value rose 4,000 percent.

—CBS News

Environmental culture is the fifth and the last quintet of the PEPSE framework of LeaderLite. Though it is the last-mentioned quintet, it is equally important as the other four. In this context, environmental culture refers to the culture of the environment that we operate in, and it could be business, technological, economic, political, natural, global or international, social and culture environment. According to Schein (1985), culture operates at many levels.

The environmental culture describes how people do things in the environment they operate at the surface level and why they do things the way they do at the root-system level. As LeaderLites, the only thing of real importance that you need to do is to create and manage culture (Schein 1985).

Kaplan, Dollar, Melian, Durme, and Wong (2016) also describes environmental culture as "the way things work around here," specifically how the values, beliefs, behaviors, artifacts, and reward systems influence people's behavior on a daily basis. Top leadership drives the environmental culture, which over time, becomes deeply embedded in the company through a number of processes, reward systems, and behaviors.

In any environmental culture, behaviors of the people may or may not improve business performance, depending on the type of environmental culture that has been established. Researchers agree that environmental culture is the issue of the CEO, and the good news is that it can be measured and improved to drive strategy (Kaplan, Dollar, Melian, Durme, and Wong 2016).

To achieve environmental culture, one needs to acquire and practice its eight moonic elements: (1) constructive culture, (2) engagement, (3) ethics, (4) problem-solving, (5) stress overload, (6) change management, (7) work diversity, and (8) adaptability (see figure 10.1).

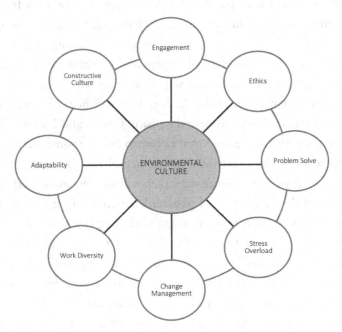

Figure 10.1. The moonic elements for environmental culture quintet.

CONSTRUCTIVE CULTURE

Research by Cooke and Lafferty (2019) shows there are three types of environmental culture: (1) constructive, where cultures promote effective goal setting and achievement, growth and learning, and teamwork and collaboration, (2) aggressive/defensive, where cultures lead to internal competition, management by exception, and short-term emphasis as opposed to long-term effectiveness, and (3) passive/defensive, where cultures lead to conformity, rigidity, and lack of team member accountability and initiative.

As a LeaderLite, creating a constructive environmental culture is the way to go. To do this, you may want to interact with people and approach tasks in ways that will help others meet their higher-order satisfaction needs. In addition, you may want the people you lead to set their own realistic goals and solve their own problems effectively, gain enjoyment from their work, produce high quality products/services, and be supportive of each other. Subsequently, allowing them to be constructive, open to influence in dealing with others, and friendly, open, and sensitive to the satisfaction of the work group will go a long way in making the environment they work in constructive and healthy. Doing these will help you to create and manage constructive environmental culture (Cooke and Lafferty 2019).

It is noteworthy to mention that failure to create a constructive culture may lead to a passive/defensive environmental culture where you find that interacting with people in ways that will not threaten their security is the order of the day. To avoid passive/defensive environmental culture, you may want to refrain from agreeing with, or gaining the approval of, or being liked by others to conform, follow the rules, and make a good impression. You may also want to discourage making people do what they are told, clear all decisions with supervisors, shift responsibilities to others, and avoid being blamed for mistakes (Cooke and Lafferty 2019).

Another type of environmental culture you may want to avoid is the aggressive/defensive environmental culture. To do this, you may want to discourage people from approaching tasks in forceful ways in order to protect their status and security. You may also want to refrain from expecting the people that you lead to gain status and influence by being critical and constantly challenging one another or take charge and control others. Finally, you may want to discourage people from making decisions autocratically, operate in a "win-lose" framework and work against their peers to be noticed, or avoid making mistakes, work long hours, and keep "on top" of everything (Cooke and Lafferty 2019).

As a LeaderLite, you need to know that environmental culture is not merely an HR issue; it is a business issue, and that calls for the CEO and the executive team to take the responsibility for an organization's culture—with HR supporting that responsibility through measurement, process, and infrastructure. It is also good to know that although environmental culture is widely viewed as important, it is still largely not well understood, and people find it difficult to measure and even more difficult to manage. Don't assume that people know and understand what environmental culture really is because a very discouraging poll shows that only 28 percent of people believe they understand their culture well, while only 19 percent believe they have the "right culture" (Kaplan, Dollar, Melian, Durme, and Wong 2016).

Finally, LeaderLites must always remember that environmental culture can determine success or failure, especially during times of change, including mergers, acquisitions, growth, and product cycles. Success or failure depends on how aligned the environmental culture is with the business's direction (Kaplan, Dollar, Melian, Durme, and Wong 2016).

ENGAGEMENT

Before we describe what engagement really is, it is important to understand that environmental culture, as described above, is intimately connected with engagement, but the two are significantly different. While environmental culture describes "the way things work around here," engagement, in contrast, describes "how people feel about the way things work around here." It is a way of portraying the level of commitment of people to the company they work for and the job that they do (Kaplan, Dollar, Melian, Durme, and Wong 2016).

Research shows that when the environmental culture is clearly aligned with the business strategy, it attracts people who feel comfortable in it, which results in a high level of engagement, and this is how environmental culture and engagement are connected. On the other hand, when programs to improve engagement are initiated, oftentimes, issues on environmental culture are discovered, encouraging the people at the top to question and change its values, incentives, programs, and structure. Another similarity between environmental culture and engagement is they both require CEO-level commitment and strong support from HR to understand, measure, and improve.

According to Bersin (2015), there are five areas of engagement: (1) meaningful work and jobs, (2) management practices and behaviors, (3) work environment, (4) opportunities for development and growth, and (5) trust in leadership. Engagement is poor when people feel uneasy or uncommitted to the work they do, resulting in high turnover, low performance, and low levels of innovation and customer service.

As a LeaderLite, you may want to focus on seeking new tools to measure and monitor engagement of people at the workplace on a detailed, real-time basis, delivering specific, actionable information to continuously improve the workplace environment (Bersin 2015).

ETHICS

There are numerous definitions of ethics. In "Ethics and Computers," a paper presented at the National Art Education Association Conference in San Francisco on March 24, 1996, Craig Roland of the University of Florida defined ethics as a system of moral principles, rules, or standards that controls the conduct of members of a group (Roland 1996). Another author, Kerns (2002), defines ethics as the situation that arises when, in the face of dilemma, one chooses to do the right or the wrong thing. He claims that ethical managerial leaders and their subordinates take the right and good path in ethical choice points.

Yet researchers like Prevost, Godward, and Dickerson (2004) define ethics as a nonspecific term for a variety of ways of understanding and examining the moral conduct of human behavior and actions. Thus, the normative aspect of ethics lies in setting standards for right or good action, and the descriptive aspect involves reporting on what people believe and how they act. A philosophical approach deals with differences between right and wrong and with the moral consequences of human actions. According to Wojtczak (2002), examples of ethical dilemmas that arise in medical practice and research include the failure to seek informed consent, disclosure of confidentiality, respect for human rights, and scientific integrity.

As a LeaderLite, you must have a philosophical or theological basis from which you derive your understanding of ethics. Without this basis, your practice of ethical behavior will be constantly changing as a result of changing circumstances and personal preferences (Hawkins 2000). Be aware that most people are confused by and suspicious of individuals who present themselves as ethical leaders, whether they are corporate CEOs or nonprofit executives. People from entirely different background and culture in other countries—or even immigrants from developing countries in America—are even more confused as they try hard to understand what ethical truly means.

It is noteworthy to mention that one of the sources of this confusion lies in the example of self-proclaimed ethical leaders, especially in developing countries, who openly engage in bribery and corruption and have self-destructed because of such moral and ethical failures (Brian 2001). It is no wonder that the ethical failures people, especially from developing countries, experience in their leaders fuel their suspicion of any leaders who make similar claims of ethical leadership.

Most people in high-velocity cultures believe stress and greed have resulted in leaders bending the rules. A research study by Aguilera and Vadera (2005) points out that 70 percent of all managers bend company rules in America. Other research by Dixon (2004) points to three reasons why 70 percent of all managers bend company rules: (1) performance-based judgment calls, (2) faulty rules and (3) social norms such as that everyone else does it. Rule bending leads to corrupt behavior, unethical decision-making, and illegal conduct.

LeaderLites have a duty to stop unethical leadership behavior; otherwise, rules, laws, and standards for right and wrong are meaningless. You need to know that good ethical leadership begins with your position on ethical issues and is guided by values such as honesty, sincerity, candor, compassion, and respect. These are termed *values* because they help guide your behavior. You can only be congruent if you live and lead in a manner that is consistent with your values (Dixon 2004).

Ethics, values, leadership, and trust are issues of immense timely importance to executives attempting to recover from a substantial downturn in the national and global economies. The challenge of promoting and maintaining ethical leadership has become ubiquitous for executives and academics in a variety of fields. In the recent past, controversy has been attached to Olympic judges. Award winning journalists have been fired for fabricating credentials, sources, and stories. Politicians have been brought before the bar of justice or tried by the court of public opinion. Church leaders have been revealed as having concealed crimes committed by their subordinates. And, of course, corporate America and Wall Street are feeling the sting of accusations that go to the heart of investor and public trust (Fulmer 2003). Even though a LeaderLite cannot personally review the behavior of the people they engage with, they do set the tone and establish expectations and standards for everyone.

Ethics training in America is very common for employees in many business organizations today; however, the same cannot be said about companies operating in developing countries. Those companies have been slower to address business ethics concerns. It can be argued that the multinational corporations in most developing countries are the only organizations that have implemented some form of business ethics initiatives. This lack of ethics training programs for employees in other companies, coupled with the fact that civil servants are not paid enough, leads to managerial leaders using their positions to provide discreet services such as cover-ups for breaches of taxation and law enforcement issues in exchange for bribes (Brian 2001).

In most developing countries, endemic corruption and misdirection of assets remain part of local business customs. Even value-based leaders, especially those who happen to be the only working members in their families, are often pressured to provide such essentials as medical support or tuition—when the only way to supplement their meager incomes is through bribery and corruption. Large companies are the victims of most fraud, which is considered acceptable practice because they are faceless benefactors (Brian 2001).

Since 2002, the governments of most developing countries have created investment policies, hoping to attract foreign investment. This did not occur probably because some multinational corporations—mostly from North America and Western Europe—are reluctant to invest in countries that will subject them to practices that would not be accepted in the United States or the West in general. For example, Reid Plastics refused to pay a $50,000 bribe to build a factory in Indonesia (Kerns 2002). A lack of ethical leadership is causing developing countries to pay a dear price. American businesses such as Reid Plastics are simply being ethical. However, with the rapid growth of globalization, business practices in developing countries need to follow the practices and values exemplified in the American legal system.

PROBLEM-SOLVING

Angle (2019) describes problem-solving as not just the process of finding solutions to difficult or complex issues, but as the act of defining a problem, determining the cause of the problem, identifying, prioritizing, and selecting alternatives for a solution, and implementing a solution. Here are the four basic steps of the problem-solving process, see figure 10.2.

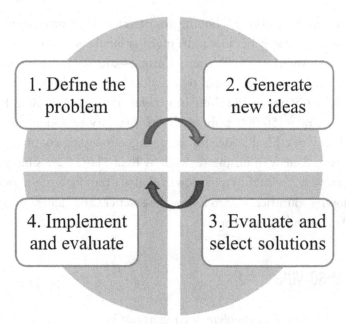

Figure 10.2. Problem-Solving Chart
adapted from Angle (2019).

1. Define the Problem

To define the problem, it is crucial to focus on diagnosing the situation and not just the symptoms. Problem-solving techniques that can be helpful in making this happen are (a) the process flowchart to identify the expected steps of the process and (b) the cause-and-effect diagrams to define and analyze the root causes of the problem (Mahanti 2019).

The first step is to review and document how the processes currently work—who does what, with what information, using what tools, communication with what organizations and individuals, in what time, using what format among others (Angle 2019).

2. Generate Alternative Solutions

The idea is to seek several problem-solving alternatives using brainstorming and team problem-solving techniques before selecting one solution. This is because when you do consider multiple alternatives, you significantly enhance the value of your ideal solution. The decision to develop a "what should be" model is critical since this target standard will the become the basis for developing a road map for investigating further alternatives (Angle 2019).

Collection of several alternative solutions to the problem should be achieved before final evaluation. It is not uncommon that in problem solving alternatives are evaluated as they are proposed. This is a mistake oftentimes the first acceptable solution that is chosen is not even the best fit and focusing on trying to get the results that we desire make us miss the potential for learning something new that will allow for real improvement in the problem-solving process (Angle 2019).

3. Evaluate and Select an Alternative

Evaluating and selecting the best alternative solution requires a great amount of problem-solving skills. To achieve this goal, skilled problem solvers consider the extent to which a particular alternative will solve the problem without causing other unanticipated problems i.e., we don't not solving one problem and creating another at the same time. In addition, there has to be a consensus toward the acceptance of the alternative. Finally, the implementation of the alternative is not just likely, but it also fits within the organizational constraints such as resources and production capabilities among others (Angle 2019).

4. Implement and Follow Up on the Solution

LeaderLite leaders must be ready at this stage to direct others to implement the solution, "sell" the solution, or facilitate the implementation with the help of others. This is because involving others in the implementation is an effective way to gain buy-in and support and reduce the resistance considerably to subsequent changes (Angle 2019).

Simple feedback channels must be built into the implementation stage regardless of how the solution is introduced to the process. This is crucial because it allows for continuous monitoring and testing of actual events against expectations. You must pay attention to whether the solution remains in place, and if it does, it is an indication that the problem-solving techniques used are most effective. You may then update problem-solving techniques used periodically to respond to future changes (Angle 2019).

WASTE REDUCTION

Waste reduction is a concept that is an integral part of lean management. The primary goal is to identify activities that cost money and resources and do not add value to the customer and figure out ways and means to eliminate them at the root-cause level so they don't appear again. For LeaderLite leaders, eliminating such wasteful activities is one of the most important prerequisites for building a successful company. This concept which is an integral part of lean thinking could help you increase profitability in the workplace (Kanbanize 2019).

Kanbanize (2019) argues that while waste is any activity that consumes resources but brings no value to the end customer, not all wasteful activities can be eliminated from the workplace because some of them are a necessity for the process to thrive. For example, testing software for reliability and accuracy is not an activity that customers are willing to pay for, but without it, the chance of delivering a low-quality product is high, which can have a negative impact on your business performance (Kanbanize 2019).

In actual fact, only a small portion of a whole work process really creates value for the customers. LeaderLites should focus on reducing wasteful activities in the workplace as much as possible because that will help them identify significant opportunities to improve the overall performance of the workplace (Kanbanize 2019).

Gitlow, Melnyck, and Levine (2015) describes waste as any activity that brings no real value to the external (end-user) customers and is not required by financial, legal, or other business reasons. Maximizing the value delivery is the main principle of lean and has always focused on maximizing the value delivery.

Kanbanize (2019) names two major types of waste:

Necessary waste. This is a non-value added (NVA) activity that is necessary to get things done in a quality manner. Such activities can be testing, planning, reporting, or other necessary activities that are considered important for the process to deliver good-quality products or services.

Pure waste. This is also a non-value added (NVA) activity, but it is unnecessary because it does not bring value to the end customer. Such an activity should be removed from the process immediately. Activities such as any form of waiting are among unnecessary activities that are considered pure waste and should be removed immediately.

Taiichi Ohno, the originator of lean management, describes three major roadblocks that can influence a company's work processes negatively: (a) Muda (wasteful activities), (b) Muri (overburden), and (c) Mura (unevenness). He categorized the seven types of waste (seven Mudas), which has become a popular practice for cost reduction and optimizing resources in numerous workplaces today (Kanbanize 2019).

In addition, Rajagopalan (2017) stated that practitioners of the Kanban approach have expanded on the standard seven types of waste in Kanban, adding the non-utilization of talents and introducing the mnemonic or memory aid, DOWNTIME, to capture these eight types of waste that LeaderLite leaders should closely monitor to increase efficiency. Here are the eight wasteful activities in detail:

1. Defects. This happens when information, products, or services are incomplete or inaccurate. Examples include (a) in production—broken parts or defected parts that need to be reworked, (b) in software development—bugs in a computer program or system that cause it to produce an incorrect or unexpected result, (c) in marketing—wrong brand communication, mistakenly branded materials, and (d) in project management—incorrect collection of data.

2. Overproduction. This wasteful activity occurs when we make more of something than needed. Examples include: (a) in production—too many items produced on a "just in case" situations, (b) in software development—producing features that nobody is going to use, (c) in marketing—performing many different marketing activities without having a clear vision and

strategy, and (d) in project management—filling an unnecessary number of documents.

3. Waiting. When the process is allowed to wait for information, equipment, materials, parts, or people. Examples include: (a) in production—waiting for goods to be delivered, (b) in software development—waiting for testing to complete, waiting for code review among others, (c) in marketing—waiting for an approval from higher management, and (d) in project management—waiting for a go-ahead green light from top executives.

4. Non-Utilized Talent. Also known as waste of intellectual capital, this wasteful activity happens when we do not properly utilize people's skills, experience, knowledge, or creativity. Examples include: (a) in production—highly skilled employees, such as engineers, having to spend a lot of time performing non-skilled operators' jobs, (b) in software development—underutilizing people's knowledge and creativity, and uneven workflow, resulting in some team members being overburdened while others are underutilized.

5. Transportation. This is the unnecessary movement of materials, information, or equipment. Examples include: (a) in production—it may mean moving parts and materials from one place to another, (b) in software development—switching between tasks too often, countless interruptions from colleagues, (c) in marketing—task switching, interruptions, unnecessarily long marketing funnel, and (d) in project management—switching tasks back and forth between team members, interruptions between tasks i.e., stop-and-go syndrome.

6. Inventory. This wasteful activity occurs when there is accumulation of parts, information, applications, among others that are beyond what is required. Examples include: (a) in production—undelivered products or parts, overstocking with equipment that may not be available in the near future, (b) in software development—undelivered code or undelivered features, (c) in marketing—fully prepared marketing campaigns that stay unlaunched and licensed tools that nobody uses, and (d) in project management—purchased

online tools that teams rarely use or office supplies that exceed needs.

7. Motion. This wasteful activity happens when there is a movement by people that is not of value to the customer. Examples include: (a) in production—unnecessary movement of employees or machinery, (b) in software development—unnecessary meetings or extra effort to find information, (c) in marketing—unnecessary meetings, extra effort to find information, attending events without clear agenda, and (d) in project management—badly structured workspaces and lack of organizational paths, too many meetings, and extra effort to find information.

8. Extra-Processing. This wasteful activity involves any steps in the process that do not add value in the eyes of the customer. Examples include: (a) in production—spending a lot of time on a given task, adding a feature that doesn't bring value to the customer, (b) in software development—unnecessary complex algorithms solving simple problems, (c) in marketing—generating countless marketing reports manually, while they can be automated, and (d) in project management—multiple levels of approval for small tasks.

The eight wastes of lean will differ from business to business. This is a never-ending list, and the seven wastes of lean will differ from one workplace to another even within the same organization—and you may even find more Muda activities that do not belong to this list. The way to do this process is to begin to explore all processes in your organization and try to find as many wasteful activities as possible. Then take the necessary steps to eliminate everything that can slow down your cycle time, damage quality, cost additional resources, or decrease profitability.

TOOLS FOR WASTE REDUCTION

Kanbanize (2019) lists tools that can guide you through the work process of identifying and eliminating wasteful activities which include:

(a) Gemba walk—a technique that gives you the opportunity to go and see where the real work occurs. This gives you the chance to observe different processes in action and the ability to see where wasteful activities occur.

(b) The five whys—a simple method of asking "why" questions used for root-cause analysis, problem-solving, and detecting waste.

(c) The A3 report—a more complicated process that encourages cross-organizational knowledge sharing and is also used for root-cause analysis, problem-solving, and detecting waste (see figure 10.3).

(d) Tague's (2015) Failure Modes and Effects Analysis (FMEA)—a risk-management tool that helps you to identify and quantify the influence of potential failures in a process. This tool analyzes potential failures using three criteria: severity (impact of the failure), occurrence (failure cause and frequency), and detection (likelihood of failure detection). Using the Risk Product Number (RPN), the product or service is assessed, and prioritized failures are addressed with mistake-proofing for preventable failures and contingency plans for unpreventable risks.

Figure 10.3. A3 Report - An appropriate tool for identifying and eliminating Muda waste.

METRIC ENHANCEMENT

Kaplan and Norton (1996) define a metric as a verifiable measure stated in either quantitative or qualitative terms that captures performance in terms of how something is being done relative to a standard, allows and encourages comparison, and supports business strategy. For example, "97 percent inventory accuracy," or "according to our customer evaluations, we are providing above-average service."

Juneja (n.d.) describes metrics as numbers that tell you important information about a process under question—accurate measurements about how the process is functioning—and provide a base for you to suggest improvements. People assert that it is when one is able to express their understanding in terms of numbers do their understanding become satisfactory and meaningful.

Deming (2000, 35) argues that metrics matter because "if you can't measure it, you can't manage it." This old adage is still accurate in today's world. In other words, if you are able to measure something, you would be in a situation to know if it is getting better or worse, which leads you to manage for improvement. Generally, if something cannot be measured, the implication is that it cannot be managed, controlled, or improved, and this is why it is crucial to come up with suitable metrics to enable you to measure the quality of deliverables in the workplace.

Since metric enhancement is mostly a quality function across all industries, it is noteworthy to define what quality really means. According to Sommerville (2004), quality is how a product or service meets the specifications of the customer. Kaplan and Norton (1996) states that quality metric data may be used to spot trends in business performance, compare alternatives, or predict business performance. However, LeaderLites should consider the costs and benefits of collecting information for a particular quality metric since collecting data will not necessarily result in higher performance levels—and higher-quality companies often use fewer metrics than their competitors.

To begin to clearly understand the concept of metric enhancement, Reh (2019) believes it is best to define a few terms:

1. Measure is a verb that means the ability to establish the measurements of something. For example, we measure the number of customer returns.
2. Measurement means the figure, extent, or amount obtained by after measuring something. For example, we collect data to determine how many customer returns we receive per week, month, or year.
3. Metric means a standard of measurement. For example, we establish defects per thousand products produced per month.
4. Benchmark is the standard by which others may be measured. For example, we compare other production lines or shifts against the benchmark of 10 percent defect rate. While a benchmark is a number, state, or condition against which future results can be compared, a metric is a quantifiable data point that can be clearly demonstrated and proven. Benchmarking metrics, then, are existing-condition data points that people can test, measure, report, and use to evaluate future performance.
5. Break points are levels where improved performance will likely change customer behavior. For example, suppose the average customer will only wait for five minutes; waiting longer than five minutes results in customer dissatisfaction, one to five minutes results in customer satisfaction, and waiting less than one minute results in customer extremely satisfied. Would you try to reduce the average wait time from four to two minutes? Maybe not.

CANDIDATES TO MEASURE

In determining the candidates to measure for metric enhancements, it is critical for LeaderLites to consider the costs and benefits of collecting information for a particular quality metric. Always remember that collecting data will not necessarily result in higher performance levels, and higher-quality companies often use fewer metrics than their competitors. It is only necessary to measure those activities or results that are important to successfully achieving your organization's goals. Metrics such as key performance indicators, also known as KPIs or key success indicators

(KSIs), help define and measure activities that support making progress toward goals at the workplace (Reh 2019).

KPIs may differ from one organization to another or even within the same organization, one department to another. A business that provides service may have as one of its KPIs the percentage of its income that comes from returning or repeat customers. Another business may measure the percentage of customer calls answered in the first minute. A software development company may count the number of defects in their code for a key performance indicator (Reh 2019).

In order to calculate the metrics in your KPIs, you may need to measure several things. For example, to measure progress toward a customer service KPI, the department will need to measure (count) how many calls it receives, measure how long it takes to answer each call, and determine how many customers are satisfied with the service they received. The head of the Customer Service Department may use those various measures to calculate the percentage of customer calls answered in the first minute and to gauge overall effectiveness in answering calls (Reh 2019).

HOW TO MEASURE, USE MEASUREMENTS, AND MEASURE TO MANAGE

LeaderLites must know that how to measure is important and what to measure is equally important. In the previous example, we can have the operator count the number of defects manually, logged and classified by each production line or shift and transfer that data on a P-chart to at the end of the day. We can also purchase a counting device and software program that counts the number of defects, classifies the failure mode, and plots the number and type of defects resulting in the updated and current P-chart at the end of each day for each production line or shift. Though the latter option could be the most expensive, it is the best option since it would deliver a good quality count and remove the human error. According to Reh (2019), collecting measurements that are current, accurate, complete, and unbiased allows managers and executives to make business decision on the go.

How to use these measurements after data collection is beneficial if management and executives are trained in the scoring and interpretation of what is measured. Most workplaces use these measurements as part of a continuous improvement plan, (CIP) such as the Shewhart cycle (see figure 10.4). The Shewhart cycle, also known as the "Plan-Do-Check-Act" (PDCA) cycle, was made popular by Dr. W. Edwards Deming, and he later attributed it to W. A. Shewhart. It is noteworthy to mention that the PDCA cycle is a form of cybernetic control—a closed system that regulates itself using a feedback loop—and it particularly lends itself to a P3 management (Reh 2019). Dunning (2017) defines the term P3 as the shorthand for public private partnership used to describe a legally binding contractual agreement between a public sector body, such as a government agency, and a private sector body, such as a business.

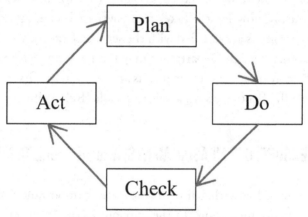

Figure 10.4. The Shewhart cycle.

There are other workplaces in different industries that use these measurements as part of other plans with different given names, including (a) Measure, Improve, Repeat (MIR) and (b) Define, Measure, Improve (DMI). However, the goal of how to use these measurements is the same: to measure the key factors and improve them along the way. Either way, it is important to communicate your metrics both up and down since the people at the very top of the organization want to know the health of the organization and those at the bottom need to know as well (Reh 2019).

Communicating your metric this way motivates people to improve on their performance. Most of all, suggestions for how to improve will also come from these very people. Using graphical presentations of your metrics, such as pie charts, line charts, key driver charts, and other graphs, helps you visually communicate your metrics quickly and easily. It is crucial to use online or hanging charts on the wall or bulletin boards in the break rooms to post team and individual results.

Now that you have your metrics in place, it is time to determine which strategies are working and which are not, and whenever you make a change to a process, use the metrics to determine whether the change improved the process or not. Make it a habit to review your metrics and use them to guide your decision-making process. When there are improvements with the metrics, share this information with all the people in the workplace. Rewarding the people who were responsible for the success is crucial—no matter how big or small the rewards are—even if it is just a verbal form of praise like "good job" or "job well done" (Reh 2019).

In order to measure to manage, Reh (2019) suggests we:

1. Measure what is important. The benchmarks committee can use a Delphi process—a technique, also known as estimate-talk-estimate (ETE), used for business forecasting—to rank the importance of various metrics and produce a list on which they would focus. Ensure your business metrics and selected benchmarks are directly tied to organizational goals. You can start by benchmarking fundamental metrics such as (a) financial, (b) market and customers, (c) business processes and operational excellence, and (d) learning and growth, and people and culture (see figure 10.5).

   LeaderLites should understand that benchmarks are a good piece of information to know when examining performance of people or processes, but it is critical not to live and die with it. After all, when you stop and think about it, a benchmark is just a pursuit to achieve somewhat better-than-average results against a number that may not even reflect a true reality.

2. Publish your metrics and benchmarks. Your metrics and benchmarks can be published via the web or mobile app, or dashboard. Doing this will motivate the people to know their current performance and how much is required of them to improve on their performances. In addition, it gives people at the workplace the opportunity to brainstorm on what they are doing wrong and

what to do better to improve their performance. Use graphical presentation of your metrics such as pie charts, line charts, key driver charts, and other graphs helps visually communicate your metrics quickly and easily.

3. Reward people for exceeding their goals. To make this happen, you have to have a more direct reward system put in place. Something as simple as an award for the team with the highest level of improvement or a lunch for all the teams with the highest level of client satisfaction would have driven behavior change. According to SYG (2019) you must create a culture of recognition (CoR) that recognizes, rewards, and motivates people at the workplace and that is woven into everything they do. Having multiple CoRs in place helps provide managers with more opportunities to praise people at the workplace and show them their appreciation, which then results in improving the employees' experiences. SYG (2019) suggests keeping CoR in place consistently influences everything and everyone in your workplace. The good news is people at the workplace will flourish in this type of environment, and businesses using this strategy are bound to see a dramatic improvement in both morale and productivity.

4. Keep tuning the metrics. This involves collecting the right data and using it to create and increase company processes over and over again. Williams (2017) claims that tuning the metrics allows the business performance metrics to produce more effective day-to-day operations.

Developing KPIs is both an art and a science and is outside the scope of this book. However, the knowledge you acquire in this publication allows you to measure activities and outputs only as a fundamental step. As previously mentioned, we can only manage what we can measure. Finally, be advised that your metrics emphasize certain activities over other equally important but unmeasured activities.

A BALANCED SCORECARD

Lim (2019) defines a balanced scorecard as a strategic management performance metric used to identify and improve several internal business functions and their resulting external outcomes. Balanced scorecards truly matter because they are used to measure and provide feedback to organizations. Data collection is extremely important in providing quantitative results because managers and executives assess and interpret the information to make healthier decisions for the organization.

Kaplan, an accounting academic, and Norton, a business executive and theorist, first introduced the balanced scorecard. Taking previous metric performance measures, Kaplan and Norton adapted them to include nonfinancial information. Today, organizations can identify factors hindering business performance easily and outline strategic changes tracked by future scorecards. One benefit of the balanced scorecard model is it helps businesses reinforce good behavior in an organization by isolating four separate areas, also called legs, that need to be analyzed: (a) learning and growth, (b) business processes, (c) customers, and (d) finance (Kaplan and Norton 1992).

CHARACTERISTICS OF THE BALANCED SCORECARD MODEL

According to Lim (2019), the balanced scorecard model is obtained by collecting information and analyzing it from four aspects of a business:

1. Learning and Growth/People and Culture. Data collected for this first leg are analyzed through the examination of training and knowledge resources. This involves the study of how well information is captured and used by employees to convert it to a competitive advantage over the industry.
2. Business Processes/Operational Excellence. Data collected for this second leg are evaluated by investigating how well products are manufactured. Analyzing operational management is the key to track any gaps, delays, bottlenecks, shortages, or waste.

3. Market/Customers. Data collected for this third leg are used to determine customer satisfaction with quality, price, and availability of products or services. Customers are voluntarily surveyed to provide feedback about their satisfaction with current products or services.

4. Financial. Data collected data, such as sales, expenditures, and income are used to establish financial performance. These financial metrics typically include dollar amounts, financial ratios, budget variances, and income targets.

In most organizations, these four legs are incorporated into the vision and strategy of the organization and require active management to analyze the data collected. This explains why the balanced scorecard is oftentimes referred to as a management tool rather than a measurement tool.

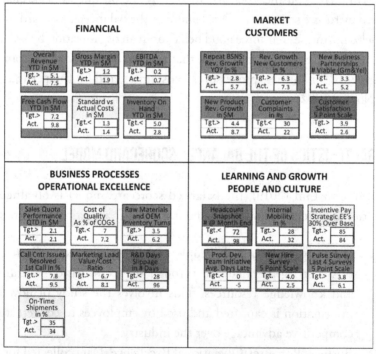

Figure 10.5. Example of a balanced scorecard.

STRESS OVERLOAD

According to the Sanford Health Newsletter (2009), although just enough stress can be a good thing, feeling overwhelmed is a different story. Stress overload isn't good for anyone. For example, feeling a little nervous about a project or a family event can motivate you to focus, but becoming exhausted can make it hard to concentrate on the tasks and determine what to do first.

LeaderLite leaders must watch for pressures that are too intense or last too long, and troubles that are shouldered alone, which can cause people to feel stress overload. Here are some of the things from SHN (2009) that can overwhelm the body's ability to cope if they continue for a long time:

- being bullied or exposed to violence or injury
- relationship stress, family conflicts, or the heavy emotions that can accompany a broken heart or the death of a loved one
- ongoing work overload, conflicts with colleagues, or job dissatisfaction
- crammed schedules, not having enough time to rest and relax, and always being on the go

Some stressful situations can be extreme and may require special attention and care. Post-traumatic stress disorder is a strong stress reaction that can develop in people who have lived through a traumatic event, such as a serious car accident, a natural disaster, or an assault (SHN staff 2009).

Some people experience anxiety that can cause them to overreact to stress, making even small difficulties seem like crises. If a person frequently feels tense, upset, or worried, it may be a sign of anxiety. Anxiety problems usually need attention, and many people turn to professional counselors for help in overcoming them (SHN staff 2009).

SIGNS OF STRESS OVERLOAD

According to SHN Staff (2009), people who are experiencing stress overload may notice some of the following signs:

- anxiety or panic attacks
- a feeling of being constantly pressured, hassled, and hurried
- irritability and moodiness
- physical symptoms, such as stomach problems, headaches, or even chest pain
- allergic reactions, such as eczema or asthma
- sleeping problems
- drinking too much, smoking, overeating, or doing drugs
- sadness or depression

Everyone experiences stress a little differently. Some people become angry and act out their stress or take it out on others. Some people internalize it and develop eating disorders or substance abuse problems. And some people who have a chronic illness may find that the symptoms of their illness flare up under an overload of stress (SHN staff 2009).

AVOIDING WORK OVERLOAD

Brearley (2019) claims work overload is a common problem in most workplace environments. But it's not just about working long hours. Work overload can also mean having too many items in your task list, which you simply never finish. I've worked in roles where I worked very long hours for long periods to finish everything. I've also managed teams where there was so much going on that it wasn't possible to finish it all. In that case, we just had to choose what wasn't going to get done. So, how do you know whether work overload is a problem for you and your team? If you look for the right signs, it's usually not hard to tell.

SIGNS OF WORK OVERLOAD

1. People Constantly Miss Deadlines

If you are in a situation where deadlines are missed consistently, you may have work overload. Usually this indicates that you don't have capacity in the team to take on the work, and people keep pushing it to the back of the queue.

2. Errors Start to Appear

In work overload situations, issues start to happen. People miss things because they take shortcuts. Nobody is focusing too hard on each task because they are busy worrying about the next one. It becomes more about ticking the task off the list than making sure it's done properly.

3. People Become Frazzled or Stop Caring

Sometimes the most dangerous part of work overload is when overloaded people start to become overwhelmed and frazzled. When there are many competing priorities, people aren't quite sure what to focus on. It also occurs because people feel upset and feel that they are letting others down. People may also give up and stop caring. They feel like they can't succeed, so why should they bother even trying? Take note of people complaining, looking stressed, being frustrated, or appearing overwhelmed. These are telltale signs of work overload. See table 10.1 for more signs and symptoms of stress overload.

HOW TO AVOID WORK OVERLOAD IN YOUR TEAM

The signs of stress overload are relatively easy to spot. But what can we do about them? It is easy to do nothing and wait for the weekend, but guess what? It will still be a problem on Monday. However, according to Brearley (2019), there some ways to avoid stress overload.

1. Avoid Work Overload by Understanding the Problem.

    One of the biggest challenges with work overload is that it's hard to measure. Just how much work can Brett the maintenance worker handle? It's hard to tell because everyone has different limits of stress they can take. Many leaders struggle to call out work overload because they feel they'll be criticized for being soft or jumping at shadows. That's why you need to understand the problem properly.

    In the areas of most concern, start to map out all the work

that people are involved in and when it's going to happen. You'll soon see if you have a problem because some people will have many priorities next to their name in a short period of time. Only once you have understood and articulated the problem properly will you be able to actually help anyone.

2. Start Saying No

One of the critical leadership skills that many people overlook is how to manage up and say no. The real problem is that many people think that saying no isn't an option. Remember that it always is and remind your team of this too. You don't want to surround yourself with people who always say yes. They will overpromise and underdeliver—and eventually burn out. You want people who push back when you are being unreasonable, and you need to do this to your boss too.

3. Give People Permission to Stop Doing Things

When you're in a work overload situation, you need to protect the well-being of the people around you. One way to do this is to give them permission to stop doing things if they're too busy. Identify some of the less important tasks that your team performs. Give your team permission to let them slip or cancel them for a month. This gives your team room to breathe, and they do not feel bad because you said it was right.

4. Keep Close to Your Team and Communicate

The last way to avoid work overload in your team is to understand what they are working on and to keep communication lines open. Make yourself available when people need to talk. Try to give your team every opportunity to raise issues if they need to. Even when everyone is busy, you need to make time for this. It may help you avoid an unfortunate burnout situation.

Work overload is never fun, and you want to avoid it in your team. Even though it seems like a good idea to push your team hard and get everything done, you need to understand the cost of doing so. There is no point in completing amazing amounts of work if everyone is burnt out and unhappy at the finish line.

The American Institute of Stress (n.d.) found that increased stress results in increased productivity, but only up to a point—after which things go rapidly downhill. However, since that point or peak may be different from one person to the another, heed to early warning symptoms and signs that suggest a stress overload is starting to push you over the hump. Such signals, see table 10.1, also differ from person to person, and they can be so subtle that they are often ignored until it is too late. Very seldom, people around you may be aware that you may be headed for trouble before you are—and you may want to listen to them. As usual, it is important to see your physician when you start experiencing any of the warning signs of stress to determine whether or not your symptoms are related to stress.

It is important for LeaderLites to know the warning signs and symptoms of stress overload in order to be proactive and have more control over it. After all, proactive people tend to be more relaxed, prepared, and positive due to the precautionary steps that they take for potential situations. Table 10.1 includes the warning signs and symptoms of stress overload to help you stay proactive.

Table 10.1
Warning Signs and Symptoms of Stress Overload

Cognitive Symptoms	Emotional Symptoms	Physical Symptoms	Behavioral Symptoms
Memory problems	Moodiness	Aches and pains	Eating more or less
Inability to concentrate	Irritability or short temper	Diarrhea or constipation	Sleeping too much or too little
Poor judgment	Agitation, inability to relax	Nausea, dizziness	Isolating yourself from others

Seeing only the negative	Feeling overwhelmed	Chest pain, rapid heartbeat	Procrastinating or neglecting responsibilities
Anxious or racing thoughts	Sense of loneliness and isolation	Loss of sex drive	Using alcohol, cigarettes, or drugs to relax
Constant worrying	Depression or general unhappiness	Frequent colds	Nervous habits (e.g., nail biting, pacing)

Originally published in *Healthy Living Magazine* by Smith, Segal, and Segal (2011) from the Office of Adult and Career Education Services, OACES, a division of the Rochester City School District.

CHANGE MANAGEMENT

Change can be particularly challenging, which makes LeaderLite even more important. Unfortunately, globalization is a constant force that is driving people across the world to change, but because change means doing something new and unknown, the natural reaction is to resist it (Kotter J. 1996). To reduce this resistance to change, you will have to learn different change strategies, such as communicating with resisting members, and involving them as the core in the implementation of the change process (Robbins 2003).

Current business practice recommends several models to support change and transformation in organizations. However, finding a model that is sufficiently effective across various types of change and transformational processes can be difficult (Lipinksi and Jamro 2017). To address this gap, LeaderLites must draw on change-management processes that are applicable to their needs.

One cannot be certain about anything in the future but change—like death and taxes. Change is inevitable in life or the workplace. Les Brown said, "Change is difficult but often essential to survival" (Hamilton 2008). LeaderLites in the workplace who have experienced change know that change can be hard and ambiguous. Dunn (2011) stated that change "involves saying goodbye to something, being unsure, and then saying hello to something else." Not knowing what lies ahead of you and the people you lead—and not being sure you can handle the unknown—leads to fear. Fear can cause people to shut down.

The good news is that not all change is bad. Many are of the mindset that change can be uncomfortable and awkward, but it can also be positive. LeaderLites are required to embrace the mindset that change is necessary and that people have to change in order to survive because their vitality depends on growth and the changes that come along with it. Positive changes, like job promotions, are easier to accept than negative changes, such as demotions or downsizing in the workplace. As a LeaderLite, you must adjust and deal with the change, whether good or bad.

This section addresses change and the need for LeaderLites to understand and handle change as part of their responsibility within an organization. This section will not make the reader a change expert. It only applies to minor changes, such as moving to a new business building or changing offices. These changes can negatively impact employees' productivity as they adjust to new and unfamiliar surroundings. Another minor change that can negatively affect employees is the arrival of new management or supervisors—even if the change is for the betterment of the organization. Change in the form of workforce reductions often occurs when the organization is facing a shortfall in income.

In a time of drastic change, the help of a change consultant may be required because implementing a massive and expansive change process can be overwhelming and can make matters even worse if it is not handled properly. It is important for LeaderLites to know their limitations when confronting change. Doing nothing when change is expected or is being choreographed can be disastrous. Nothing remains the same; even organizations must change. As a LeaderLite, you must have witnessed change in the workplace at some point in your lives. If you do not respond to change, your department or organization will struggle and eventually die. LeaderLites must acknowledge that changes in the workplace occur more frequently than you may think, and you must adapt to them quickly. A key part of this depends on how well you understand the change process. If in doubt, consult a change expert (Cummings, Bridgman, and Brown 2016).

For your information, there are numerous change models. Some include (a) the Eight-Stage Change Process by John Kotter (1996), (b)

Learning Organization by Peter Senge (1980), (c) managing transitions by William Bridges (1980), and (d) Deep Change by Robert Quinn (1996). While all these change models are good, I will introduce another that can be used on a daily basis: the Unfreezing/Refreezing Change Model by Kurt Lewin (Cummings, Bridgman, and Brown 2016).

According to Cummings, Bridgman, and Brown (2016), Kurt Lewin's change model consists of three stages of change: (1) unfreeze, (2) change, and (3) refreeze. If you have a large ice cube and want to change the shape to an ice ball, what do you do? Some might think chipping the corners of the ice cube with a chisel gradually and gently might achieve the desired result, but this approach might crack the ice cube into pieces. A second and more noninvasive option is to first melt the ice to make it amenable to change (unfreeze), then, using a spherical container, mold the iced water into the desired shape (change), and finally, solidify the new shape (refreeze). See figure 10.2 (Glaser, Russo, and Eckler 1988).

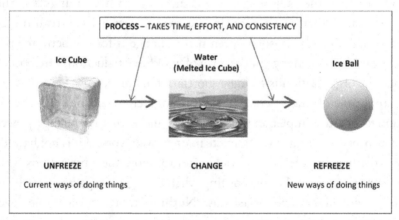

Figure 10.6. The three stages of Kurt Lewin's change model.

As a LeaderLite, you must look at change as a process with distinct stages, and if you do, it will prepare yourself for what is coming and create a plan to manage the transition—looking before you leap, so to speak. All too often, people go into change blindly, causing unnecessary turmoil and chaos (Glaser, Russo, and Eckler 1988).

To begin any successful change process, you must start by understanding why the change must take place. As Lewin stated, before change can occur, motivation for change must be generated. In addition, one must be helped to reexamine many cherished assumptions about oneself and one's relations to others (Glaser, Russo, and Eckler 1988). This is the unfreezing stage from which change begins, according to Glaser, Russo, and Eckler (1988).

Glaser, Russo, and Eckler (1988) argued that change is influenced by two opposing forces—*driving forces* and *resisting forces*. Driving forces initiate change and keep it going. These forces may be external and/or internal; for example, there is pressure to use modern technology. On the other hand, resisting forces act against the driving forces for change. They are usually internal; for example, a design group fears new ideas and prefers to do things the way they have always been done.

To make the change process easier on you, here are some strategies for successful change. There may be one or many driving forces initiating change in your organization. Groups will usually respond to a driving force by showing resistance. If you push, people push back. Resistance to change is normal and can be expected. Change is more easily accepted by decreasing resisting forces than by increasing the driving forces. Success will only come by removing the resisting force. According to Glaser, Russo, and Eckler (1988), the following strategies can be used to decrease the resisting forces to change:

> *Communication*: Providing adequate information to members of the organization in need of change helps gain their support; doing so makes the purpose of the change clear. Fear of change can be as disturbing as the change itself.

> *Participation*: Involve everyone in planning and making the change. It is much easier to support an initiative in which you have a stake. If possible, committees using small groups of people should be set up to review and make recommendations for change. Surveys and newsletters can also be effective tools.

> *Support*: Be prepared to spend extra time with members who have difficulty accepting the change. Ensure that you, as the person initiating the change, are perceived as trustworthy and credible.

Negotiation: Work out a win/win situation for all parties involved. Match the personal goals of the members to the objectives of the change. The change will be resisted if it blocks personal goals.

The change process. The following model for change can be used to understand and plan for change. It uses the analogy of an ice cube to explain the change process of an organization. The ice cube in its original shape represents the current state of the organization. In order to change, the ice cube must be unfrozen, molded to its new shape, and then refrozen. Similarly, in order to change positively, the organization must melt any forces that resist change and create a climate of acceptance and trust that will reinforce or refreeze the new state of the organization (Glaser, Russo, and Eckler, The force field problem-solving model 1988). See figure 10.7 for the unfreezing/refreezing model of change.

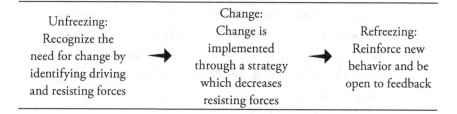

Figure 10.7. The unfreezing, change, refreezing change model.

As a LeaderLite, you will constantly encounter forces that drive you to make changes periodically, but because change means doing something new and unknown, the natural reaction for people is to resist it. Use change strategies such as communicating with resisting people and involving them can reduce resistance to change. If possible, use the Change Style Indicator assessment, CSI, by Musselwhite and Ingram (2003) to measure yourself and others' preferred style in approaching and addressing change. This assessment will provide you with insights on personal preferences for managing through change and provide context for how those around them might perceive and respond to their preferred style.

CSI helps you classify people's preferred style, on a continuum, in approaching change as (1) conservers, (2) pragmatists, and (3) originators. The *conserver* is the term that is used to refer to the change style of an individual who prefers incremental change and tends to favor maintaining the current status quo through the better use of resources. The *originator* is the term that is used to refer to an individual who prefers a faster, more radical approach to change, though systemic transformations that target efficiency and effectiveness. The *pragmatist* is the term that is used to refer to the change style of an individual who prefers functional change, which will be most effective in a specific situation, determined through an objective analysis of the circumstances (Musselwhite and Ingram 2003).

As a LeaderLite, you will be experiencing constant and continuing change as a powerful and natural force for good. Using CSI, you will understand the human response to change—and that may be your greatest challenge and most valuable resource. Because change is here to stay, regardless of how people experience change or how they feel about it, by understanding our change preferences and the preferences of others, we can become better able to lead, manage, and assist others through the inevitable changes in our lives and organizations (Alievo 2018).

It is noteworthy to mention that changes do not need to be radical; rather, small changes introduced often are better than large changes rarely introduced. Organizations will fade and fall behind or will not survive at all if they fail to understand the need for change or are inept in their ability to deal with change (Glaser, Russo, and Eckler 1988).

LEADING THE CHANGE

There may be times when you will be called upon to lead an expansive and large-scale change. It is noteworthy to mention that an expansive and a large-scale change requires a change agent with your attributes. As a LeaderLite, you are capable of handling the change because LeaderLite leaders possess the leadership qualities and knowledge that you can draw from to make expansive and large-scale change happen.

In addition, according to Ball (2001), certain situations that "call upon all the skills, experiences, and knowledge that can be mustered from multiple disciplines" (15) to keep a business on the path to achieving its goals. This bold statement implies that lacking a multidisciplinary approach renders a consultant incapable, which is untrue. Though there is a belief that many consultants are unusually skilled and often unusually well credentialed in their fields, these kinds of credentials are not a requirement (Holtz 1999). This is true and very evident since nowadays, "the demand for advice, help, and convenience is so great that even the most mundane of skills can be put to work as the basis for a successful independent consulting practice, if you structure your service and marketing properly" (Holtz 1999, 32).

What happened to the concept where specialization increases efficiency through division of labor? The scope of competence standard limits what an individual within the profession may do, and I believe that there may be certain skills and knowledge that—if applied without training—could be unethical and could harm the company. Nonetheless, bringing in experts in the field could be beneficial to the company. One should consider the phrase *primum non nocere* ("first, do no harm") when operating from their scope of competence; otherwise, one may end up providing services that could harm organizations. All your skills, knowledge, and experience can be adequate to resolve all the change issues at hand, but having perfect skills but a lack of help-seeking from experts in certain areas of the field may be unethical and unprofessional.

As a LeaderLite leader, your approach toward expansive and large-scale change could be drawn from many disciplines—the moonic elements. Using interpersonal and group dynamics, you may be able to guide and facilitate activities in a rapidly changing environment that can help keep the company on course. If you possess some clinical experiences, you can respond effectively to the challenges, such as management's reaction to a leader with whom they could play out both conscious and unconscious hostilities (Levinson 2002 as cited in Ball 2001). The conventional wisdom is that implementing expansive and large-scale change in organizations may not initially go smoothly because there is always room for improvement and fine-tuning after evaluation.

LEADERLITE LEADERS AS PROCESS CONSULTANTS AND COLLABORATORS

Ed Schein (1998) defines process consultation as: "the creation of a relationship with the client that permits the client to perceive, understand, and act on the process events that occur in the client's internal and external environment in order to improve the situation as defined by the client" (20).

To enable you to consult as well as collaborate with the global workplace, you will use the key elements of Ed Schein's (1998) process consulting techniques in approaching the expansive and large-scale change process:

1. *Always try to be helpful.* You will have the people at the workplace to have the perception that you are intervening only to help cut cost, improve morale, or increase employee productivity or otherwise (Schein 1998).

2. *Always stay in touch with the current reality.* It is of utmost importance that you, the consultant, become aware of the situation and how fluid the learning process can be. You may have to strive to become highly familiar with your own insights into what is going on and your own impact on the system at the workplace (Schein 1998).

3. Access your ignorance. Process consultation as a philosophy acknowledges that you, the consultant, are not an expert on anything but how to be helpful and starts with total ignorance of what is actually going on in the system at the workplace. By accessing your ignorance, you can genuinely understand the problem and what kind of help is needed, and then you can begin to think about recommendations and prescriptions (Schein 1998).

4. *Everything you do is an intervention.* Shaking hands, saying hello, and even your very presence at the workplace for meetings are a set of interventions that must be guided primarily by their presumed impact on the workplace system (Schein 1998).

5. *It is the client who owns the problem and the solution.* The cornerstone of the process consulting approach you may use is about working with the people at the workplace to help them find their own

solutions to workplace challenges rather than being told what to do and how to do it (Schein 1998).

6. *Go with the flow.* As the consultant, you must be willing and able to adapt to the culture at the workplace as you find it as well as the personality traits of the leaders and managers at the workplace. Any interventions that yield results that are not conducive to the culture at the workplace will not fit the workplace culture and will, therefore, not be refrozen even if initially adopted (Schein 1998).

7. *Timing is crucial.* It is important to ensure that you are alert to those moments when something truly transformational becomes possible—after all, opportunity comes to those who wait and are ready. The right moment to intervene is difficult to predict, but it is not so difficult to predict that such a moment will surely come one day. It is always advisable that you do the preparatory work so that what really counts is the moment (Schein 1998).

8. *Be constructively opportunistic with confrontive interventions.* Another course of action is always looking for opportunities for small changes that are capable of achieving significant results (Schein 1998).

9. *Everything is data; errors will occur and are the prime source for learning.* This is a fact of any diagnosis. But this does not give you the license to do a sloppy job at the onset. What this means is you have to understand that when unexpected and undesirable outcomes occur, you should avoid the defensive, shameful, or guilty attitudes. In other words, you must be ready to stand by your mistakes, apologize if you can, and preserve the people at the workplace's understanding of what is wrong and what needs to get better (Schein 1998).

10. *When in doubt, share the problem.* It is good to use the philosophy that you, the consultant, are not the expert, the person in charge, or the authority. Instead, you will help the people at the workplace find the solution to improve the situation as defined by them. Though your focus is clearly on the moment-to-moment experience of employees, there comes a time when you will get stuck. The next thing to do may not clear. When that happens, it is best to share the problem with the people at the workplace (Schein 1998).

Globalization is a constant force driving the global workplace to change, but because change means doing something new and unknown, the natural reaction is to resist it—and that will be anticipated and needs to be addressed (Kotter 1996). To reduce this resistance to change, it is best to use change strategies such as communicating with resisting members and involving them as the core in the implementation of the change process (Robbins 2003).

SELECTING THE APPROPRIATE CHANGE MODEL

Since culture, on a societal level, is the collective programming that leads to differential behavior of peoples of different societies, it is deep-rooted and difficult to change (Hofstede and Bond 1998). It helps to provide stability to a nation of people, but on the other hand, for other nations such as the developing countries, it is also a major barrier to change. The need for change in other cultures is widely recognized and acknowledged, but the reality of creating that change, and more important, making the change stick, are extremely difficult. There are numerous change models that can help guide and instruct the implementation of major change of this kind, but it is of utmost importance that the selected change model be grounded in both theory and professional practice in order to create a change, especially in the cultures of developing countries.

In the endeavor to gain insight into possible solutions to the change problem, the LeaderLite leader must analyze several theoretical change-strategy models and then find the one approach that may be useful in describing you own philosophy and system for leading cultural and management style change. The models that you may analyze may include: (a) the unfreezing/refreezing model for change by Glaser and Lewin (1988), (b) the eight-stage process of creating major change by Kotter (1996), (c) the process for creating and sustaining major change in an organization by Senge (1999), (d) Deep Change: Discovering the Leader Within, by Quinn (1996), and (e) the strategy for coping with difficult changes by Bridges (1980).

Each of the models mentioned in the previous chapter addresses expansive and large-scale change process from differing perspectives, yet all are useful for thinking about change in a peculiar application—either on an individual or organizational basis. However, I consider Kotter's (1996) eight-stage process of creating major change appropriate for expansive and large-scale change because to make a change to a system that has existed for several years, especially in the global workplace in developing countries, it is important that the change model be grounded in both theory and practice. I personally find this model to be that. Thus, it is noteworthy to mention that you should adopt this model as your philosophy and system for proactively leading the change.

Since there is no second chance to give a good first impression, I will recommend that on your first day of meeting with the executive team at the workplace, you make it very clear to them that expansive change is a large-scale and system-wide jolt that can be extremely difficult, and it requires senior-level commitment (Senge 1999). The core challenge is for you as a LeaderLite leader to get the right people in place with trust, emotional commitment, and teamwork to guide a difficult change process (Kotter and Cohen 2002). Thus, you must demand of them to take the Change Style Indicator (CSI) assessment—an assessment instrument designed to measure one's preferred style in approaching change and dealing with situations involving change. One's score on this instrument will place them on a change style continuum, ranging from a conserver style to an originator style. A third style, the pragmatist, occupies the middle range of the continuum. The three styles display distinct differences and preferences when approaching change (Musselwhite and Ingram 2003).

Have this self-scoring assessment completed and scored as soon as possible. Based on the scores, you may want to form a team comprising of people who are: (a) strong originators, if any, because such individuals challenge the paradigm and prefer change that is expansive, (b) strong conservers, if any, because such individuals accept the paradigm and prefer change that is incremental, and (c) strong pragmatists, if any, because such individuals explore the paradigm and prefer change that is functional. In addition, you may find individuals who are moderate conservers, meaning their approach to change could swing between accepting the paradigm and preferring change that is incremental to exploring the paradigm and preferring change that is functional, as worthy to be part of the team (Musselwhite and Ingram 2003).

A combination of all the three types of change styles is an indication that you have a blend of each preference in the coalition team, which will result in improving teamwork, interpersonal communication and understanding, avoiding unnecessary conflicts, and reducing dysfunctional meetings, making sure that all perspectives are included when resolving issues, enabling the group's creativity—increasing collaboration, getting to the win-win solution more quickly (Musselwhite and Ingram 2003).

THE EIGHT-STAGE PROCESS OF CREATING MAJOR CHANGE

For expansive change, John Kotter (1996), in his book *Leading Change*, developed a model based on his experience in observing change efforts in many organizations, this eight-stage model for implementing change. Each stage is associated with one fundamental error that undermines transformation efforts. Have an agreement with the coalition team to meet for at least sixteen consecutive days (approximately two days for each stage of the process) to address the issues with this eight-stage process of creating major change.

Prior to the start of the deliberations in implementing the change process, you have to meet with all members of the team and emphasize that they follow through on the process religiously. In other words, all the stages must be worked through in order, and completely, to successfully accomplish the change process. You may have to caution the team members that short-circuiting the process, which mostly happens when people are under the pressure to show results sooner than the process requires, could be disastrous.

During the meeting, you will have to explain to the members that, for example, when one skips the warm-up or defrosting activities (the first four steps), one rarely establishes a solid enough base on which to proceed—thus the earlier stages are not reinforced, and that results in the sense of urgency dissipating or the guiding coalition breaking up. Finally, you may want to advise them that, without follow through, which takes place in the final step, one will never get to the finish line and make the required changes stick. Here are the eight steps (Kotter 1996):

Step 1: Establishing a Sense of Urgency.

In order to achieve a sense of urgency, you will be examining realities and identifying crisis in the very system in which you need to make the significant change. Establishing a sense of urgency is critical to gaining cooperation in the change process. This requires the aggressive removal of sources of complacency, setting higher expectations than normal for the members of the organization, and following through with accountability for results (Kotter 1996).

To achieve this goal, you may want to challenge the coalition team to meet, work together, and brainstorm to create dynamic presentations with compelling objects that people can actually see, touch, and feel and to provide evidence from outside the organization that change is required. As a LeaderLite leader, you may want to recommend that they find cheap and easy ways to avoid complacency (Kotter and Cohen 2002). And you may want to demand that you receive this information by the second day of the series of meetings.

Step 2: Creating the Guiding Coalition

This step involves putting together a group to lead change and making the group work like a team. As a LeaderLite leader, you must emphasize the point that the guiding coalition is a critical enabler of the change process because a collaborative coalition can process more information more quickly and speed the implementation of change by building trust and relying on position, power, expertise, credibility, and leadership (Kotter 1996).

Next you may want to challenge the team to meet and find ways and means to help communicate the vision, execute the change plan, generate and sustain a sense of urgency, walk the talk, and lead by example (Kotter 1996). You must request that you receive this information on the fourth day of meeting.

You may also want to caution the team that conflicts may arise in the course of their meetings, and if handled properly, they will bring good ideas out of people. On the other hand, if not controlled properly, it could be destructive (Robbins 2003). You may find it necessary to also instill into the team the use of collaboration to find an integrative solution when both sets of concerns are too important to be compromised by gaining commitment, incorporating concerns into consensus, and by working through feelings that have interfered with a relationship. Since this stage involves individual members with individual differences getting together very frequently to find solutions to issues pertaining to the change process, it is necessary to have an agreement with the team members to have me do a four-hour training with the members of the executive team on conflicts and conflict resolution—and also the art of giving and taking criticisms. This enhances the teamwork spirit needed in the group.

Finally, you must demand that they use the five practices of exemplary leadership model to help them become successful leaders with certain leadership traits. I will, therefore, apply the set of five practices in the leadership challenge: (a) modeling the way, (b) inspiring a shared vision, (c) challenging the process, (d) enabling others to act, and (e) encouraging the heart (Kouzes and Posner 2003). The application of such leadership practices will eventually help form the desired new behavior of the team, make them very powerful to guide big changes, and make the team members start to work together well (Kotter and Cohen 2002).

Step 3: Developing a Vision and Strategy

This step involves creating a vision and strategy to implement the vision. The change vision helps define the reality of where the organization will be in the future (Kotter 1996). First of all, you will have to demand that the team meet and come out with a good vision statement that is short, concise, and straight to the point—and also good enough to make the employees remember it at all times. Secondly, you must insist that the vision be a clear understanding of what they must do to attain the vision and why it is important to them and the organization. Next, you must request that you receive this information by the sixth day of meetings.

Step 4: Communicating the Change Vision

This step involves more than just making people know and understand the change vision by a single policy speech or a notice board bulletin. In this regard, you will demand of the team members to walk the talk and lead by example so that organizational members can develop trust that the change is real because it is an essential part of communicating the change vision. You must demand that they meet and come up with multiple channels of communicating the change (Kotter 1996) by the eighth day of deliberations.

You may also ask them to keep this change communication simple and heartfelt, find out what people are really feeling, and speak to anxieties, confusion, anger, and distrust. You must also recommend they rid communication channels of junk so important messages can get through and use new technologies to help people see the vision (Kotter and Cohen 2002). Finally, you may want to advise them to keep this process in a loop until the people begin to buy into the change—and it shows in their behavior (Kotter and Cohen 2002).

Step 5: Empowering Broad-Based Action

This step involves getting rid of obstacles and changing systems that undermine the vision. Empowerment is a form of sharing power than can energize individuals to perform, freeing them to use their abilities more fully. When people are empowered, there is true alignment toward a common vision and a common mission, and synergies are created. Within an organization, it is paramount that cross-functional members be empowered to represent fully their core organization and make decisions related to their areas of expertise (Kotter 1996).

To achieve this step, you must demand that the team members meet and identify and remove key obstacles that stop people from acting on the vision— and you should receive this information by the tenth day of deliberations. You must also recommend that, if needed, they can bring in experienced change leaders to bolster confidence that the job can be done, create recognition and reward systems that inspire, promote optimism, and build self-confidence. It is essential to give constructive feedback and help disempower managers to experience powerfully the need for change (Kotter 1996). In addition, you may want to advise them to be on the alert and check if workers are beginning to feel able to act and acting on the vision (Kotter and Cohen 2002).

Finally, you may want to demand that they construct a system of rules or principles that guide them in making decisions about what is right or wrong, and these could include the ethics of respect, the ethics of virtue, and the ethics of duty (Hinman 2003).

Step 6: Generating Short-Term Wins

This step involves planning for visible improvements or wins, creating those wins, and visibly recognizing and rewarding people who make wins possible. Early success in the change process is important because it provides visible evidence that the changes are working, and it undermines cynics and self-serving resisters who might thwart progress (Kotter 1996).

In this regard, you may need to demand the team comes up with ways and means to produce short-term wins by the twelfth day of deliberations, which is fast enough to energize the change helpers, enlighten the pessimists, defuse the cynics, and build momentum for the effort. This will make them successful at motivating the employees—accounting for their individual's intensity, direction, and persistence of effort toward attaining a goal (Robbins 2003).

Step 7: Consolidating Gains and Producing More Change

This involves hiring and promoting managers who can implement change and reinvigorating the process with new projects. As change takes hold, it is the right time to recommend that they meet, identify, and begin periodic purging of the remnants of old paradigms. You may also advise that they use the increased credibility to challenge all systems, structures, and policies that no longer fit the change vision. In their meetings, they should identify opportune times to reinvigorate the process with new projects, themes, and change agents (Kotter 1996). Then you need to demand that you receive this information by the fourteenth day of deliberations. Finally, advise them to be on alert, look for people who are trying to fulfill the vision, and find out if fewer people are resisting the change.

Step 8: Anchoring New Approaches in the Culture

This last and equally important step involves developing leadership succession and articulating the connection between behavior and success. Kotter (1996) said ways to anchor new approaches in the culture are:

Creating better performance through customer- and productivity-oriented behavior, more and better leadership, and more effective management; articulating the connections between new behaviors and organizational success; and developing means to ensure leadership development and succession. (21)

To achieve this goal, you may need to challenge the team to create a supporting structure that provides roots for the new ways of operating, and you should receive that information by the sixteenth day of deliberations. You will have to advise the team members very strongly to refrain from declaring victory too soon, use new employee orientation, use the promotion process, and tell vivid and compelling stories to reinforce visibly the vision. Finally, you will have to recommend that they ensure that there is the desired new behavior with which people formulate a culture of new and winning behavior despite the pull of tradition and turnover of change leaders.

WORKPLACE DIVERSITY

Kayla Kozan (2019) defines workplace diversity as the understanding, accepting, and valuing differences between people of different races, ethnicities, genders, ages, religions, disabilities, and sexual orientations, as well as differences in personalities, skill sets, experiences, and knowledge bases.

LeaderLite leaders tend to be proponents of training and development programs as a vehicle for changing behaviors in the workplace. Some of you probably may have encountered a diversity awareness training program in your current or previous workplace that failed to provide any positive results and rarely resulted in the transfer of immediately useful information to the organization. You may have wondered why the training program did not achieve its goals, though the training program by itself was superb, if the learners demonstrated their knowledge by performing various role-plays.

In a research conducted by Gebert, Beungeler, and Heinitz (2017), it was found that corporate diversity training programs often are not as effective as people would think, despite organizations investing considerable time and money into these trainings to reduce discrimination. This research delved into the underlying barriers to learning that may cause diversity training to fail. One barrier that makes a lot of sense involves trainees' tendency to keep their thoughts to themselves when they are likely to lead to latent conflict, thus hindering learning. This research also showed why the currently dominant diversity-training models are insufficient to overcome such a barrier to learning.

Also, research has shown that economic indicators can create backlash and resistance in managers, and the manner by which these indicators are presented to managers indeed affects their reception of the intended message. Why does almost every organization seek to conduct diversity training in the workplace? The answer is very simple. According to Jones, King, Nelson, Geller, and Bowes-Sperry (2013), most management of organizations conduct diversity training programs not necessarily to increase the employees' cultural awareness, knowledge, and skills, thereby increasing the inclusion of different identity groups, and by promoting better teamwork, but rather to benefit the organization by protecting against them against civil rights violations.

You may also want to know that despite all the benefits of diversity training programs, social categorization and similarity-attraction theories suggest that diversity can undermine group performance through reducing cohesion, trust, and communication and increasing intergroup bias and conflict (Jones, King, Nelson, Geller, and Bowes-Sperry 2013).

You may find people out there who believe that race does not and should not matter in the workplace. Such people are said to hold colorblind racial attitudes, according to Barzantny (2007). There are three aspects of color blindness in the well-known twenty-item Colorblind Racial Attitudes Scale: (a) racial privilege, (b) institutional discrimination, and (c) blatant racial issues. Racial privilege assesses one's lack of awareness of the existence of White privilege in the United States, including its role in determining who is successful, who gets opportunities and social services, and who gets sent to prison. Institutional discrimination indicates limited awareness of the implications of institutional forms of racial discrimination, such as affirmative action and immigration and language policies. Blatant racial issues indicate a more general unawareness of racism and racial discrimination as a current problem in United States at large, including in public schools.

Finally, you may want to know that discrimination against women persists around the globe, and it remains a major obstacle to economic development in emerging and developing countries. Coming from Ghana, in West Africa, I can relate to these gender-based discriminatory sentiments that face women in most emerging and developing countries of the world today. According to Shirodkar (2013), women in such countries are searching for a place to connect, to fill the emotional void created by the increased isolation, invisibility, and constant stress.

As a LeaderLite leader, you may want to look into how to improve women's rights, especially in developing countries and ensure greater gender diversity at the workplace. As suggested by Shirodkar (2013), you may want to incorporate constitutional changes in policies, rules, and regulations in the organizations to foster greater representation of women at the workplace, and most of all, conduct periodic training and development in changes in psychological mindset among both men and women in the workplace.

ADAPTABILITY

Adaptability skills are one of the most important abilities needed to be successful at the workplace. It allows you to fit the changed circumstance in the work environment. Andresen and Gronau (2005) define adaptability, in the field of organizational management, as the ability to change something or oneself to fit to occurring changes. Valchev (2020) defines adaptability in the workplace as the ability to change in order to be successful in a new and different business situations and work assignments. An adaptable LeaderLite leader is the individual who is able to learn from experience and deal well with the problems of business or personal life.

An adaptable person is able to learn from experience and deal with the problems of business or personal life. Flexibility and adaptability are among the most required employability skills and abilities by companies.

If you want to be adaptable, you have to be able to evaluate and adjust to the different roles, responsibilities that you have each day (Valchev 2020).

Adaptability skills are some of the most valuable abilities that a person can possess because these skills allow you to survive, develop, create, learn and to achieve success. You have to be open to changes without fear but with positive thinking and desire to learn (Valchev 2020).

Being adaptable requires a range of adaptability skills. Here a list from Valchev (2020) of some of them:

1. Self-Management Skills

    Self-management skills are some of the most important and difficult to learn abilities. Self-management skills definition refers to the ability to control our feelings, emotions, and activities. These qualities are the basis of learning to cope with changes because our feelings and emotions have a huge impact on our ability to adapt. Effective self-management has the power to change dramatically almost every aspect of our lives. Some of the most important skills in this category are self-confidence, time management, organization skills, and self-motivation.

2. Decision-Making Skills

    Decision-making skills are essential skills that refer to adaptability. We have to make decisions and choices everywhere and almost all the time in our personal and business lives. Some of them are easy to make and require a short decision-making process, and others are the hardest choices in our lives. The world of work is changing constantly.

    Examples of decision-making skills and tools are the ability to gather and select information; finding possible options and solutions; analysis skills; selecting the best option, the ability to evaluate your plan and using different types of software such as risk-management tools, decision-making tools, project planning software, and time-management tools.

KEEPING CALM IN THE FACE OF DIFFICULTIES

Keeping calm in the face of difficulties is one of the best and most important adaptability skills that a person can possess. All of us come across something unexpected or something that frustrates our goals. During these situations, we need to stay calm and self-confident. If we manage to do this, we will be able to be effective in our jobs and maintain good business and personal lives.

POSITIVE THINKING AND OPTIMISM

Positive thinking allows you to use the power of optimism. Positive thinking doesn't mean that you keep your head in the sand and stay away from difficult situations. Positive thinking means that you are able to see a new situation and unpleasant changes in a more positive and productive way. Optimism and positive thinking are adaptable skills that are crucial for every type of success—business and personal.

BE OPEN TO NEW IDEAS AND CHANGES

You have to clearly understand that changes are normal. They are some of the most interesting and exciting parts of life. You don't have to fear changes; you have to accept and welcome them. If you are open to new ideas and changes, you will be able to manage them in a way that is profitable to you.

KNOWLEDGE OF NATIONAL CULTURE

LeaderLite leaders need to know that the business cultures of people from different nationalities can be vastly different. Cross-cultural researchers (Hofstede 1980 2001; Ronen and Shenkar 1985; Trompenaars 1994) have stressed that cultures in developing countries differ significantly from each other. Nonetheless, in the global workplace, numerous people from different cultures occupy management, professional, and related occupations in global workplace. As a LeaderLite leader, you must have the knowledge of national culture from different cultures across the globe to be able to lead and manage people in the global workplace.

Culture, on a societal level, is the collective programming that leads to the differential behavior of peoples of different societies. Culture is deep-rooted and difficult to change (Hofstede 2001). Unfortunately, people from other cultures entering the American business environment in multinational corporations around the world tend to have severe, chronic problems that prevent them from adapting easily to American business culture.

People may come from a business system that is generally autocratic— endorsing hierarchy and not requiring subordinates' participation in decision-making—rather than generally participative. If subordinates' participation is requested, and hierarchy is not endorsed in making decisions, these people may find themselves in a system that practices a generally participative style of management.

However, people from other cultures who furthered their educations in the United States prior to entering corporate America may find "their everyday lives can be a struggle and challenge, but the advantage of having access to good education has helped their adjustment" (Luther 2005, May, 1). LeaderLite leaders must be aware that the transition of those from other cultures different, generally autocratic to generally participative styles of leadership, can be a process full of frustration, anxiety, and concerns that you may need to be fully address. To do so, you may need learn and understand the research study based on the theoretical framework developed by Hofstede (2001) and presented in chapter 3. Otherwise, you may find yourself in a difficult scenario.

APPENDIX 10.1.
ENVIRONMENTAL CULTURE QUESTIONNAIRE

ENVIRONMENTAL CULTURE QUESTIONNAIRE (ECQ)

Instructions: The purpose of this questionnaire is to measure environmental culture in leadership. This questionnaire should be completed by you using the following scale to indicate the degree to which you agree or disagree with each of the 12 statements below.

_____ (leader's name)

Key: 1 = Totally disagree   2 = Disagree a little   3 = Neutral opinion
      4 = Agree a little   5 = Totally Agree

1. I do interact with people and approach tasks in ways that will help them meet their goals. 1 2 3 4 5

2. I want the people that I lead to set their own realistic goals. 1 2 3 4 5

3. I want the people that I lead to solve their own problems effectively. 1 2 3 4 5

4. I gain enjoyment from the people I lead to work and produce high quality products/services. 1 2 3 4 5

5. I strive to make the people that I lead be supportive of each other. 1 2 3 4 5

6. I allow the people that I lead to open to influence in dealing with others, and be friendly, open. 1 2 3 4 5

7. I want the people that I lead to be sensitive to the satisfaction of the work group. 1 2 3 4 5

8. I understand how my workplace environmental culture is clearly aligned with the business strategy 1 2 3 4 5

9. I like people in the workplace to feel comfortable in it. 1 2 3 4 5

10. I know how environmental culture and engagement are connected. 1 2 3 4 5

11. I know when programs to improve engagement are initiated, oftentimes, issues on environmental culture are discovered 1 2 3 4 5

12. I encourage the people at the top to question and change its values, incentives, programs, and structure. 1 2 3 4 5

13. I commit and offer strong support from HR to understand, measure, and improve engagement in the workplace environment. 1 2 3 4 5

14. I focus on seeking new tools to measure and monitor engagement of people at the workplace. 1 2 3 4 5

15. I do set standards for right or good actions. 1 2 3 4 5

16. I have a philosophical basis from which I derive my understanding of ethics. 1 2 3 4 5

17. I would rather fall with respect and admiration than succeed by fraud. 1 2 3 4 5

18. I hardly bend the rules. 1 2 3 4 5

19. Ethics, values, and trust are issues of immense timely importance to me. 1 2 3 4 5

20. I use a model in problem-solve before implementing a solution. 1 2 3 4 5

21. Eliminating wasteful activities is one of my most important prerequisites for building a successful workplace. 1 2 3 4 5

22. I use metric as a verifiable measure to capture performance. 1 2 3 4 5

23. I believe in rewarding people for exceeding their goals. 1 2 3 4 5

24. Key Performance Indicators, KPIs, are important goals at the workplace. 1 2 3 4 5

25. I have this natural feeling that one wants to serve first, leader later. 1 2 3 4 5

26. Finding about my strengths and weaknesses is crucial for understanding my inner self and how it affects others around me. 1 2 3 4 5

27. I do like change and help people to reduce their resistance to change. 1 2 3 4 5

28. I understand, accept, and value diversity in the workplace. 1 2 3 4 5

29. I do know business cultures of people from different nationalities can be vastly different. 1 2 3 4 5

30. I refrain from control of others, rather influence them to change. 1 2 3 4 5

SCORING

Add up the scores on all the 30 items.

SCORING INTERPRETATION

- *High range:* A score between 120 and 150 means you have an extreme desire to acquire and practice constructive environmental culture.

- *Moderate range:* A score between 90 and 120 means you have a very much desire to acquire and practice constructive environmental culture.
- *Low range:* A score between 60 and 90 means you have a moderate desire to acquire and practice constructive environmental culture.
- *Extremely low range:* A score between 30 and 60 means you have a little desire to acquire and practice constructive environmental culture and you need to seek help.

REFERENCES

Aguilera, R., and Vadera, A. (2005, August). A multi-level theory of organizational deviance: Corruption and corporate governance in a comparative perspective. *Paper presented at the Annual meeting of the American Sociological Association.* Marriott Hotel, Loews Philadelphia Hotel, PA.

Alcorn, R. (2015, November 11). *Is There a Difference Between Happiness and Joy?* Retrieved from Eternal Perspective Ministries: Retrieved from Eternal Perspective Ministries: https://www.epm.org/blog/2015/Nov/11/difference-happiness-joy

Alievo. (2018). *Change Style Indicator.* Retrieved from Alievo.com: https://www.alievo.com/our-services/assessment-tools/change-style-indicator/?lang=en

Andresen, K., and Gronau, N. (2005). An Approach to Increase Adaptability in ERP Systems. In *Managing Modern Organizations with Information Technology: Proceedings of the 2005 Information Resources Management Association International Conference 2005.*

Angle, A. S. (2019). *Unleash quality: Build a winning strategy for a culture of quality that will unleash your growth and profit potential.* Milwaukee, WI: Quality Press.

Avedian, A. (2014). *Anger management essentials* (1st ed.). Glendale, CA: Anger Management Essentials.

Ball, K. L. (2001). Managing in ongoing crises: A psychologist-manager case study. *The Psychologist-Manager Journal, 5*(1), 15–20. doi:10.1037/h0095898

Barzantny, C. (2007). Managing diversity: Toward a globally inclusive workplace. *Academy of Management Learning and Education,* 285–286. doi:10.5465/AMLE.2007.25223469

Baumeister, R., Vohs, K., Aaker, J., and Garbinsky, E. (2013). Some key differences between a happy life and a meaningful life. *The Journal of Positive Psychology, 8*(6), 505–516. doi:10.1080/17439760.2013.830764

Bersin, J. (2015, January 16). Becoming irresistible: A new model for employee engagement. *Deloitte Review, 16.* Retrieved from Dupress.com: http://dupress.com/articles/employee-engagement-strategies/

Brian, D. (2001). The future of business ethics in Africa. *International Business Ethics Institute, 4*(1), 14.

Bridges, W. (1980). *Transitions: Making sense of life's transitions.* Reading, MA: Perseus Books.

Brown, S. L. (2012, December 18). *Joy -vs- happiness*. Retrieved from Psychology-today.com: https://www.psychologytoday.com/us/blog/pathological-relation-ships/201212/joy-vs-happiness

Coaching Positive Performance. (n.d.). *Building a support network*. Retrieved from Coachingpositiveperformance.com: https://www.coachingpositiveperformance.com/building-a-support-network/

Cooke, R. A., and Lafferty, J. C. (2019). *Organizational Culture Inventory*. Mount Prospect, IL: Human Synergistics International.

Cummings, S., Bridgman, T., and Brown, K. (2016). Unfreezing change as three steps: Rethinking Kurt Lewin's legacy for change management. *Human Relations, 69*(1), 33–60. doi:10.1177/0018726715577707

Deming, W. E. (2000). *The new economics for industry, government, education* (2nd ed.). Boston, MA: MIT Press.

Dictionary.com. (2015). Retrieved from Dictionary.com: https://www.dictionary.com/browse/trust?s=t

Discovery Learning Inc. (2008). *Change style indicator*. Greensboro, NC: Discovery Learning Inc.

Dixon, D. L. (2004). Lead with integrity. *Executive Excellence, 21*(10), 19–20.

Dunn, S. (2011). How to manage a transition successfully. *Human Performance and Achievement Resources*.

Dunning, D. (2017, September 26). *What Is a P3 Project?* Retrieved December 23, 2019, from Bizfluent.com: https://bizfluent.com/info-12202156-p3-project.html

Fabrega, M. (n.d.). *17 ways to be kind to yourself*. Retrieved from Daringtolivefully.com: https://daringtolivefully.com/how-to-be-kind-to-yourself

Frankl, V. E. (2006). *Man's search for meaning*. Boston, MA: Beacon Press.

Fulmer, R. M. (2003). *Dialogue with four executives: Daniel Burnham, Nancy McGaw, Mila Baker, and Blair Shepard*. Retrieved from Gbr.pepperdine.edu: http://gbr.pepperdine.edu/033/conversation.html#note1

Gebert, D., Beungeler, C., and Heinitz, K. (2017). Tolerance: A neglected dimension in diversity training? *Academy of Management Learning and Education, 16*, 415–438. doi:10.5465/amle.2015.0252

Gitlow, H. S., Melnyck, R. J., and Levine, D. M. (2015). *A guide to six sigma and process improvement for practitioners and students: Foundations, DMAIC, tools, cases, and certification* (2nd ed.). Old Tappan, NJ: Pearson FT Press.

Glaser, R., and Lewin, K. (1988). *The Force Field Problem Solving Model.* West Chester, PA: Organizational Design and Development, Inc.

Glaser, R., Russo, E., and Eckler, M. (1988). *The force field problem solving model.* West Chester, PA: Organizational Design and Development, Inc.

Glaser, R., Russo, E., and Eckler, M. (1988). *The force field problem solving model.* West Chester, PA: Organizational Design and Development, Inc.

GoodTherapy. (2019). *Hopelessness.* Retrieved from GoodTherapy.org: https://www.goodtherapy.org/blog/psychpedia/hopelessness

Graham, R. (2019, October 12). Ellen DeGeneres is killing us with her kindness. *Boston Globe.* Retrieved from https://www.bostonglobe.com/opinion/2019/10/12/degeneres-killing-with-her-kindness/XdKK562OPOkPOePuhiTiNI/story.html

Greater Good Magazine. (2019). *What is mindfulness?* Retrieved from Greatergood.berkeley.edu: https://greatergood.berkeley.edu/topic/mindfulness/definition

Greenleaf, R. K. (1977). *Servant Leadership: A Journey Into the Nature of Legitimate Power and Greatness.* Mahwah, NJ: Paulist Press.

Gupta, S. (2016). Why America's Nurses Are Burning Out? *Everyday Health.*

Hall, K. (2017, December 4). *The importance of kindness.* Retrieved from Psychologytoday.com: https://www.psychologytoday.com/us/blog/pieces-mind/201712/the-importance-kindness

Hamilton, R. M. (2008, November 23). *Dictionary of Quotes.* Retrieved from Dictionary-quotes.com: https://www.dictionary-quotes.com/change-is-difficult-but-often-essential-to-survival-les-brown/

Hawkins, J. (2000). *What exactly does ethical leadership mean these days?* Retrieved from Lead-edge.com: www.lead-edge.com

Hedegaard H, Curtin SC, and Warner, M. (2018). Suicide mortality in the United States, 1999–2017. *NCHS Data Brief* (330).

Hereford, Z. (n.d.). *Perspective.* Retrieved from Essentiallifeskills.net: https://www.essentiallifeskills.net/perspective.html

Hersh, E. (2019). *Why is finding meaning in life and work so important?* Retrieved from Positiveroutines.com: https://positiveroutines.com/finding-meaning/

Hinman, L. M. (2003). *Ethics: A pluralistic approach to moral theory.* Belmont, CA: Thomson Learning/Wadsworth.

Hofstede, G., and Bond, M. H. (1998). The Confucius Connection: From Cultural Roots to Economic Growth. *16*(4), 4.

Holtz, H. (1999). *The concise guide to becoming an independent consultant.* Toronto, Canada: John Wiley and Sons, Inc.

Jones, K. P., King, E. B., Nelson, J., G. D., and Bowes-Sperry, L. (2013). Beyond the business case: An ethical perspective of diversity training. *Human Resource Management, 52,* 55–74. doi:10.1002/hrm.21517

Juneja, P. (n.d.). *What are Metrics and Why are they Important?* Retrieved December 23, 2019, from Managementstudyguide.com: https://www.managementstudy-guide.com/what-are-metrics.htm

Kanbanize. (2019). *7 wastes of lean: How to optimize resources.* Retrieved from Kanbanize.com: https://kanbanize.com/lean-management/value-waste/7-wastes-of-lean/

Kaplan, M., Dollar, B., Melian, V., Durme, Y. V., and Wong, J. (2016). *Shape culture.* Retrieved from Deloitte.com: https://www2.deloitte.com/us/en/insights/focus/human-capital-trends/2016/impact-of-culture-on-business-strategy.html

Kaplan, R. S., and Norton, D. P. (1992). The balanced scorecard - Measures that drive performance. *Harvard Business Review* (January–February). Retrieved from https://hbr.org/1992/01/the-balanced-scorecard-measures-that-drive-per-formance-2

Kaplan, R. S., and Norton, D. P. (1996). *The balanced scorecard: Translating strategy into action* (1st ed.). Watertown, MA: Harvard Business Review Press.

Kerns, C. (2002). *GBR Conversation with Joe Rokus.* Retrieved from Gbr.pepperdine.edu: http://gbr.pepperdine.edu/021/print_Rokus_conversation.html

Khazan, O. (2018, August 16). It Pays to Be Nice. *The Atlantic.* Retrieved from https://www.theatlantic.com/business/archive/2015/06/it-pays-to-be-nice/396512/

Kotter, J. (1996). *Leading change.* Boston, MA: Harvard Business School Press.

Kotter, J. P., and Cohen, D. S. (2002). *The Heart of change: Real-life stories of how people change their organizations* (1st ed.). Boston, MA: Harvard Business School Press.

Kouzes, J., and Posner, B. (2003). *Encouraging the heart: A leader's guide to rewarding and recognizing others.* San Francisco, CA: Jossey-Bass.

Kozan, K. (2019, February 13). *6 Best Workplace Diversity Trends for 2019.* Retrieved November 12, 2016, from Ideal.com: https://ideal.com/workplace-di-versity-trends/

Lim, S. (2019, April 19). *Balanced Scorecard.* Retrieved December 17, 2019, from Investopedia.com: https://www.investopedia.com/terms/b/balancedscorecard.asp

Lipiński, R., and Jamro, K. (2017). Information Flow Model: a Versatile and Effective Change Management Model. *International Conference On Intellectual Capital, Knowledge Management and Organizational Learning*, (253–259).

Mahanti, R. (2019). *Data quality: Dimensions, measurement, strategy, management, and governance*. Milwaukee, WI: ASQ Quality Press.

McGraw, P. C. (2014, April). *Dr. Phil: The powerful ability that will help you manage your life*. Retrieved from Oprah.com: http://www.oprah.com/spirit/develop-perspective-how-to-see-someone-elses-point-of-view

Musselwhite, C., and Ingram, R. (2003). *Change style indicator: Facilitator guide*. Greensboro, NC: Discovery Learning, Inc.

Perspective. (2019). In Merriam-Webster.com. Retrieved from https://www.merriam-webster.com/dictionary/perspective

Prevost, T., Godward, S., and Dickerson, C. (2004). *Definitions*. Retrieved from Cirem.co.uk: http://www.cirem.co.uk/definitions.html#e

Quinn, R. (1996). *Deep change: Discovering the leader within*. San Francisco, CA: Jossey-Bass Inc., Publishers.

Rajagopalan, S. (2017, February 27). *The costs of non-delivery and non-conformance*. Retrieved December 10, 2019, from Scrumexpert.com: https://www.scrumexpert.com/knowledge/the-costs-of-non-delivery-and-non-conformance/

Rath, T. (2007). *StrengthsFinder 2.0*. New York, NY: Gallup Press.

Reh, F. J. (2019, January 8). *Using metrics to measure business performance: You can't manage what you don't measure*. Retrieved December 15, 2019, from Thebalancecareers.com: https://www.thebalancecareers.com/you-can-t-manage-what-you-dont-measure-2275996

Robbins, S. (2003). *Organizational Behavior* (10th ed.). Saddle River, NJ: Prentice-Hall Inc.

Roland, C. (1996). *Some definitions*. Retrieved from Grove.ufl.edu: http://grove.ufl.edu/~rolandc/definitions.html

Schein, E. H. (1985). *Organizational culture and leadership: A dynamic view*. San Francisco, CA: Jossey-Bass.

Schein, E. H. (1998). *Process consultation revisited: Building the helping relationship (Addison-Wesley Series on Organization Development)*. Midway Drive Kent, OH: Prentice Hall.

Seaward, B. L. (2018). *Managing stress: Principles and strategies for health and well-being* (9th ed.). Burlington MA: Jones and Bartlett Learning, LLC.

Selye, H. (1978). *The Stress of Life Paperback*. London, UK: McGraw-Hill.

Senge, P. (1980). *Transitions: Making sense of life's transitions.* Reading, MA: Perseus Books.

Senge, P. (1999). *The dance of change.* New York, NY: Doubleday.

Shirodkar, P. (2013). Unclogging the MENtal block: Ensuring greater gender diversity at the workplace. *Journal of Commerce and Management Thought, 4*(2), 339–355. Retrieved from Journal of Commerce and Management Thought IV - 2.

Smith, M., Segal, R., and Segal, J. (2011, December). *Signs and Symptoms of Stress Overload.* Retrieved from OACES: https://oaces.net/healthy-living/signs-and-symptoms-of-stress-overload/

Sommerville, I. (2004). *Software Engineering (7ʰ Edition) 7ʰ Edition.* Boston, MA: Addison Wesley.

Spears, L. C. (2004). Practicing servant-leadership. *Leader To Leader 2004*(34), 7–11.

Support Network. (2019). *In Cambridge Dictionary.* Retrieved from https://dictionary.cambridge.org/us/dictionary/english/support-network

SYG. (2019). *Employee Recognition Programs.* Retrieved December 24, 2019, from Select-Your-Gift.com: https://www.select-your-gift.com/employee-recognition?msclkid=0837b6ed14841e56acc6e8ef963d7ad4

Tague, N. R. (2015). *The quality toolbox* (2ⁿᵈ ed.). Florence, KY: Cengage Learning.

Taylor, G. (2019, July 25). *10 symptoms of stress.* Retrieved from Facty.com: https://facty.com/ailments/stress/10-symptoms-of-stress/1/

The American Institute of Stress. (n.d.). *What is stress?* Retrieved from Stress.org: https://www.stress.org/what-is-stress

Valchev, M. (2020). Adaptability Skills. Retrieved from https://www.business-phrases.net/adaptability-skills/

Williams, A. (2017, April 4). *11 key business performance metrics for better operations.* Retrieved December 24, 2019, from Alistemarketing.com: https://alistemarketing.com/blog/business-performance-metrics/

Wojtczak, A. (2002). *Glossary of medical education terms.* Retrieved from Iime.org: http://www.iime.org/glossary.htm

THE CASE FOR LITE LEADERSHIP

No dream is too big. No challenge is too great. Nothing we want for our future is beyond our reach.

—Donald Trump

Donald John Trump (born June 14, 1946) is the 45th and current president of the United States. Before entering politics, he was a businessman and television personality. Trump was born and raised in the New York City borough of Queens and received a bachelor's degree in economics from the Wharton School. Forbes estimates his net worth to be $3.1 billion.

—*The Washington Post*

For decades, the world has been becoming such a troublesome environment, and workplaces have become dark and confused. The whole world seems to be tumbling into crisis, but none of the problems seem to be addressed or solved. No single leader is capable or willing to bring leadership, knowledge, and different cultures together to resolve problems at their root. Here are a few areas of darkness that we live in today.

CYBERSPACE

Balkhi (2014) argues that *cyberspace*, a growing community where everyone is able reach out to one another regardless of time and distance, has become a new way of life. However, cyberspace today is being used by some individuals for their own dubious schemes, and they target unsuspecting individuals, companies, banks, and even military and government agencies' trade secrets and intellectual property. Hardy and Williams (2014) stated that activity like this is referred to as cyberterrorism when it is motivated by a political, religious, or ideological cause and intended to threaten a government or a section of the public to varying degrees, possibly seriously interfering with infrastructure.

According to Mardisalu (2020), IBM and Ponemon Institute's *Cost of a Data Breach Report* found that the average cost of a data breach for organizations worldwide is $3.6 million, which amounts to a 6.4 percent increase from the previous year. However, data breaches are more costly in the U.S., reaching an average of $7.91 million. The cost of cybercrime is expected to exceed $2 trillion globally in 2019.

POLITICAL VIOLENCE

Political violence can be described as violence used by individuals, organizations, or governments to achieve political goals. Such violence includes war, police brutality, counterinsurgency or genocide, rebellion, and rioting. In addition, refusing to alleviate famine or otherwise deny resources to politically identifiable groups within their territories, through nonaction, can also be characterized as a form of political violence because this can result in deaths. Political violence resulting in deaths, injury, or loss of property is not uncommon in many countries today (*Political Violence*, n.d.).

Political violence amounted to some 9,842 incidents globally in Q1 2019, a 13 percent increase over Q4 2018 and a 2 percent decrease year over year. Some of the political violence included a 44 percent quarterly increase in oil and gas sector attacks in Colombia, a sharp rise in attacks and war incidents in Myanmar, a twofold increase in unrest incidents in Nigeria due to presidential, parliamentary, gubernatorial, and state assembly polls that were postponed, and a rise in unrest incidents in Russia from six in Q3 2018 to twenty-seven in Q1 2019 (Control Risks 2019).

POVERTY

Peer (2018) stated that high unemployment and poverty can lead to depression, homicide, suicide, alcohol abuse, and even violence in the home and workplace if uncontrolled. There is tremendous global progress in ending extreme poverty; however, contaminated water, malaria, poor nutrition, and lingering effects of war have taken a toll on numerous people in the world. One quarter of the world has risen out of extreme poverty since 1990. Today, less than 10 percent of the world lives in extreme poverty, surviving on $1.90 a day or less, and the number of children dying—mostly from preventable causes such as poverty, hunger, and disease—is less than half of what it was, dropping from more than thirty-five thousand a day to less than fifteen thousand.

While progress continues, help is needed today more than ever to curtail conflict, poor governance, and natural disasters, especially in sub-Saharan Africa, which has seen an increase in people living in poverty. The World Bank (n.d.) argued that, despite progress made in alleviating poverty in the world, access to good schools, health care, electricity, safe water, and other critical services remains elusive for numerous people, especially those in rural areas and villages. The lack of education, access to basic utilities, health care, and security reveals a world in which poverty is a much broader, more entrenched problem.

The World Bank (n.d.) revealed that there are people in poverty who have worked so hard to get themselves out of it, but such a jump can be temporary because economic shocks, food insecurity, and climate change threaten to rob them of their hard-won gains and force them back into poverty. This is where Lite leaders with the moonic element of emotional intelligence are called to come to reward and create conditions that will help them to prosper in the future. It will be critical to find ways to tackle these issues as we make progress toward 2030. The intent of the Lite leader is to help quicken the process of alleviating poverty and make sure good schools, health care, electricity, safe water, and other critical services become unquestionable rights. These are not privileges; these are basic needs that have to be fulfilled at all times.

GREED

The people of the world are divided into two: the wise and the fools. There are good leaders who are wise, and there are bad leaders who are fools. However, if the wise will not rule, the only alternative left is the fools, and that is most of the root cause of the quest for *greed*—the selfish desire to acquire more privilege, wealth, or power, leaving the others with little or nothing, helpless and suffering.

Wise leaders begin with the natural feeling that they want to serve, serve first, and make sure other people's highest-priority needs are being served. By doing so, these leaders grow as persons, become healthier, wiser, freer, and more autonomous, and are more likely to become servants. Too often, foolish leaders want to lead first, most likely because of the need to assuage an unusual power drive, because of greed, or because they want to acquire material possessions (Greenleaf 1977).

RELIGIOUS FREEDOM

Merriam-Webster (2004b) defined *religious freedom* as a right of an individual or group to practice their religion or exercise their beliefs without intervention by the government, and to be free of the exercise of authority by a church through the government.

Yet, eleven Christians are martyred each day around the world, and approximately 80 percent of the world's population lives in countries where religious liberty is threatened, restricted, or even banned (Woodward and Jordahl 2019). President Donald Trump, in his address to the United Nations in 2019, asked the rest of the international community to join in the effort to protect individuals and groups who are persecuted for their faith (Trump 2019). Addressing the United Nations as the first leader to touch such a sensitive yet important topic is a sign of courage, a moonic element of the personal leadership quintet of PEPSE Lite leadership.

MENTAL ILLNESS

The Mayo Clinic (n.d.) described *mental illness*, also called mental health disorders, as a wide range of mental health conditions that affect mood, thinking, and behavior. Mental health concerns are not uncommon among many people; however, when these mental health concerns—and their signs and symptoms—cause frequent stress and affect a person's ability to function, it becomes mental illness. Depression, anxiety disorders, schizophrenia, eating disorders, and addictive behaviors are examples of mental illnesses.

Mental illness can be managed with a combination of medication and psychotherapy, which can help reduce the signs and symptoms remarkably. However, when it is not properly managed, it can make people miserable and cause problems in their daily lives, such as at school, at work, or in relationships.

In 2017, approximately 970 million people in the world suffered from mental illness. This represents 13 percent of the world population—12.6 percent of males and 13.3 percent of females. Anxiety disorders are the number one mental illness in the world, affecting about 284 million people, which represents 3.8 percent of the world population—2.8 percent of males and 4.7 percent of females. Depression is the second most common mental illness in the world, affecting about 264 million people, which represents 3.4 percent of the world population—2.7 percent of males and 4.1 percent of females. Alcohol use disorder is the third most common mental illness in the world, affecting some 107 million people, which represents 1.4 percent of the world population—2 percent of males and 0.8 percent of females (Ritchie and Roser 2018).

It may seem that the direct death toll from mental health and substance use disorders is typically low; however, significant numbers of indirect deaths through suicide and self-harm are attributed to mental health disorders. Meta-analyses in high-income countries suggest that up to 90 percent of suicide deaths result from underlying mental and substance use disorders (Ritchie and Roser 2018).

Today's leaders may not be doing enough to curtail this deadly mental malady. It is also noteworthy to mention that a study by the Central Florida Intelligence Exchange (2013) found that 79 percent of the fourteen mass shootings that occurred between 2011 and 2013 were committed by individuals then suffering from mental illness, and only three of the shooters had no history of mental illness.

DISEASES

Merriam-Webster (2004a) defined *disease* as a condition of the living body or animal or plant or of one of its parts that impairs normal functioning and is typically manifested by distinguishing signs and symptoms.

Most people think the deadliest diseases in the world are the fast-acting, incurable ones that periodically grab headlines. In fact, these types of diseases don't even rank in the top ten causes of worldwide deaths. Approximately 56.4 million people died worldwide in 2015 due to diseases that progressed slowly, and this represents 68 percent of the total global deaths that year. Luckily, these diseases are partially preventable given a good and healthy environment, access to preventive care, and quality of health care (Pietrangelo and Holland 2019). Making Lite leaders available in situations such as this could help lower their risk.

The World Health Organization (2018) reported that there were 56.9 million deaths in 2016, and about 54 percent of them were caused by the top ten deadliest diseases. Ischemic heart disease is the world's biggest killer, and stroke is second. Together, they have remained the leading causes of death globally in the past fifteen years, accounting for a combined 15.2 million deaths in 2016 (WHO 2018). The third largest global killer is chronic obstructive pulmonary disease, which claimed some three million lives in 2016 (WHO 2018). Lower respiratory infections are the fourth on the list of deadliest diseases worldwide, and they have remained the deadliest communicable disease, causing three million deaths worldwide in 2016 (WHO 2018).

Alzheimer's disease and other types of dementia are the world's fifth biggest killer, causing some 1.9 million deaths in 2016, which is more than double compared to 2000, when these diseases ranked fourteenth on the list (WHO 2018). Trachea, bronchus, and lung cancers rank sixth, causing approximately 1.7 million deaths in 2016 (WHO 2018). In 2016, 1.6 million people were killed due to diabetes mellitus, making it the seventh biggest killer, up from less than one million in 2000 (WHO 2018). Surprisingly, road injuries killed 1.4 million people, about 74 percent of whom were men and boys, making them the eighth biggest global killer in 2016 (WHO 2018).

Though diarrheal diseases decreased by almost one million between 2000 and 2016, they still caused 1.4 million deaths in 2016, putting them at ninth on the list (WHO 2018). Likewise, the number of tuberculosis deaths decreased during the same period, but 1.3 million people were still killed, and making tuberculosis the tenth most deadly disease in 2016 (WHO 2018). It is noteworthy to mention that HIV/AIDS, which killed one million people in 2016 compared with 1.5 million in 2000, is no longer among the world's top ten causes of death (WHO 2018).

With a lack of Lite leaders, honesty—a moonic element of the personal leadership quintet of the PEPSE Lite Leadership—is elusive. Andrew Jeremy Wakefield, a British gastroenterologist at the Royal Free Hospital in London, along with twelve coauthors, published a 1998 paper in *The Lancet* claiming a link between the measles, mumps, and rubella (MMR) vaccine and autism. In addition, Wakefield et al. (1998) went on to recommend that the combination MMR vaccine be suspended in favor of single-antigen vaccinations given separately over time. Meanwhile, Wakefield himself had filed for a patent for a single-antigen measles vaccine in 1997, and so would seem to have a potential financial interest in promoting this view (The College of Physicians of Philadelphia 2018).

Wakefield's publication immediately drew worldwide attention and frightened parents, who began to delay or completely refuse vaccination for their children. The rates of MMR vaccination dropped significantly, and over the next twelve years, further research into the possibility of a link between MMR and autism intensified. The results of several relevant, well-designed studies were unable to confirm Wakefield's findings, and they found no link between MMR and bowel disease or MMR and autism.

In 2004, Dr. Richard Horton, then editor of *The Lancet*, found out that Wakefield had a selfish and excessive desire for money motivated by naked ambition and greed, and he had been paid by attorneys seeking to file lawsuits against vaccine manufacturers. Horton also claimed in television interviews that Wakefield's research was "fatally flawed." *The*

Lancet formally withdrew the paper itself, and most of the coauthors of the fake study publicly retracted their interpretation (Laurance 2004).

Finally, Britain's General Medical Council banned Wakefield in May 2010 from practicing medicine in Britain after finding evidence that he committed research fraud by falsifying data about the conditions of the children used in his research. The lesson learned is that, due to the lack of honesty and pursuit of greed by Wakefield and his gang, there is still public doubt that causes one of the most powerful weapons we have against human disease (i.e., MMR vaccination) to be less used for its purpose today. This has resulted in outbreaks of measles and mumps in the United States and in the stubborn persistence of polio in Pakistan, Afghanistan, and Nigeria. This resistance to vaccinate children because of the fear of autism still exists today, and it has contributed to the deaths of more than 11,300 people due to Ebola in West Africa alone. Disinformation such as this has the power to maim children, kill health workers, and stoke public health disasters across the world (Nathe 2018).

This is not the end of disinformation, also known as "fake news," but with the internet-powered self-misdiagnosis to misguided policies, especially in family planning and mental health, to name a few among many, the risks still exist today.

NUCLEAR WEAPONS

Nuclear warfare has become a major cause of concern for the whole planet, and a large number of countries have acquired powerful nuclear weapons, which can be a threat for the entire human race (Kumar 2019). However, these countries advocate possession of such weapons with the argument that they are necessary to protect their peace and sovereignty from enemies with similar powers.

The most important job description of a Lite leader is to listen to people as they cry for help for the disarmament of nuclear weapons for the simple reason that "every gun that is made, every warship launched, every rocket fired signifies in the final sense a theft from those who hunger and are not fed, those who are cold and are not clothed."

According to the International Campaign for the Abolishment of

Nuclear Weapons (2012), opinion polls show that a majority of people in seven of the nine nuclear-armed nations support the prompt negotiation of a treaty to eliminate nuclear weapons in their entirety. If this is the democratic wish of the people of the world, why hasn't it been accomplished? The answer is not far-fetched.

It is because the traditional and conventional leadership styles have done the best for humankind over the past decades. They have helped humankind develop the internet, go to space, and create nuclear bombs, and they have helped feed humanity to a large extent. However, the choices these leaders with traditional and conventional leadership styles have taken mostly were at the expense of humanity. Training and cultivating Lite leaders in connectedness can help lead and educate the leaders of today to watch and listen very closely to the people they serve. If leaders serve first (Greenleaf 1977), one of the moonic elements of the Lite leadership, poverty will be wiped from the surface of this earth. Lite leaders also do problem-solving with the win-win approach in mind.

GLOBAL WARMING

There is a gradual increase in the average temperature of the earth's atmosphere and its oceans, which could permanently change the earth's climate. This concept of global warming has aroused a heated debate among climate scientists across the world on whether global warming is real; some call it a hoax. Despite the differences among climate scientists, the scientific consensus is that the average temperature of the Earth has risen between 0.4 and 0.8 °C over the past hundred years.

It is believed that the primary source of the global warming that has occurred over the past fifty years is the increased volume of carbon dioxide and other greenhouse gases released by the burning of fossil fuels, land clearing, agriculture, and other human activities. The Intergovernmental Panel on Climate's scientists who carry out global warming research have recently predicted that average global temperatures could increase between 1.4 and 5.8 °C by the year 2100, and it could result in increased sea levels due to the melting of the polar ice caps, as well as increased frequency and severity of storms and other severe weather events (Live Science 2019).

On one hand, Lite leaders believe the scientific term "global warming" sounds too political and divides the global community. On the other hand, *stewardship*, a theological belief that humans are responsible for the world and should take care of it, is a term that both sides of the global warming debate could embrace. Educating the global community on environmental stewardship instead of global warming will eliminate the political implications that global warming has and yield the same effect on both sides, achieving the same goal that both school of thoughts strive to achieve, and bringing the two sides to agree on one thing: taking care of the planet Earth.

REFERENCES

Balkhi, S. (2014, May 11). *25 biggest cyberattacks in history*. Retrieved from https://list25.com/25-biggest-cyber-attacks-in-history/

BusinessDictionary.com. (n.d.). *Political violence*. Retrieved September 17, 2019, from http://www.businessdictionary.com/definition/political-violence.html

Central Florida Intelligence Exchange. (2013, July 15). *Acts of violence attributed by behavioral and mental health issues* [Case study analysis]. Retrieved from https://info.publicintelligence.net/CFIX-MentalHealthViolence.pdf

The College of Physicians of Philadelphia. (2018, January 25). *Do vaccines cause autism?* Retrieved from https://www.historyofvaccines.org/content/articles/do-vaccines-cause-autism

Control Risks. (2019, April 30). *CORE political violence and violent organised crime report Q1 2019*. Retrieved from https://www.controlrisks.com/our-thinking/insights/reports/core-incident-report-q1-2019

Greenleaf, R. K. (1977). *Servant leadership: A journey into the nature of legitimate power and greatness*. Mahwah, NJ: Paulist Press.

Hardy, K., and Williams, G. (2014). What is 'cyberterrorism'? Computer and internet technology in legal definitions of terrorism. In T. Chen, L. Jarvis, and S. Macdonald (Eds.), *Cyberterrorism* (1–23). New York, NY: Springer. doi:10.1007/978-1-4939-0962-9_1

The International Campaign to Abolish Nuclear Weapons. (2012). *Nuclear weapons spending: A theft of public resources*. Retrieved from https://www.icanw.org/nuclear_weapons_spending_a_theft_of_public_resources

Kumar, S. (2019, June 19). *Top 10 nuclear power countries in the world 2019*. Retrieved from https://www.indiasstuffs.com/nuclear-power-countries-in-the-world/

Laurance, J. (2004, September 20). Health check: How was the MMR scare sustained for so long when the evidence showed that it was unfounded? *The Independent*. Retrieved from https://www.independent.co.uk/life-style/health-and-families/health-news/health-check-how-was-the-mmr-scare-sustained-for-so-long-when-the-evidence-showed-that-it-was-33294.html

Live Science. (n.d.). *Global warming: News, facts, causes and effects*. Retrieved from https://www.livescience.com/topics/global-warming

Mardisalu, R. (2020, January 6). *14 most alarming cyber security statistics in 2020*. Retrieved from https://thebestvpn.com/cyber-security-statistics-2020/

Mayo Clinic. (n.d.). *Mental illness*. Retrieved from https://www.mayoclinic.org/ diseases-conditions/mental-illness/symptoms-causes/syc-20374968

Merriam-Webster. (2004a). Disease. In *The Merriam-Webster Dictionary*. New York, NY: Merriam-Webster.

Merriam-Webster. (2004b). Religious Freedom. In *The Merriam-Webster Dictionary*. New York, NY: Merriam-Webster.

Nathe, M. (2018, January 19). *10 global health issues to watch in 2018*. Retrieved from https://www.intrahealth.org/vital/10-global-health-issues-watch-2018

Peer, A. (2018, November 21). *Global poverty: Facts, FAQs, and how to help*. Retrieved from https://www.worldvision.org/sponsorship-news-stories/global-poverty-facts

Pietrangelo, A., and Holland, K. (2019, July 10). The top 10 deadliest diseases. *Healthline*. Retrieved from https://www.healthline.com/health/top-10-deadliest-diseases

Ritchie, H., and Roser, M. (2018, April). *Mental health*. Retrieved from https://ourworldindata.org/mental-health

Trump, D. J. (2019, September 24). *Remarks by President Trump to the 74th Session of the United Nations General Assembly*. Retrieved from https://www.whitehouse.gov/briefings-statements/remarks-president-trump-74th-session-united-nations-general-assembly/

Wakefield, A. J., Murch, M. B., Anthony, A., Linnell, J., Casson, D. M., Malik, M., ... Walker-Smith, J. A. (1998). RETRACTED: Ileal-lymphoid-nodular hyperplasia, non-specific colitis, and pervasive developmental disorder in children. *The Lancet, 351*(9103), 637–641. doi:10.1016/S0140-6736(97)11096-0

Woodward, C., and Jordahl, S. (2019, September 24). Trump praised for advancing religious freedom at U.N. *OneNewsNow*. Retrieved from https://onenewsnow.com/persecution/2019/09/24/trump-praised-for-advancing-religious-freedom-at-un

The World Bank. (n.d.). *Poverty*. Retrieved October 3, 2019, from https://www.worldbank.org/en/topic/poverty/overview

World Health Organization. (2018, May 24). The top 10 causes of death. Retrieved from https://www.who.int/en/news-room/fact-sheets/detail/the-top-10-causes-of-death

12

LITE LEADERSHIP IN THE VUCA WORLD

Nothing can stop the man with the right mental attitude from achieving his goal; nothing on earth can help the man with the wrong mental attitude.

—Thomas Jefferson

Thomas Jefferson was a founding father of the United States who wrote the Declaration of Independence. As US president, he completed the Louisiana Purchase. As the third president of the United States, Jefferson stabilized the US economy and defeated pirates from North Africa.

—Biography.com (n.d.)

While the benefits of Lite leadership are evident to most organizations, leaders today have taken to using the military acronym VUCA—volatility, uncertainty, complexity, ambiguity—to describe the world in which they operate. They may ask, in a VUCA world, what is the point of Lite leadership when your competitors are not as holistic as Lite leaders? The intent of Lite leadership is to change one leader at a time and put the right people—the Lite leaders—in the right positions. Even the fattest budgets and the most brilliant non-holistic people who lead corporate organizations today are unable to find the best leadership practice to bring harmony to the workplace, while at the same time creating wealth for the organization.

A refreshingly different approach to VUCA is to make this holistic leadership practice—Lite leadership—a part of the strategic planning for the organization. Bonn and Christodoulou (1996) asserted that strategic planning is not about predicting the future, per se, since no one can do that. Rather, strategic planning is preparing for the future by making a series of estimates or educated guesses about what will happen. Despite living in a VUCA world, strategy does still have a purpose, but building one in a VUCA environment requires more nuanced thinking. Bennett and Lemoine (2014) provided a guide (see figure 1) to identifying, preparing for, and responding to events in each of the four VUCA categories.

	Complexity	Volatility
How well can you predict the results of your actions? + ... **−**	**Characteristics:** The situation has many interconnected parts and variables. Some information is available or can be predicated, but the volume or nature of it can be overwhelming to process. **Example:** Doing business in many countries, all with unique regulatory environments, tariffs, and cultural values. **Approach:** Restructure, bring on or develop specialist, and build up resources adequate to address the complexity.	**Characteristics:** The challenge is unexpected or unstable and may be of unknown duration, but it is not necessarily hard to understand; knowledge about it is often available. **Example:** Prices fluctuate after a natural disaster takes supplies offline. **Approach:** Build in slack and devote resources to preparedness—for instance, stockpile inventory or overbuy talent. These steps are typically expensive; investment should match the risk.
	Ambiguity	Certainty
	Characteristics: Casual relationships are completely unclear. No precedents exist; facing "unknown unknowns." **Example:** Moving into immature or emerging markets or launching products outside core competencies. **Approach:** Experiment. Understanding cause and effect requires generating hypotheses and testing them. Design experiments so that lessons learned can be broadly applied.	**Characteristics:** Despite a lack of other information, the event's basic cause and effect are known. Change is possible but not a given. **Example:** A competitor's pending product launch muddies the future of the business and the market. **Approach:** Invest in information—collect, interpret, and share it. This works best in conjunction with structural changes, such as adding information analysis networks, which can reduce ongoing uncertainty.
	− How much do you know about the situation? +	

Figure 12.1. Responding to events across the four VUCA categories.

According to Porter (2011), there are three key principles that define *strategic planning*: (a) it is the creation of a unique and valuable position involving a different set of activities, (b) it requires one to make trade-offs in competing (i.e., choosing what not to do), and (c) it involves creating "fit" among a company's activities. Most managers under pressure are forced to improve productivity, quality, and speed using tools such as total quality management, benchmarking, and reengineering to achieve dramatic results. However, these gains rarely translate into sustainable profitability. Although necessary to superior performance, such operational effectiveness is not sufficient because its techniques are easy to imitate. By contrast, the essence of strategy planning is choosing a unique and valuable position rooted in systems of activities that are much more difficult to match (Porter 2011).

While the benefits of effective strategic planning are evident to most businesses, small business owners often plan poorly. Many contend that the daily demand of running their businesses reduces their time available for effective strategic planning. Since strategic planning drives the allocation of resources (time and personnel), it is practiced in every organization—large and small. Small organizations that ignore strategic planning do so at their peril (Cordeiro 2013).

BENEFITS OF STRATEGIC PLANNING

The benefits of strategic planning can be categorized into four groups, which will be described in the following sections.

UNDERSTANDING THE ENVIRONMENT, INCLUDING GAPS

Effective strategic planning assists organizations in developing clear assessments of their competitive environment—their current competitors, potential new competitors, and internal resources, especially scarcities (Cordeiro 2013). Drucker (2001) argued that all organizations face outside pressures from emerging issues and trends related to globalization, technology, competition, government policies, and others. Effective strategic planning helps organizations analyze, understand, and react to these issues (Cordeiro 2013).

FOCUS RESOURCES ON SPECIFIC GOALS

There are many pressures and rapid changes that organizations of all sizes face that stretch the limits of resources and can leave them in shambles. Oftentimes, this may lead to a dilution of efforts, a misallocation of people and financial resources, a scattered approach to customer service, and ultimately, a loss of competitive advantage in the marketplace. However, strategic planning provides a mechanism to focus and direct the efforts of employees despite the many pressures and changes organizations may face (Drucker 2001).

MAINTAIN AND IMPROVE COMPETITIVE POSITION

To survive, all organizations must have a long-term competitive advantage—the ability to deliver services or products "by implementing a strategy that competitors are unable to duplicate of find too costly to try to imitate" (Grieve 2009, 9).

PREPARE FOR FUTURE ENVIRONMENTS

Allocating resources based on environmental analysis and strategic planning assists organizations in preparing for future environments. Fitzroy and colleagues noted that in past decades, many large firms developed sophisticated models in an attempt to accurately forecast revenues, expenses, and profits; however, turbulence in the business environment has limited most models' applicability (Cordeiro 2013).

LEADING IN A VUCA WORLD

One school of thought argues that the concept of VUCA may mean the world is a crazy place could be misleading. To this end, VUCA combines four distinct types of challenges that demand four distinct types of responses, and although it is difficult to know how to approach a challenging situation in a VUCA world, there are still opportunities to business plan strategically to succeed. A second school of thought postulates that the VUCA world offers no choice to businesses because it is not possible to prepare strategically for a world that is volatile, uncertain, complex, and ambiguous. To the first school of thought, this is a way to use VUCA as a crutch to throw off the hard work of strategy and planning (Bennett and Lemoine 2014).

No matter how the concept of VUCA is viewed, it is apparent that traditional leadership skills are insufficient to weather an increasingly volatile, uncertain, complex, and ambiguous VUCA world. Johansen and Euchner (2013) discussed five skills that provide competitive advantage in a VUCA world. The most basic of the five leadership skills is the *maker instinct*, or the inner urge that we all have to build or grow things. What is new about this skill is not the urge to make, but the ability to create communities of makers to affect much larger impacts. The second is *clarity*, or the ability to see through messes and contradictions to a future that others cannot yet envision. Often, the challenges of the VUCA world will not have clear solutions, thus requiring the third skill called *dilemma flipping*, which is the ability to turn difficult problems into smaller micro-tasks, presenting new opportunities. To make the most of micro-tasking requires a fourth skill known as *smart mob organizing*, which involves bringing groups of people together to work toward a productive goal, empowered and amplified by media platforms to solve pressing business and societal issues in an adaptive way while using minimal resources. The fifth skill is called *bio-empathy*, which refers to a leader's ability to empathize with the principles of nature and take the interconnected systematic metaphor presented by natural systems to reorganize and guide effective teams. However, to create these pooled resources, leaders must develop a complex and challenging leadership skill known as *commons creating*—the ability to develop a common cause with others for mutual benefit through sharing of assets (Johansen and Euchner 2013).

The idea of VUCA is that leaders can no longer sit back and work a five-year strategic plan. Instead, they need to operate with the assumption that things may change at any moment, and they cannot necessarily predict how their actions will impact those unanticipated changes. It is still useful to look at a SWOT (strengths, weaknesses, opportunities, and threats) analysis, but businesses need to go one step further and have a what-if conversation with their employees. They must create what-if scenarios in each element of SWOT and discuss what will happen if they are wrong—as well as what might happen if the team hits it out of the park. Businesses must create three budgets each year—one the organization expects to meet, and then a best- and worst-case scenario. Such a strategy would certainly address the complexities of a VUCA world (Kleiman 2016).

VUCA 2.0

All in all, the VUCA world will get worse in the future. With the events of 2016—Brexit, the election of Donald Trump, threats from terrorists and cybercriminals, and climate change—business leaders have entered a new era requiring new ways of leading. George (2017) labeled this VUCA 2.0, now standing for vision, understanding, courage, and adaptability. These rapid-fire changes are putting extreme pressures on business leaders to lead in ways not taught in business schools (George 2017). Traditional management methods seem no longer sufficient to address the volume of change in the VUCA world because business is not running as usual any longer. George's VUCA 2.0 examines the different ways of leading in a VUCA world.

VISION

This is the ability to see through the chaos to have a clear vision for an organization. Leaders must define the true north of the organization:

its mission, values, and strategy. Leaders should create clarity around this true north and refuse to let external events pull them off course or cause them to neglect or abandon their mission, which must be their guiding light.

UNDERSTANDING

With their vision in hand, leaders need an in-depth understanding of their organization's capabilities and strategies to take advantage of rapidly changing circumstances by playing to their strengths while minimizing their weaknesses. Leaders need to tap into myriad sources covering the full spectrum of viewpoints by engaging directly with customers and employees to ensure they are attuned to changes in their market.

COURAGE

Now more than ever, leaders need the courage to step up to these challenges and make audacious decisions that embody risks and often go against the grain. They cannot afford to keep their heads down, using traditional management techniques while avoiding criticism and risk-taking. This era belongs to the bold—and not the meek or timid.

ADAPTABILITY

This is the ability for leaders to be flexible in adapting to this rapidly changing VUCA environment. Instead of long-range plans, businesses are required to adopt flexible tactics that require rapid adaptation to changing external circumstances—without altering strategic course.

CONCLUSION

George's (2017) advice in his VUCA 2.0 approach to business leaders today is the most pragmatic solution to the VUCA world. Business leaders who stay focused on their missions and values and have the courage to deploy bold strategies that build on their strengths will ultimately be the winners. On the other hand, those who abandon core values or lock themselves into fixed positions and fail to adapt will wind up the losers.

REFERENCES

Bennett, N., and Lemoine, G. J. (2014). What VUCA really means for you. *Harvard Business Review*, *92*(1/2), 27. Retrieved from https://hbr.org/2014/01/what-vuca-really-means-for-you

Biography.com. (n.d.). Thomas Jefferson. Retrieved April 14, 2020, from https://www.biography.com/us-president/thomas-jefferson

Bonn, I., and Christodoulou, C. (1996). From strategic planning to strategic management. *Long Range Planning, 29*(4), 543–551. doi:10.1016/0024-6301(96)00046-5

Cordeiro, W. P. (2013). Small businesses ignore strategic planning at their peril. *Academy of Business Research Journal, 3*, 22–30.

Drucker, P. F. (2001). *The essential Drucker.* New York, NY: HarperCollins.

George, B. (2017, February 17). VUCA 2.0: A strategy for steady leadership in an unsteady world. Retrieved October 3, 2017, from https://www.forbes.com/sites/hbsworkingknowledge/2017/02/17/vuca-2-0-a-strategy-for-steady-leadership-in-an-unsteady-world/#3bfc8c5013d8

Grieve, H. R. (2009). Bigger and safer: The diffusion of competitive advantage. *Strategic Management Journal, 30*, 1–23. doi:10.1002/smj.721

Johansen, B., and Euchner, J. (2013). Navigating the VUCA world. *Research-Technology Management, 56*, 10–15. doi:10.5437/08956308x5601003

Kleiman, L. (2016, September 2). *This VUCA world—Will we ever get control?* [Blog post]. Retrieved from https://blog.shrm.org/blog/this-vuca-world-will-we-ever-get-control

Porter, M. E. (2011). What is strategy? In *HBR's 10 must reads: On strategy* (1–38). Boston, MA: Harvard Business Review Press.

13

HOW TO LEAD AND MANAGE PEOPLE

INTRODUCTION

An organization cannot get very far in accomplishing its goals without its employees. This is so true because the people who work as employees in the organization are the most important puzzle piece in the organization. Knowing how to motivate them to perform the best work they can to help the organization reach its objectives becomes a significant part of leading and managing them. Knowing when to motivate them is more significant. There is a delicate balance of knowing how to motivate them and knowing when to intervene to keep them motivated or when to let them fly on their own (Daviault and Campbell 2017). First of all, we need to know the difference between leaders and managers.

THE DIFFERENCE BETWEEN LEADERSHIP AND MANAGEMENT

According to Daviault and Campbell (2017), leading and managing people requires possessing all the tools to perform as individuals while remaining present to support them in their tasks. Moreover, leading and managing people are two different skills, but both come with many responsibilities and challenges. First, let us look at the differences and similarities between these two roles of leaders and managers.

Operational definition of terms is a description of term as applied to this topic. The importance of defining the terms used in this topic is to clarify them in order to avoid possible variations in interpretation. "The only definition of a leader is someone who has followers" (Drucker 1996, 8). According to this definition, managers do have followers, so managers are leaders. "Managers work toward the organization's goals, using its resources in an effective and efficient manner" (Bennis and Nanus 2004, 75). According to this definition, since leaders do work toward the organization's goals, leaders are also managers.

Thus, it is of utmost importance that the two roles though different in some ways are very similar in many ways. When you assume a role as a leader, you must add the role of manager and vice versa. While managing people will require helping people to adhere to the rules, regulations, and principles to achieve the goal and objectives of the organizations, leading people will require some intervention when situations change as expected in this VUCA (volatile, uncertain, complex, and ambiguous) world environment.

To lead and manage people in organizations, it is important to know what research leader and management styles and theories are required to help one to perform these roles effectively and efficiently. It is important to not just know but understand what these theories represent in leading and managing people. Here are the major theories.

THE THREE BASIC FORMS OF LEADERSHIP AND MANAGEMENT STYLES

Martin (1995) identified three basic forms of leadership: (a) authoritarian, (b) participatory, and (c) delegative or laissez-faire. A leader commands one of these behaviors and never all of them at the same time. These studies also supported the concept that, in the long term, the combination of the democratic and participatory forms of leadership are the most productive because subordinates always participate in the decision-making process.

Despite its extensive use across a variety of settings, including work, school, and family, using only one form of these styles makes the leader inflexible because leaders are constantly challenged to use all forms of the basic traditional leadership styles (autocratic, participative, and delegative) when appropriate. This approach, often called situational leadership, demands of its leaders to be autocratic sometimes, other times participatory, and sometimes laissez-faire, depending on the situation. It is well known that situational leadership has stood the test in the marketplace and is frequently used for training leaders within several organizations, including more than four hundred of the Fortune 500 companies (Hersey and Blanchard 1988).

Common leadership styles include authoritarian or autocratic, participative or democratic and delegative, and laissez-fair. Effective leaders generally incorporate all three styles, using one more predominately. Ineffective leaders use one style exclusively, typically autocratic.

The authoritarian leadership style creates clear and concise expectations about what needs to be accomplished, when it needs to be accomplished, and how it needs to be accomplished. Authoritarian leadership concentrates on the decisions and commands of the leader. Use this style if you want to make decisions independently with little input from followers (*The Resourceful Manager* 2006).

The participative leadership style is recognized as the most effective style. Democratic leaders provide direct feedback to followers while participating in group activities. This leadership style encourages input and participation from followers in the decision-making process. Use this style if you want to control the final say over decisions. Research has shown that followers are more motivated and creative as a result of feeling engaged (*The Resourceful Manager* 2006).

Use this style if you want your followers to make decisions, but then you, the leader, remain responsible. This style is considered the least effective of the three, as followers generally lack guidance and direction. Delegative leadership leads to followers blaming one another for mistakes and refusing to accept responsibility (*The Resourceful Manager* 2006).

From these three basic forms of leadership have sprung various leadership theories, but the major theories of leadership that have dominated much of our thinking in the past century are: (a) trait theories, in which emphasis is placed on identifying the qualities of great persons; (b) behavioral theories, where the focus is exclusively on what leaders do and how they act, there being two general kinds of behaviors, task behaviors and relationship behaviors; (c) contingency theories; (d) dyadic theories, an approach to leadership that attempts to explain why leaders vary their behavior with different followers; and (e) transformational leadership (Northouse 2004).

LEADERSHIP THEORIES

Things have changed, and now almost every book on leadership practice has its own take on what constitutes a good and effective leader. The major theories of leadership that dominate much of our thinking today are:

THE LEADERSHIP TRAIT APPROACH

This leadership trait approach reinforces the notion that leadership is an art rather than a science, that people are born with those traits, and that only great people possess them (Bass and Avolio 1994). According to Northouse (2004), this approach emphasizes certain personality traits that contribute to the leadership process, including intelligence, alertness, insight, responsibility, initiative, persistence, self-confidence, and sociability.

Trait theorists would argue that you can spot a potential leader just by their looks, manner, or education level. Trait theory assumes that leaders share certain physical, psychological, and sociological characteristics that determine their effectiveness. Use this approach if you have above average height and good looks, intelligence or charisma, and sociological characteristics that include education level or socioeconomic class.

THE LEADERSHIP SKILLS APPROACH

The leadership skills approach points out that leadership is a science and not an art—and that it is a set of skills and abilities that can be learned and developed. Katz's (1974) work suggested that effective leadership depends on three basic personal skills: technical, human, and conceptual. Use this style if you have a technical skill, knowledge about, and competency and proficiency in a specific work or activity, are able to get along with people and communicate and work within teams, and understand and decide the best actions and measures that have to be taken in a particular field of work. Northouse (2004) believes that great leaders are not born with innate leadership qualities; they must learn and acquire the knowledge and abilities necessary for effective leadership.

THE LEADERSHIP STYLE/BEHAVIOR APPROACH

The leadership style/behavior approach focuses exclusively on what leaders do and how they act. According to researchers of the style approach, leadership is essentially composed of task behaviors and relationship behaviors: what leaders do and how they act. In other words, there are two general kinds of behaviors—task behaviors and relationship behaviors—within this style of leadership.

Use this leadership style/behavior approach if you want to help group members achieve their objectives and help subordinates feel comfortable with themselves, with each other, and with the situation in which they find themselves (Northouse 2004).

THE SITUATIONAL LEADERSHIP APPROACH

The situational leadership approach tends to match leadership actions with leadership situations. For example, a supervisor will have to be adaptable and flexible to change according to the needs of the group rather than staying in one mode (Martin J. 1995). In the situational approach, leaders are challenged to use all four forms of the basic traditional leadership styles when appropriate.

Use this approach if you are capable of being autocratic sometimes, and at other times, variously democratic or laissez-faire, depending on the situation.

TRANSFORMATIONAL LEADERSHIP THEORY

Transformational leadership theory, as its name implies, is a process that changes and transforms individuals and influences followers to accomplish more than is normally expected of them. In fact, it is one of the most well-known leadership theories with the so-called new leadership paradigm (Northouse 2004). Use the transformational leadership style if you want to inspire workers to find better ways of achieving a goal or if you want to mobilize people into groups that can get work done. It is also useful if you are a leader and want to raise the morale, well-being, and motivation level of a group through excellent rapport. They are also good at conflict resolution.

HOW TO LEAD AND MANAGE PEOPLE

Now that you know the difference between leadership and management, the leadership theories, and the three basic forms of leadership and management styles, you are ready to learn the skills in leading and managing people. In my view, you cannot lead people without knowing how to manage them—and you cannot manage people without knowing how to lead them. Leading and managing skills are intertwined. Knowing when to lead and not manage people and knowing when to manage them and not lead them are the keys to be successful. Obviously, knowing when to use the finest combination of both leadership and management skills is ultimately the way to be effective in leading and managing people in an organization.

The question of what makes a good leader is widely debated. It is clear that the ability to lead effectively relies on a number of key skills, but different leaders have very different characteristics and styles. There is, in fact, no one right way to lead in all circumstances, and one of the main characteristics of good leaders is flexibility and the ability to adapt to changing circumstances. Leadership skills are highly sought after by employers as they involve dealing with people in such a way as to motivate, enthuse, and build respect (Skills You Need 2017).

How to lead and manage people in an organization is widely debated. However, it is clear that effectively leading and managing people in an organization requires numerous characteristics and styles. In my view, leading and managing people in organizations requires the following eleven sets of skills.

MASTERY OF EMOTION—EMOTIONAL INTELLIGENCE

To lead and manage people, you must first and foremost learn to master your emotions. Robbins (1992) defines emotions as any of the feelings of joy, sorrow, fear, hate, and love, and the only reason anyone does anything is to change the way they feel. For example, if you want to make more money, lose weight, or buy a new item of clothing, you're doing it because of what you think it will give you, which is a certain emotion. It is worth noting that you can always change your emotional state no matter how you are feeling today (Robbins 1992).

Leaders and managers must always be upbeat in order for their followers to continue to follow them. There are three factors that determine what you feel from moment to moment. Tony Robbins (1992) and other psychologists call it the "emotional triad." At any time, your emotional state is controlled by your (a) physiology (your body), (b) focus, and your (3) language or words. Using the emotion triad, see figure 1, can keep leaders and managers emotionally stable.

PHYSIOLOGY

According to Robbins (1992), emotion is created by motion. Whatever you're feeling right now is related to how you are using your body. If you start to feel emotionally down, you might want to stand up, reach your arms up in a big swinging motion, and breathe in deeply. If that does not work, try to smile or march in place. These will get you back to your emotional equilibrium because the way you use your body biochemically changes how you feel.

FOCUS

To feel happy, focus on things in your life that will make you feel happy. You may want to ask yourself, "What am I happy about in my life right now?" You may also try remembering happy moments from the past, like a fun birthday, wedding, or graduation. Whatever you focus on, you will feel. When you are feeling down, change your focus, find reasons to be grateful, and picture your world as it would be (Robbins 1992).

LANGUAGE

Your words and language patterns also change how you feel. If you say things like, "I feel very tired" or "This is too hard," you will literally feel tired or think what you're trying to do is too hard. It simply doesn't put you in an empowering state. All words have different emotional states associated to them. Certain phrases are disempowering, which will affect how you feel from moment to moment. Being aware of your vocabulary, statements, phrases, and metaphors is crucial to controlling your state of mind. Use words and language that will encourage and empower you to move on and pay attention to the words you repeat to yourself (Robbins 1992).

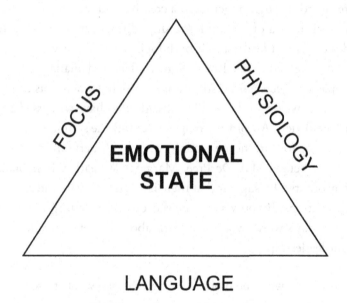

Figure 13.1 The emotion triad.

SERVE FIRST

The business environment is changing, and leaders and managers had better start changing their traditional ways of doing business, which is no longer cost effective. Today, according to Spears (2004), the traditional, autocratic, and hierarchical modes of leadership and management are yielding to a different way of working—one based on teamwork and community, one that seeks to involve others in decision-making, one strongly based in ethical and caring behavior, and one that is attempting to enhance the personal growth of workers while improving the caring and quality of our many institutions. This emerging approach to leadership and service is called *servant-leadership.*

The word *servant* is construed to mean "personal or domestic attendant," people who serve or wait on others, or people who perform household duties for others (servant, n.d.). On the other hand, the word *leader* is construed to mean a person who rules, guides, or inspires others; a head of an institution (leader, n.d.). Thus, these two words, servant and leader, are usually thought of as being opposites. However, these two opposites words brought together in a creative and meaningful way create the paradoxical idea of servant-leadership. Spears (2004) argues that the basic idea of servant-leadership is both logical and intuitive.

During the Industrial Revolution, leaders and managers tended to view people as objects, and institutions considered workers as cogs within a machine. However, in the past few decades, we have witnessed a shift in that long-held view. According to Spears (2004) the standard practices are rapidly shifting toward the ideas put forward by Robert Greenleaf, Stephen Covey, Peter Senge, Max De Pree, Margaret Wheatley, Ken Blanchard, and many others who suggest that there is a better way to lead and manage our organizations. If you want to be successful in leading and managing people in today's world, you must learn about Robert Greenleaf's model of servant-leadership.

> It begins with the natural feeling that one wants to serve, to serve first. Then conscious choice brings one to aspire to lead. The difference manifests itself in the care taken by the servant—first to make sure that other people's highest priority needs are being served. The best test is: Do those served grow as persons; do they, while being served, become healthier, wiser, freer, more autonomous, more likely themselves to become servants? (Greenleaf 1977, 4)

If you want to lead and manage people successfully, be a servant-leader" and learn to serve first. It begins with the natural feeling that one wants to serve first. Then conscious choice brings one to aspire to lead. That person is sharply different from one who is leader first—perhaps because of the need to assuage an unusual power drive or to acquire material possessions. The leader-first and the servant-first are two extreme types. Between them, there are shadings and blends that are part of the infinite variety of human nature. The difference manifests itself in the care taken by the servant-first to make sure that other people's highest priority needs are being served. In serving first, leaders and managers grow as persons, they become healthier, wiser, freer, more autonomous, and they are more likely to become servants. This will benefit the least privileged in society or at least cause them not to be further deprived (Greenleaf 1977).

To use this, Greenleaf (1977) suggests you focus primarily on the growth and well-being of people and the communities to which they belong. While traditional leadership generally involves the accumulation and exercise of power by one at the "top of the pyramid," servant leadership is different. You must be ready to share power, put the needs of others first, and help people develop and perform as highly as possible.

In examining Greenleaf's (1977) writings, Spears (2004) identified ten core characteristics of servant leadership that should be learned, and with practice, they will help anyone lead and manage people more effectively.

ACTIVE LISTENING

Servant leadership requires leaders to actively listen to other people—and not just be good at communication and decision-making. Listening is about focusing on what the team is saying and using this information for guiding the group toward its objectives. An effective leader should also identify the things that are left unsaid, as well as the inner voices. To be an active listener, you should focus on the spoken word, regularly venture amongst the team, and assess the mood in the room because conflicts can often be sensed, and unhappiness felt without someone having to voice it out (Spears 2004).

In order to improve your listening skills, you should learn more about being attentive. This can be improved by understanding body language better and by improving the ability to give and receive feedback (Spears 2004).

EMPATHY

Active listening and the ability to empathize go hand in hand. Since the focus of servant leadership is to serve others, you must be able to accept and recognize the individual values and feelings people have. Even when someone is underperforming at work, a servant leader should be able to love and understand them as a human. In a business environment, empathy is often hard to achieve because the focus is on company objectives and performance, but with servant leadership, the focus shifts to the individual employee and their well-being. An empathetic leader wouldn't just accept any behavior or performance, but instead of simply dismissing the team member, the leader would try to understand the behavior.

In order to improve your ability to be empathetic, when having a conversation, you should try to put your own viewpoints aside and openly listen to what the other person is saying. You need to be inquisitive and learn more about different ways of doing things. Instead of rejecting an idea or a thought, learn more about it to understand where the person suggesting it is coming from (Spears 2004).

HEALING

According to Spears (2004), servant leadership emphasizes the emotional health of an individual, together with mental and physical well-being. A servant leader should focus on their potential to heal the self and others. In a business context, healing would be achieved by ensuring there are enough support options employees can use. This could mean access to counseling, provision of proper health care facilities, a strong health and safety culture, and focus on self-development through courses and training.

In order to improve your healing abilities, you should make the above resources a priority, but you can also help people achieve the wholeness by using the right approach. Ensure you don't focus on just work-related things in your conversations with people, but also get to know how the person is doing. Make sure you read self-development guides and provide tips on what you've learned to your team. Ensure you are doing well mentally and physically to guarantee you have the strength to help others (Spears 2004).

AWARENESS

Spears (2004) argues that servant leadership requires awareness, both in terms of general awareness and self-awareness. Self-awareness in particular requires the leader to see their own emotions and behaviors in the context of how they affect the rest of the team. Through self-awareness, you become better at noticing what the people around you are doing—and you can fix problems quicker. Self-awareness is tightly connected to the feedback culture within the organization. It is important that employees are able to provide feedback, not just on themselves and each other, but also the management and leadership.

The secret to becoming more aware is taking a closer look inside you. Finding about your strengths and weaknesses is crucial for understanding your inner-self and how it affects those around you. You can learn more about yourself through personality tests, such as Myers-Briggs. But more importantly, a good leader seeks for feedback from the team to learn more about how they are perceived and how their actions are influencing others (Spears 2004).

PERSUASION

According to Spears (2004), servant leadership doesn't rely on authority to get things done. Instead, the concept uses persuasion in order to make a decision. A servant leader seeks consensus rather than compliance, which is perhaps the biggest difference from traditional authoritarian models. Greenleaf (1977) wrote that a fresh look is being taken at the issues of power and authority and that people are beginning to learn that the ability to relate to one another creates a less coercive and more creative supporting environment. In a large part, persuasion in business is highlighted by the organization's need to "make their case." Employees should be involved in the decision-making and understand what the objectives are and why since this can help influence them in to act a positive manner.

In order to become more persuasive, which is an important tool, there are a few ways to master it. You can improve your body language, communication, and ability to sense the right time to talk and listen. Finally, you should aim to be the expert in your field, which can guarantee that the team looks up to you and feels inspired by you. Showing enthusiasm and expertise with your actions will inspire others (Spears 2004).

CONCEPTUALIZATION

Greenleaf (1977) said that a servant leader is able to conceive solutions to problems, which are not presently there. This kind of conceptualization requires the leader the look beyond simple day-to-day realities. While it's important for a leader to be on top of the day-to-day operations and ensure that they are efficiently implemented and achieved, the leader must also look beyond short-term objectives and develop a visionary strategy for the future.

The most efficient way to improve your ability to conceptualize is through improving your business acumen. You need to improve your understanding of the industry and the organization by reading relevant reports, books, and industry blogs. This can help you see where the industry and organization are heading and better prepare yourself for the future.

FORESIGHT

Another relating point to conceptualization is the concept of foresight. Servant leadership requires the ability to foresee likely outcomes through the understanding of the past. There are three key points to foresight in leadership:

- the ability to learn from past experiences
- the ability to identify what is currently happening
- the ability to understand the consequences of specific decisions

For both Spears and Greenleaf, foresight is tightly related to intuition. It's an area where leadership studies have not yet ventured in more detail.

In order to improve foresight and become better at predicting the future, you should improve your analytical skills. This can be done by focusing on your decision-making process and by following up on the decisions you've made. In short, you need to develop a deeper understanding of the consequences of your decisions.

STEWARDSHIP

Stewardship in servant leadership relates to taking responsibility of your actions and those of the team. The main assumption is to commit to serve the needs of others first. For Greenleaf, this means that the organization holding their trust in the leader—and the entire organization is serving the wider community. Stewardship requires openness and persuasion. It's not about controlling the actions; it is about allowing yourself to be accountable.

In order to include greater stewardship in your leadership, you should start by understanding your own values and how they guide you in your leadership roles. Furthermore, study how those values align with the values of the organization or the team you are leading. Remember that you shouldn't be afraid of pointing out situations when the two don't align.

COMMITMENT TO THE GROWTH OF PEOPLE

The servant leadership model focuses on the intrinsic value people offer outside of their contributions as employees. Therefore, the aim of a servant leader is to help people realize their potential beyond just the ability to do the job well. Servant leadership requires the commitment to help people realize the personal and professional development potential—and support it. Greenleaf said, "The secret of institution building is to be able to weld a team of such people by lifting them up to grow taller than they would otherwise be."

In order to show your commitment to the growth of people, you can set an example as a leader by investing in your own personal and professional development. If you are constantly seeking to grow, you provide motivation to the team around you to do the same. In addition, you must also discuss personal and professional goals with your team. By understanding which things they want to develop, you can help provide the tools and routes for them to achieve these objectives. Learn more about how to grow your people and the benefits associated with it.

BUILDING COMMUNITY

Finally, servant leadership relies on the creation of a community and a sense of togetherness within the organization. With the above in mind, businesses could foster a sense of community by focusing on team building. By creating effective and caring teams, the organization as a whole will become more caring.

In order to support community building, you want to ensure different people within the organization interact with each other. Organizing social events and get-togethers is important. You want to encourage diversity and the flow of opinions within the organization as much as possible.

SOLVING CONFLICTS

Generally, *conflict* refers to some form of friction, disagreement, or discord arising within a group when one or more members' beliefs or actions are either resisted or deemed unacceptable to one or more members of another group (Holt 2017). Putnam and Poole (1987) provided a more specific definition of conflict as "the interaction of interdependent people who perceive opposition of goals, aims, and values, and who see the other party as potentially interfering with the realization of these goals" (Putnam and Poole 1987, 552).

To lead and manage people, it is crucial to understand that no two people think the same—no matter how much they have in common. This requires understanding that conflict will inevitably occur between people in the workplace. The only way of getting around it is to not find way out or be angry and feel threatened. Sometimes it may be hard to get resolution on a conflict, making matters worse. Yet, instead of seeing conflict as a threat, reframe it and see conflict as an opportunity and a sign of growth for you as a leader.

Miller (2015) highlighted three general characteristics of conflict: (a) incompatible goals, (b) interdependence, and (c) interaction. *Incompatible goals* arise when two or more people utilize different approaches to achieve specific goals. Incompatibility, however, is not a sufficient condition for organizational conflict to occur. Instead, conflict arises only when the organizational members' behaviors are *interdependent*. *Interaction* involves the expression of incompatibility and "highlights the importance of communication in the study of conflict" (Miller 2015, 159). Additionally, conflict can arise at three organizational levels: (a) between the organization's members, known as *interpersonal conflict*, (b) between members of the same group, known as *intragroup conflict*, or (c) between members of two or more groups, known as *intergroup conflict* (Miller 2015).

Furthermore, Miller (2015) noted that individuals seldom move suddenly from peaceful coexistence to conflict-ridden relationships. Rather, people move through phases as conflict develops and subsides. Pondy (1967) put forth five phases characterizing organizational conflict:

- *Latent conflict*: Individuals interact in interdependent relationships conducive to developing incompatible goals.
- *Perceived conflict*: One or more individuals perceive the situation to be characterized by incompatibility and interdependence.
- *Felt conflict*: Individuals begin to personalize perceived conflict by focusing on the conflict issue and planning conflict management strategies.
- *Manifest conflict*: Conflict is enacted through communication. Interaction may involve cycles of escalation and de-escalation as various strategies are used.
- *Conflict aftermath*: The conflict episode has both short- and long-term effects on the individuals, their relationships, and the organization (Miller 2015).

RELATIONAL FACTORS

The relationship between the conflict parties (e.g., supervisor-subordinate, colleague-colleague) appears to strongly impact the conflict management process. One important characteristic of the relationship between the conflict parties is *power* or the hierarchical position individuals occupy within an organization (Miller 2015). Relational factors include (a) supervisor versus subordinate, (b) subordinate versus supervisor, and (c) colleague versus colleague. Conflict-management styles can help you analyze how relational factors influence the conflict management process. Thomas (1976) described two dimensions of conflict-management styles, *concern for self* and *concern for others,* and identified five conflict styles that would fall at various points on this conflict grid (see figure 13.2).

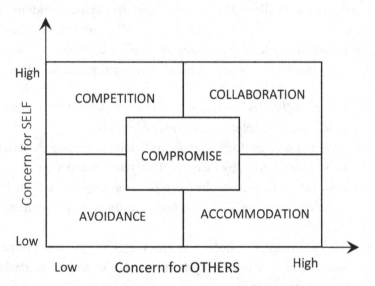

*Figure 13.2 Thomas's (1976) five conflict
management styles plotted on two axes: (a)
concern for self and (b) concern for others.*

This model is useful in understanding how relational factors influence conflict-management processes utilize the five styles of (a) competing, (b) collaborating, (c) avoiding, (d) accommodating, and (e) compromising.

The *competition style* depicts those high in concern for self, which is characterized by a drive to maximize individual gain—even at others' expense. This style contrasts with the *collaboration style*, which constructs solutions to conflict to meet the needs of all parties involved. The *avoidance style* depicts someone who is low in concern for self and disengages from conflict, and the *accommodation style* sacrifices self-interests to satisfy others' needs. Finally, the *compromise style* straddles the midpoint between concern for self and concern for others, and it involves compromising to arrive at a resolution of conflict (Thomas K. W. 1976).

Putnam and Poole (1987) reviewed the literature on hierarchical level and conflict styles and generally recommend that you use (a) competitive styles when dealing with subordinates, (b) accommodation or collaboration when dealing with superiors, (c) accommodation or avoidance styles when dealing with peers, and (d) compromise styles when the conflict grinds into a deadlock, yet a resolution is necessary. At that point, a third party is normally involved to help mediate the necessary concessions.

It is also important to understand that, according to Thomas and Kilmann (1974), no two individuals have exactly the same expectations and desires, making conflict a natural part of our interactions with others. Additionally, Holt (2017) recently published an article explaining that conflict in the workplace often occurs due to a lack of communication, and if not confronted, it can cause major problems for a business. Many employers mistake disagreements with conflicts; in contrast to conflict, disagreements are differences in opinion that could, but do not always, lead to conflict. Handling disagreements and other forms of possible conflict quickly can be healthy, but ignoring them may be very destructive and result in detrimental outcomes to organizations, including rapid turnover rates, loss of productivity, and absenteeism. The cost of turnover in the workplace is, of course, extraordinary.

Researchers such as Dana (2005) have found out that 60–80 percent of all conflicts in organizations in the United States come from strained relationships between employees (i.e., relational factors). Ilgaz (2014) also found that a typical manager spends 25–40 percent of their time dealing with workplace conflicts, amounting one to two days out of every workweek. Further, Fortune 500 senior executives spend 20 percent of their time in litigation activities (Ford 2000). Moreover, the number of employees seeking mental health consultation for work-related conflict has increased from 23 percent in 1999 to close to 30 percent in 2001 (Shepell 2002). Workplace conflict is a decisive factor in more than 50 percent of employee departures (Johnston 2011), and more than 50 percent of employers report being sued by an employee (Armour 2001).

Unresolved conflict represents the largest reducible cost in many businesses, yet it remains largely unrecognized (Dana 2005). However, to be successful in leading and managing people, you need to adopt the collaborative style where both you and your followers win. Also, make sure your organization adopts conflict-management processes, such as mediation and arbitration, to reduce relational conflicts. Doing so will help you and your organization report a 50–80 percent reduction in litigation costs (Stipanovich 2004), which is a good reason to consider conflict-management processes.

ETHICAL SKILLS

Based on my previous knowledge and experience in leading and managing people for several years, and that which I derived in the readings of several books, this topic has afforded me the opportunity to engage with and clarify my perspectives of leaders and managers. Block (2011) suggests that to be successful in leading and managing people, a person needs to influence and not control their followers. Furthermore, ethics are critically important in leading and managing people, and a lack of ethics can put your reputation at risk (Greiner and Poulfelt 2010).

One important ethical guideline to adhere to is the need to be authentic—putting into words what you experience with your followers (Block 2011) and doing what you say you will do (Kouzes and Posner 2002). Block (2011) asserted that "this is the most powerful thing you can do to have the leverage you are looking for and to build client commitment" (37). Also make sure that your mission statements, vision, values, and strategy are fully aligned at all times. It is best to refrain from doing things to make short-term profits that could put your reputation at risk (Greiner and Poulfelt 2010).

Professional and ethical behaviors you should be committing to gain leverage include getting involved; sticking to the assigned role; reaching out for responsibility; doing whatever it takes to get the job done; being a team player; being observant, honest, and loyal; really listening to the client's needs; and taking pride in your work (Greiner and Poulfelt 2010). If you adhere to these ethical principles, you will be effective in leading and managing people.

WOMEN, PEOPLE OF COLOR, AND FOREIGN-BORN LEADERS

I believe that leading and managing people must be different for women, people of color, and foreign-born people because traditional notions of leading and managing are largely derived from a White, usually urban, male context, thus making them potentially inappropriate and possibly ineffective for them (Ruderman and Ohlott 2005). Note that the measurement tools used for the leading and managing process were developed by mostly European American males and may therefore contain substantial measurement bias when applied to other ethnic groups. In addition, these leadership and management processes are often interpreted based on norms obtained mostly from European American male participants, and if used without consideration of the people's ethnic backgrounds, these could lead to ineffective or risky leading and managing people in minority populations (Thyer, Padgett, and Royse 2016).

CHALLENGES FACED BY NONMAINSTREAM LEADERS AND MANAGERS

The prevalence of nonmainstream leaders and managers has steadily increased throughout the United States over the past two decades, but there are particular challenges they must deal with. One out of the many challenges that non-mainstream leaders and managers face is the fact that the small things they say and do can make a difference in how people in the organization who are mainstream perceive them. For example, when mainstream people notice subtle differences, they might be apt to attribute them to personality, gender distinctions, or, worse, a character flaw (Hyun 2002).

Ruderman and Ohlott (2005) state that the number of women and minority and foreign-born leaders and managers in leadership and managerial roles has increased significantly; however, these leaders often do not have the leadership-development techniques to address their particular needs. A special unique challenge is that nonmainstream leaders and managers differ in their communication preferences and styles. Master your conflict-management styles in order to handle this challenge properly; otherwise, these can create conflict between the sexes socially, professionally, and intimatelyInvalid source specified.. Moreover, you must note that even the most progressive modern organizations have been created by and for white male, and thus tend to have systems, policies, norms, and structures that favor the male life experience. In addition, these leaders must be sensitive to the behaviors and values that regard the "norm" at work and tend to favor traits and characteristics traditionally associated with white maleness, while undervaluing traits and characteristics traditionally associated with women, people of color, and foreign-born leaders and managers (Ruderman and Ohlott 2005).

If you are a woman, leading and managing people, you must note that for the most part, you will encounter gendered environments. In most organizations, the standards of success are measured in male terms; therefore, women are typically isolated from formal networks. Furthermore, wage and salary structures are different for traditionally male work versus work that is traditionally female. In addition, while the same norms might accept certain male managers' behaviors, female managers' behaviors might be rejected by the same norms in the same organization—and different norms apply to the demonstration of vulnerability as well (Ruderman and Ohlott 2005). Leaders and managers must recognize that ongoing discrimination exists for women and minorities in managerial roles.

CONCLUSION

After reading this, you may need to add a few skills to your toolbox to help you make that necessary change to lead and manage people more effectively. Change is one of the few things about which we can be certain. Change can be positive and lead to rewards, but it can also be uncomfortable and awkward. Only when the individual who has to effect change is shown the vision that will make life for them happier and better do they accept it easily. Whether change is good or bad, it requires one to adjust and deal with it (Byvelds and Newman 1997). If leaders and managers do not change, they will struggle and eventually lose their jobs, be demoted, or become frustrated at work. They must recognize that change is necessary and be better in leading and managing people more effectively.

Research shows that leaders and managers who are women, people of color, and other nonmainstream people can be challenging because traditional notions of leading and managing are largely derived from a White, usually urban, male context, thus making them potentially inappropriate and possibly ineffective for women, those of Latino/a origins, African Americans, Native Americans, as well as Asians/Asian Americans, and other ethnic minorities (Ruderman and Ohlott 2005).

Women, people of color, and other nonmainstream leaders and managers today are faced with a multitude of problems when they lead and manage people in organizations. The most important of these is the ability to recognize and make the necessary changes to assimilate into organizational culture. Coming from a nonmainstream culture where values are pronounced and very different, their lack of trust in the business system could lead to low morale and low productivity, creating the potential of diminished profits. Fortunately, a research study by Annan (2008) indicates a general willingness on the part of nonmainstream leaders and managers, especially foreign-born leaders and managers, to change and assimilate. However, this change comes rather slowly and painfully. Nonetheless, with some coaching and mentoring struggles and concerns during the change process, mistakes can be minimized.

Finally, studies point to the fact that where culture is interwoven into the fabric of management philosophy, the result tends to be successful; where local culture is absent, and the leadership and management technique is alien to the environment, either wholesale failure or underperformance is the result (Versi 2004). In other words, if foreign-born leaders and managers interweave their culture into their organizational management philosophies, they will be very successful. On the other hand, if foreign-born leaders and managers in organizations are encumbered with their leadership and management techniques conceived in an era that has long been discarded into the rubbish bin of history (Versi 2004)—and if they do not discard the old ways of doing business—their struggles and concerns will be monumental and have serious consequences.

REFERENCES

Annan, B. (2008). *Immigrants in U.S.: Insights, Views and Approaches.* Los Angeles, CA: Sharp Image.

Armour, S. (2001, March 27). *Workers win more lawsuits, awards. USA Today.* Retrieved from http://www.usatoday.com/

Avedian, A. (2014). *Anger management essentials: A workbook for people to manage their aggression.* San Bernardino, CA: Anger Management Essentials.

Bass, B. M., and Avolio, B. J. (1994). *Improving organizational effectiveness through transformational leadership.* Thousand Oaks, CA: Sage Publications.

Bennis, W., and Nanus, B. (2004). Management versus leadership. In Jossey-Bass Publishers (Ed.), *Management skills: A Jossey-Bass reader* (1st ed., 41–52). San Francisco, CA: Jossey-Bass.

Betancourt, H., and Lopez, S. R. (1993). The study of culture, ethnicity, and race in American psychology. *American Psychologist, 48,* 629–637.

Block, P. (2011). *Flawless consulting: A guide to getting your expertise used (3rd ed.). San Francisco, CA: Pfeiffer* (3rd ed.). San Francisco, CA: Pfeiffer.

Byvelds, R., and Newman, J. (1997). Understanding change. *Factsheet, 91*(14), 57.

Commonwealth of Australia. (2009). Educators' guide to the early years learning framework. *Commonwealth of Australia,* 23.

Community Toolbox. (2017). Tools to change our world. Retrieved November 22, 2017, from http://ctb.ku.edu/en/table-of-contents/culture/cultural-competence/culturally-competent-organizations/main

Dana, D. (2005). *Managing differences: How to build better relationships at work and home.* St. Louis, MO: MTI Publications.

Daviault, C., and Campbell, C. (2017). *Leading and managing people.* Retrieved November 5, 2017, from https://oeru.org/oeru-partners/oer-foundation/leading-and-managing-people/

Drucker, P. F. (1996). Leaders are doers. *Executive Excellence, 13*(4), 8.

Ford. (2000, July). *Workplace conflict: Facts and figures. Retrieved from http://mediate.com/articles/Ford1.cfm.* Retrieved from http://mediate.com/articles/Ford1.cfm

Greenleaf, R. K. (1977). *Servant Leadership: A Journey Into the Nature of Legitimate Power and Greatness.* Mahwah, NJ: Paulist Press.

Greiner, L., and Poulfelt, F. (Eds.). (2010). *Management consulting today and tomorrow*. New York, NY: Routledge.

Hersey, P., and Blanchard, K. H. (1988). *Management of organizational behavior: Utilizing human resources* (5th ed.). Englewood Cliffs, NJ: Prentice Hall.

Holt, M. (2017). Risks of not confronting conflict in the workplace. Retrieved November 14, 2017, from Retrieved from http://www.chron.com/

Hyun, J. (2012). Leadership principles for capitalizing on culturally diverse teams: The bamboo ceiling revisited. *Leader To Leader 2012*(64), 14–19. doi:10.1002/ltl.20017

Ilgaz, Z. (2014, May 15). *Conflict resolution: When should leaders step in?* Retrieved from Washington Business Journal: https://www.forbes.com

Johnston, E. (2011). *Workplace conflict is expensive [Blog post]*.

Katz, R. L. (1974). Skills of an effective administrator. *Harvard Business Review* (September-October 1974), 90–101.

Kitayama, S. (2002). Culture and basic psychological processes—Toward a system view of culture: Comment on Oserman et al. (2002). *Psychological Bulletin, 128*, 89–96.

Kouzes, J. M., and Posner, B. Z. (2002). *The leadership challenge*. (3rd, Ed.) San Francisco, CA: Jossey-Bass.

Martin, J. (1995). On the quest to become a leader. *Tribune Business Weekly, 6*(31), 1.

Martin, M., and Vaughn, B. (2007). "Cultural and Global Competence: The nuts and bolts of diversity and inclusion. (Billy Vaughn, Ed.) *Strategic Diversity and Inclusion Management magazine*, 31–38.

McNamara, C. (2003). *Basics -- definitions (and misconceptions) about management*. Retrieved November 5, 2017, from http://www.managementhelp.org/mgmnt/defntion.htm

Miller, K. (2015). *Organizational communication: Approaches and processes*. Stamford, CT: Cengage Learning.

Northouse, P. (2004). *Leadership theories and practice* (3rd ed.). Thousand Oaks, CA: Sage Publications, Inc.

Pondy, L. R. (1967). Organizational conflict: Concepts and models. *Administrative Science Quarterly, 12*, 296–320. doi:10.2307/2391553

Putnam, L. L., and Poole, M. S. (1987). Conflict and negotiation. In F. M. Jablin, L. L. Putnam, K. H. Roberts, and L. W. Porter, *Handbook of organizational communication*. Newbury Park, CA: Sage.

Reference.com. (2017). *What is cultural competence?* Retrieved November 22, 2017, from Reference.com: https://www.reference.com/world-view/cultural-competence-6c8402e708ab401a

Robbins, T. (1992). *Awaken the giant within: How to take immediate control of your mental, emotional, physical, and financial destiny.* New York: Free Press.

Royse, D., Thyer, B. A., and Padgett, D. K. (2006). *Program evaluation: An introduction.* Belmont, CA: Cengage.

Royse, D., Thyer, B. A., and Padgett, D. K. (2016). *Program evaluation: An introduction to an evidence-based approach* (6th ed.). Boston, MA: Cengage Learning.

Ruderman, M. N., and Ohlott, P. J. (2005). Leading roles: What coaches of women need to know. *LIA, 25*(3).

Shepell, W. (2002, November 15). *Workplace trends linked to mental health crisis in Canada [Press release].* Retrieved from https://www.shepellfgiservices.com/newsroom/pr-nov152002.asp

Skillsyouneed. (2017, November 14). Leadership skills. Retrieved from https://www.skillsyouneed.com/leadership-skills.html

Spahr, P. (2014). What is transformational leadership? How new ideas produce impressive results. *Leadership Is Learned.* Retrieved November 16, 2017, from https://online.stu.edu/transformational-leadership/

Spears, L. C. (2004). Practicing servant-leadership. *Leader To Leader 2004*(34), 7–11.

Stipanovich, T. J. (2004). ADR and the "vanishing trial": The growth and impact of alternative dispute resolution. *Journal of Empirical Leal Studies* (1), 843–912. doi:10.1111/j.1740-1461.2004.00025.x

Stogdill, R. M. (1974). *Handbook of leadership: A survey of theory and research.* New York: Free Press.

The New International Webster's Vest Pocket Dictionary. (2003). Peru: Trident Press International.

The Resourceful Manager. (2016). The resourceful manager's guide to leadership. Malvern, PA: Resourceful Manager.

Thomas, K. W. (1976). Conflict and conflict management. In M. Dunnette, *Handbook of industrial and organization psychology* (889–935). Chicago, IL: Rand McNally.

Thomas, K. W., and Kilmann, R. H. (1974). *Thomas-Kilmann conflict mode instrument.* Palo Alto, CA: Consulting Psychologists Press.

Thomas, R. R. (2000). Coaching in the midst of diversity. In M. Goldsmith, L. Lyons, and A. Freas, *Coaching for Leadership: How the world's greatest coaches help leaders learn* (349–358). San Francisco, CA: Jossey-Bass.

Versi, A. (2004). A management revolution is needed. *African Business, 303*(13).

Zigarmi, D., Fowler, S., and O'Connor, M. (2017). DISC profile 2011 [Software]. Retrieved November 17, 2017, from https://www.discprofile.com/

PROGRAM EVALUATION

Measuring training results is important, and it can be frustrating and illusive at times. However, "in developing countries as in fully developed nations, this issue is a hot topic" (Phillips 1996, 314). No wonder, "chief executives and top administrators, struggling to make their organizations lean, profitable, and viable are demanding accountability with all expenditures. They are encouraging, and sometimes requiring, the Human Resources Department, HRD, staff to measure training results" (Phillips 1996, 315). To illustrate how to evaluate programs, I will use the *five levels of evaluation* approach in evaluating the African Participative Leadership Training Program (APLTP).

ADVANTAGES AND DISADVANTAGES OF DEVELOPING A NEW INSTRUMENT

Thousands of testing and measuring instruments are available today. Finding the right psychological test or measure for your research needs can be a challenging task since there is no one source to consult, and the source you choose to consult may only include a test description or review and not an actual copy of the test. The availability of psychological tests and measures depends on whether or not they are published (Gleeson Library, n.d.).

ADVANTAGES AND DISADVANTAGES OF EXPENDING
EFFORT TO SEARCH FOR AN INSTRUMENT

Most instrument developers require advance payment to use their instruments, but you will save yourself the development time since many measurement tools have already been created. The benefit of using an existing instrument is convenience. On the other hand, it can be difficult to find an existing instrument that aligns exactly with a program's specific objectives.

When selecting a measurement tool, the most important factor to consider is how well the instrument aligns to the program's learning objectives. Alignment is crucial because it relates directly to the utility of the information gained from assessment. The more aligned the instrument is to the program's objectives, the more direct the inferences into the program's effectiveness. Poor alignment may result in the assessment providing weak or limited information about the program (The Center for Assessment and Research, n.d.). Nonetheless, searching for the perfect instrument may be a futile task since the chances of finding a seamless alignment are slim.

Some instruments must be purchased directly from the test publisher or author. Other instruments are available free of charge. Also, scoring or analyzing data from certain instruments requires time and energy or employing others for assistance. For each potential instrument, one must consider what resources would be necessary to fully implement use of the instrument for a program's assessment. Even if an instrument is available free of charge, it is still helpful to contact the test author to request the use of their scale (The Center for Assessment and Research, n.d.).

Like most things, instruments can be of either high or low quality. The better the instrument's quality, the more useful and trustworthy the scores obtained using it. It is imperative that high-quality instruments are used for assessment work. If you do not trust the instrument's scores, it will be difficult to make decisions about a program by using them. Thus, an instrument's quality should be evaluated before deciding on it, potentially making the search more time-consuming and frustrating (The Center for Assessment and Research, n.d.).

ADVANTAGES AND DISADVANTAGES OF DEVELOPING A NEW INSTRUMENT

It is important to keep in mind that although instrument development is a resource-intensive endeavor, in the end, you will own the instrument. Thus, the advantage of creating a new instrument is that you can customize it to achieve very strong alignment. Developing a new instrument enables the researcher quality control. As noted earlier, the better the instrument's quality, the more trustworthy the scores obtained. Developing such a high-quality instrument could be time-consuming and complex; however, the researcher will not have to search endlessly and settle for an instrument with untrustworthy scores, making it hard to base program decisions on them (The Center for Assessment and Research, n.d.).

Although developing one's own instrument enables the person to control the quality, one can become stuck on developing an unnecessarily high-quality instrument. There are several factors to consider for arriving at a high-quality instrument. The Center for Assessment and Research (n.d.) stated that evidence about the quality of an instrument is typically called *validity evidence*, a term that includes content validity, internal consistency validity, and external validity. Again, the higher the quality of the instrument, the more useful the assessment results will be—an argument for the resource-intensive endeavor of developing one's own instrument. Deciding whether to use an existing instrument or create a new one is a matter of balancing resources and convenience with quality and alignment to the program's learning objectives.

THE MOST COMMON REACTIONS TO BEING EVALUATED

The evaluation process invariably poses a potential threat to those being evaluated. Oftentimes, the person being evaluated fears negative evaluation: being labeled or identified as inadequate or incompetent. Knowing the feelings of those being evaluated is key in designing and conducting successful evaluation activities, particularly if those not involved in the planning of an evaluation are suspicious of its "real purpose" or "hidden agenda" (Royse, Thyer, and Padgett 2016).

Many times, staff become angry and perhaps scared when they feel they are being scrutinized, especially when there is no examination throughout the administrative hierarchy. However, staff will feel less threatened when they feel that the problems lie not with their functioning, but at the administrative level, and that the evaluation will help rectify this problem. Persons under evaluation often believe that evaluation is purely subjective, according to the evaluators' ideas and inclinations; therefore, managers must be mindful of anyone fearing job loss or other repercussions from an evaluation (Royse et al. 2016). According to Lopiano and Zotos (2013), fear of job loss or other negative repercussions stems from the common belief that managers use evaluation punitively to highlight weaknesses and demonstrate their own power. Royse et al. (2016) stated that evaluators should not underestimate the amount of power that they are perceived to have by the person within the organization being evaluated. Thompson (as cited in Royse et al. 2016) described the evaluator as a "power broker" because they can speak and act for others in a position of authority for those who are unable or reluctant to do so on their own.

Other staff members may view the evaluator as a "hired gun" who has come into the organization to do away with certain staff by documenting their inefficiency or ineffectiveness. Those in this school of thought believe that the evaluator takes orders from those who did the hiring and may not be interested in hearing the "truth," given their ties to those paying the consulting fees (Royse et al. 2016).

Lopiano and Zotos (2013) further stated that employees are kept in the dark about what evaluation tools will be used, if any, and what will be measured until they walk into the evaluation meeting. Even when they do not fear job loss, they may feel unjustly singled out, making them less cooperative than the evaluator might desire (Royse et al. 2016). Some may also act viciously and cause confusion, and others may quite pleasantly refuse to complete the requisite questionnaires or forms.

WHAT AN EVALUATOR CAN DO TO MAKE EVALUATION EFFORTS LESS THREATENING

There are several ways an evaluator can make evaluation efforts less threatening. For example, the evaluator should meet with the employees being evaluated to emphasize the importance of the program evaluations. If possible and if approved by the client, evaluators can request that the client send the persons being evaluated a copy of the instrument and explain that the evaluator will be completing the instrument in consultation with them at the evaluation meeting and will be open to any questions to suggestions. This may help reduce employee anxiety and fear and make the evaluation process less threatening (Lopiano and Zotos 2013).

Prior to beginning the program evaluation, it would be helpful to emphasize the program's accomplishments and positive comments. Encouraging the persons being evaluated to disagree if they believe the assessment is incorrect and remaining open to discussing those items of disagreement can also help the evaluator make assessment efforts less threatening (Lopiano and Zotos 2013).

It is worth noting that program evaluations in the United States "most often have been designed to White, usually urban, English speakers—thus making them potentially inappropriate and possibly ineffective for Hispanics, African Americans, and Native Americans, as well as Asian and other ethnic minorities" (Royse et al. 2016, 370). Furthermore, Branson, Davis, and Butler (as cited in Royse et al. 2016) asserted that these measurement tools were developed by European Americans and may therefore contain substantial measurement bias when applied to other ethnic groups. In addition, these tests are often interpreted based on norms obtained mostly from European American subjects, which could lead to ineffective or risky treatment of minority populations.

Another effort an evaluator can make to facilitate a less threatening program evaluation process—especially to people of color—would be for evaluators to view the world through cultural lenses shaped to a large extent by teachings that have been acquired from our families and close friends (Royse et al. 2016). Lopiano and Zotos (2013) stated that since evaluation is purely subjective according to the evaluator's ideas and inclinations, it is important for evaluators to make sound judgments in their findings when applying their results to other groups. To make program evaluations less threatening to people of color, involving others who do not share the evaluator's same cultural experiences in the evaluation process as well as pilot testing procedures and instructions with groups of clients who resemble the targeted group are two ways to increase cultural sensitivity and make the program more threatening (Royse et al. 2016).

Occasionally, evaluators find themselves in an undesirable political environment that could threaten the program evaluation process. It is therefore not surprising to note that evaluators can become uncomfortable in their role and may have a tendency to rush through the process without accomplishing their specific objectives (Lopiano and Zotos 2013). This is more evident when evaluators find themselves conducting program evaluations in the political arena. Royse et al. (2016) noted that employees may presume the evaluator to have "influence" within the administration that the evaluator does not, in fact, feel. It can also be expected that political pressures will vary in strength, depending on what is at stake. Political and other factors can definitely impact the evaluator's judgment and threaten the evaluation process. As such, another effort an evaluator can do to make program evaluation less threatening is to remain sensitive to the political factors at play and refrain from being too accommodating or unfair to any single group. In such situations, Royse et al. (2016) recommended that the evaluator share the rough draft of a final report with a trusted colleague who would be in a position to detect any lack of objectivity or balance and make the program evaluation less threatening.

LEARNING ABOUT PROGRAM EVALUATION

Completing a program evaluation assignment helps one better understand program development evaluation, especially using the major content areas for evaluation reports outlined in Royse et al. (2016). The assignment will also help deepen your appreciation for writing evaluation reports. Below is my draft of a small evaluation report of a fictitious program.

EXECUTIVE SUMMARY

The evaluation report on the continuous improvement process (CIP) program examined quality differences between a manufacturing company and its supplier, and how these quality differences affect the company's ability to manufacture quality products for its customers. The program evaluation adopted a mixed-methods approach, which included objective (quantitative) intervention—the statistical process control (SPC)—and subjective, interpretive, constructive (qualitative) interventions—root-cause analysis (RCA). The data were analyzed in accordance with the CIP. Using the SPC, the findings most notably demonstrated that the manufacturing supplier's processes were out of control and the process incapable. However, the supplier is eager to establish quality control in the manufacturing processes and remain competitive. Responses from the RCA meetings indicate that (a) normal machine and tooling wear, (b) improper equipment adjustments, (c) an inexperienced operator unfamiliar with process, and (d) variability in operator-controlled settings caused samples to fall outside the SPC's control limits. This indicates the need for a drastic change in the processes that were deemed out of control. Through statistical measurement of SPC, all of the eight manufacturing processes were found to have out-of-control parts. By establishing an SPC program and a preventative maintenance operator training, all manufacturing processes eventually fell statistically within process control limits and were deemed quality assured.

INTRODUCTION

In this section, the implementation of CIP on a manufacturing organization will provide insights into how manufacturing organizations can thrive and remain competitive.

DESCRIPTION OF THE PROBLEM, ITS CONTEXT, AND ITS SIGNIFICANCE

A manufacturing company has been having quality problems with its supplier for several years. Despite several attempts to work as a team to resolve the constant quality problems, the supplier continues to ship poor quality parts to the manufacturing company.

PROGRAM DESCRIPTION AND QUESTIONS TO EXPLORE

The manufacturing company has recently acquired a large account with a big organization, and quality is a top priority for them if they are to keep this account. The manufacturing company decided to bring me in as a consultant to help alleviate the quality problem. The CIP program has been in operation for more than a year, but a few company staff members have been complaining about the quality problems since acquiring this new big account and fear losing it if these quality problems are not resolved. Despite the poor quality, the manufacturing company wants to continue to work with the supplier because of the relationship they have had for several years. They want to help them improve their quality procedures rather than dropping them as a supplier. They are committed to making the program successful and want a consultant to make that happen.

PURPOSE OF THE EVALUATION

The purpose of this evaluation was to determine whether program activities have been implemented as intended and if they have resulted in certain outputs. One approach to achieving this is to use the *logic model*, "a systematic and visual way to present and share your understanding of the relationships among the resources you have to operate your program, the activities you plan, and the changes or results you hope to achieve" (W. K. Kellogg Foundation 2004, 1). To achieve this purpose, we started by reviewing the activities and output components of the logic model (see figure 1).

LITERATURE REVIEW

This section includes a review of selected literature detailing the history and current state practices in American business organizations.

THEORETICAL/HISTORICAL FOUNDATION OF THE PROGRAM

CIP involves an ongoing effort to improve products, services, or processes. These efforts can either seek "incremental" improvement over time or "breakthrough" improvement all at once. Processes are constantly evaluated for their efficacy and flexibility. The Institute of Quality Assurance offered a broader definition, definition of CIP:

> Continuous improvement as a gradual never-ending change which is ... focused on increasing the effectiveness and/or efficiency of an organization to fulfil its policy and objectives. It is not limited to quality initiatives. Improvement in business strategy, business results, customer, employee, and supplier relationships can be subject to continual improvement. Put simply, it means "getting better all the time." (Fryer, Antony, and Douglas 2007)

A SURVEY OF RELEVANT LITERATURE

At its core, CIP includes *RCA*, a method of problem solving used for identifying the root causes of problems (Wilson, Dell, and Anderson 1993), and a preventive maintenance program that provides insight into how manufacturing firms can maximize overall equipment effectiveness to increase plant and equipment productivity. CIP helps facilitate a company's goal to reduce manufacturing costs and promote employee and equipment productivity. CIP can also be viewed as a management philosophy going against the adage that "if it ain't broke, don't fix it." In contrast, at CIP, most things can be improved. Thus, no system is developed; instead, all systems are in the process of developing.

METHODOLOGY

The systematic, theoretical analysis of the methods applied to this evaluation report are stated in this section. This analysis comprises the methods and principles used in the evaluation (Irny and Rose 2005).

EVALUATION DESIGN AND DATA COLLECTION PROCEDURES

In *process evaluation*, data are collected to get an initial impression about the quality of the program and determine whether activities are achieving the desired effect. Data are collected from the manufacturing processes and evaluated to determine the main areas of waste. Not all dimensions are monitored, however, due to the expense, time, and production delays that would incur (Quality-One, n.d.). Specifically, a process evaluation may have the following overarching purposes or goals: (a) program description, (b) program monitoring, and (c) quality assurance (Royse et al. 2016).

DESCRIPTION OF SAMPLING PLAN, PARTICIPANTS, AND RECRUITMENT METHODS

To further illustrate, I used a flowchart to provide a visual demonstration of the program's steps in sequential order. Elements include (a) the sequence of actions, (b) materials or services entering or leaving the process (inputs and outputs), (c) decisions that must be made, (d) people who become involved, and (e) time involved at each step and/or process measurements. This flowchart helped me understand how the process works, document the process and study ways to improve it, and then communicate to the ad hoc committees how the process works (Royse et al. 2016).

DEPENDENT VARIABLES OPERATIONALIZED AND DESCRIPTION OF INSTRUMENT

SPC is an industry-standard methodology for measuring and controlling quality during the manufacturing process. Quality data are obtained in the form of product or process measurements in real-time during manufacturing. This data is then plotted on a graph with predetermined control limits. Control limits are determined by the capability of the process, whereas specification limits are determined by the client's needs (InfinityQS, n.d.).

PROCEDURES FOR DATA COLLECTION AND ANALYSIS

Before implementing the SPC quality system, the manufacturing process is evaluated to determine the main areas of waste, such as rework, scrap, and excessive inspection time. It would be most beneficial to apply the SPC tools to these areas first. Again, not all dimensions are monitored during SPC, given the expense, time, and production delays that it creates. Data are then collected and monitored on the key or critical characteristics (Quality-One, n.d.).

DATA COLLECTION

SPC data is collected in the form of product dimension measurements at some workstations and in process instrumentation readings at others. The data are then recorded and tracked on the SPC charts. Depending on the workstation, some of the data collected are recorded as individual values and an average of a group of readings. Some of the variable data are recorded as individuals on a moving range chart, and others are recorded in subgroups of five and plotted on an X-bar–R chart (Quality-One, n.d.).

ANALYZING THE DATA

The data points recorded on a control chart should fall between the control limits, provided that only common causes and no special causes have been identified. Common causes fall between the control limits, while special causes are generally outliers or are otherwise outside the control limits. For a process to be deemed in statistical control, there should be no special causes in any of the charts. A process in control will have no special causes identified in it, and the data should fall between the control limits. In this case, however, the SPC charts did fall outside of the control limits in all the eight manufacturing processes, suggesting that none of the manufacturing processes are in a state of control and are producing low-quality parts.

RESULTS (FINDINGS)

The results of the program evaluation revealed that the supplier perceives itself to be able to run high-quality manufacturing processes if provided adequate knowledge, tools, and CIP techniques. In the brainstorming interviews for the RCA, the suppliers were fully focused and engaged throughout the process. After replacing worn-out parts on the machines at specific workstations, training operators on the controlled settings, and training operators on normal measurement variation, the SPC charts fell within the control limits. This ensures that the supplier is now producing parts that are up to the manufacturing company's standards (Quality-One, n.d.).

FACTUAL INFORMATION PRESENTED (INCLUDING TABLES, CHARTS)

Through the statistical measurement of Cpk, the process capability index, all of the eight manufacturing processes were measured to assess how close each process was running to its specification limits relative to the natural variability of the process. The larger the index, the less likely it is that any item will fall outside the specifications (iSixSigma, n.d.). Four manufacturing processes (numbers 3, 5, 6, and 8) were found to have out-of-control processes. The remaining four manufacturing processes (Numbers 1, 2, 4, and 7) were in statistical control and had Cpk values of 1.92 and above (see Table 1).

An RCA revealed the following causes for why samples fell outside the SPC control limits: (a) normal machine and tooling wear, (b) improper equipment adjustments, (c) inexperienced operator unfamiliar with process, and (d) variability in operator-controlled settings. In response, the team worked to develop and implement an autonomous preventive maintenance procedure to help maximize overall equipment effectiveness by increasing plant and equipment productivity. Training in the manufacturing processes' operator-controlled settings helped curb the other workstations' variability. After this intervention, all of the eight manufacturing processes became statistical in control, and process capable (see table 2).

STATISTICAL AND CLINICAL OR PRACTICAL SIGNIFICANCE

The Process Excellence Network (2013) defined *continuous improvement* as the ongoing effort to improve products, services, and processes by making small, incremental improvements within a business. It is based on the belief that these incremental changes will add up to major improvements over time, and it is as much about tactics (i.e., specific improvements) as it is about changing organizational culture to focus on opportunities for improvement rather than problems.

DISCUSSION

Explanation of Findings

One important finding from the program evaluation was that there seems to be inadequate support to implement a continuous improvement program. Indeed, the supplier seems to have to do this to maintain the account with the manufacturer for survival. In order to anchor the new approaches in culture (Kotter 1996), emphasis was placed on changing the leadership team's mindset during the evaluation program—to "walk the talk." The Process Excellence Network (2013) asserted that leaders must exhibit behaviors that demonstrate support for the initiative and for the behaviors they wish all employees to emulate.

Another finding was that the supplier's team does not seem to have the time to implement the needed changes. Instead, the team is often caught fixing a series of "fires" that constantly distract members from solving the root causes of their problems. This program evaluation emphasized that the team should focus on "fire prevention" rather than "firefighting," which will enable members to work smarter rather than harder. This can be done by training the supplier's leaders on the concept of failure modes and effects analysis for a period of two weeks.

APPLICATION TO AGENCY, PROGRAM, OR PRACTICE

To ensure continuous improvement programs' success, there must be an unrelenting, unwavering focus on improvement, which is critical to maintaining and sustaining process improvements. Changes need to maintain momentum to ensure that they do not grind to a halt through fatigue or resistance (Process Excellence Network 2013).

LIMITATIONS OF THE EVALUATION

Program evaluations of this type—continuous improvement process—are a change process. Such change requires (a) establishing a sense of urgency, (b) creating the guiding coalition, (c) developing a vision and strategy, (d) communicating the change vision, (e) empowering broad-based action, (f) generating short-term wins, (g) consolidating gains, and (h) anchoring new approaches in culture (Kotter 1996). One limitation to this CIP evaluation program is that it lacks the authority to empower the broad-based action required to solidify the change process. Block (2011) stated that "a consultant is a person in a position to have some influence over an individual, a group, or an organization but has no direct power to make changes or implement programs." (2). Thus, without the necessary authority required, this change may not last very long.

REFERENCES

Block, P. (2011). *Flawless consulting: A guide to getting your expertise used* (3rd ed.). San Francisco, CA: Pfeiffer.

The Center for Assessment and Research. (n.d.). Overview of selecting, designing instruments. *The Program Assessment Support Service*. Retrieved from https://www.jmu.edu/assessment/_files/PASS_Instruments.docx

Fryer, K. J., Antony, J., and Douglas, A. (2007). Critical success factors of continuous improvement in the public sector: A literature review and some key findings. *Total Quality Management, 19*, 497–517. doi:10.1108/09544780710817900

Gleeson Library. (n.d.). *Tests, measures, instruments and surveys*. Retrieved from http://psychologyresearchhelp.wiki.usfca.edu/Tests,+Measures,+Instruments+%26+-Surveys

InfinityQS. (n.d.). What is statistical process control? Retrieved from https://www.infinityqs.com/resources/what-is-spc

Irny, S. I., and Rose, A. A. (2005). Designing a strategic information systems planning methodology for Malaysian Institutes of Higher Learning (isp- ipta). *Issues in Information Systems, 6*, 325–331. Retrieved from http://www.iacis.org/iis/iis.php

iSixSigma. (n.d.). *Capability indices/process capability*. Retrieved from https://www.isixsigma.com/tools-templates/capability-indices-process-capability/

Kotter, J. P. (1996). *Leading change*. Boston, MA: Harvard Business Review Press.

Lopiano, D. A., and Zotos, C. (2013). *The athletics director's handbook: A comprehensive practical guide to the management of scholastic and intercollegiate athletics programs*. Champaign, IL: Human Kinetics.

Phillips, J. J. (1996). Measuring the results of training. In Robert L. Craig (Ed.), *The ASTD Training and Development Handbook: A Guide to Human Resource Development* (4th ed., 313–341). New York: McGraw-Hill.

Process Excellence Network. (2013, February 19). *4 factors that make a continuous improvement program successful*. Retrieved from http://www.processexcellencenetwork.com/innovation/articles/continuous-improvement-4-factors-that-make-a-conti

Quality-One. (n.d.). *Statistical process control: Collecting and recording data*. Retrieved from http://quality-one.com/spc/#Why

Royse, D., Thyer, B. A., and Padgett, D. K. (2016). *Program evaluation: An introduction to an evidence-based approach* (6th ed.). Boston, MA: Cengage Learning.

Wilson, P. F., Dell, L. D., and Anderson, G. F. (1993). Root cause analysis: A tool for total quality management. *ASQ Quality Press* (8–17). Milwaukee, WI: ASQ Quality Press.

W. K. Kellogg Foundation. (2004). *Evaluation handbook.* Retrieved from http://www.wkkf.org/knowledge-center/resources/2006/02/WK-Kellogg-Foundation-Evaluation-Handbook.aspx

Table 14.1
State of Manufacturing Process

Workstation No.	State of Statistical Control	Cpk	Remarks
1	Yes	1.94	
2	Yes	1.96	
3	No	—	Not in a state of control
4	Yes	1.92	
5	No	—	Not in a state of control
6	No	—	Not in a state of control
7	Yes	1994	
8	No	—	Not in a state of control

Note: For those manufacturing processes without Cpk values assigned, the process capability index could not be measured, as the manufacturing process was not in control (iSixSigma, n.d.).

Table 14.2
State of Control Post-Intervention

Workstation No.	State of Statistical Control	Cpk	Remarks
1	Yes	0.72	Process in control Cpk < 1.33; Process capable
2	Yes	0.81	Process in control Cpk < 1.33; Process capable
3	Yes	0.62	Process in control Cpk < 1.33; Process capable
4	Yes	0.89	Process in control Cpk < 1.33; Process capable
5	Yes	0.78	Process in control Cpk < 1.33; Process capable
6	Yes	0.91	Process in control Cpk < 1.33; Process capable
7	Yes	0.77	Process in control Cpk < 1.33; Process capable
8	Yes	0.9	Process in control Cpk < 1.33; Process capable

Note: After the intervention, all eight manufacturing processes became statistical in control and process capable.

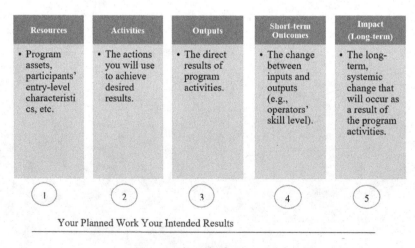

Figure 14.1 The basic model.

Printed in the United States
by Baker & Taylor Publisher Services